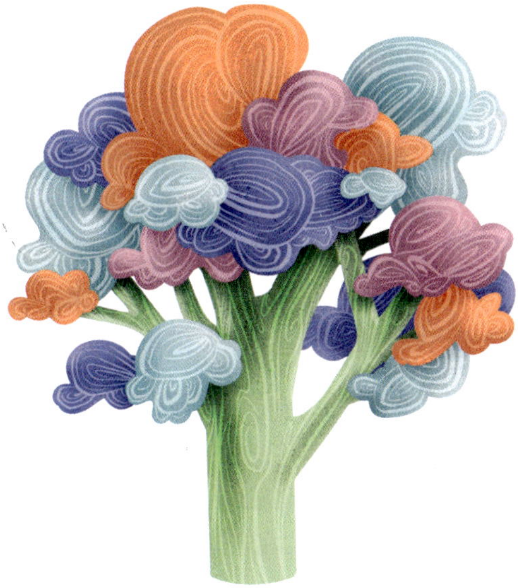

KAUAI TREE PUBLISHING

Copyright © 2019 Robert W. McCarthy. All Rights Reserved.

Without limiting rights under copyright reserved above, no part of this publication may be reproduced, stored in or introduced into a retrieval system, or transmitted in any form by any means (electronic, mechanical, photocopied, recorded, or otherwise), without the prior written permission of both the copyright owner and the publisher of this book, except in the case of brief quotations embodied in critical articles or reviews.

Title: 3-Dimensional Bodywork
A Systematic Approach to Myofascial Network Release for Massage Therapists
Author: Robert W. McCarthy
Publisher: Kauai Tree Publishing
Book website: 3DimensionalBodywork.com
Email contact: citizenrob@hotmail.com
Identifiers: ISBN: 978-1-7334392-0-6 (print); 978-1-7334392-1-3 (e-book)
First Edition: December 2019. Printed in the United States of America
Library of Congress Control Numbers: 2019916176

Design and illustration by Liza Mana Burns, LizaManaBurns.com

Graphics, diagrams, and photographs licensed by Shutterstock for commercial use are so noted, along with the credited artist/photographer. Images provided as a courtesy by Tama Starczak are so noted. Author headshot photography credit Taylor Sherrill. All other photographs were taken by the author, are the property of the author, and remain under the copyright of the author and publisher.

This book is presented solely for educational and entertainment purposes. This publication is written and published to provide accurate and authoritative information relevant to the subject matter presented. It is published and sold with the understanding that the author and publisher are not engaged in rendering legal, medical, or other professional services by reason of their authorship or publication of this work. If medical or other expert assistance is required, the services of a competent professional person should be sought. While best efforts have been used in preparing this book, the author makes no representations or warranties of any kind and assumes no liabilities of any kind with respect to the accuracy or completeness of the contents. Furthermore, the author specifically disclaims any implied warranties of merchantability or exercise fitness efficacy or therapeutic efficacy. The author shall not be held liable or responsible to any person or entity with respect to any loss or incidental or consequential damages caused, or alleged to have been caused, directly or indirectly, by the information or programs contained herein. No warranty may be created or extended by sales representatives or written sales materials. Mentions of any persons, resources, websites, and associations does not imply an endorsement.

Printed in the United States of America

I dedicate this book to my wife,
Barbara "Bar" Comess, M.D., whose Sisyphean, arcane work as a pathologist has allowed me to indulge in a pursuit of
fitness and therapy

FOREWORD

AT THE OUTSET, author Rob asks massage and other manual therapists and bodyworkers a crucial question: "Wouldn't it feel better (and be more therapeutic) if a client were stretched and massaged at the same time, especially if limbs and body were three-dimensionally and optimally positioned?"

If you answered "yes" like I did, then be prepared to start a most wonderful, new journey of learning how to integrate one of the most important "missing links" in your practice. Even if you do some assisted stretching with your clients, this is different and certainly much more effective than traditional stretching most of us first learned years ago.

This book, like its author, is thorough and well-organized, full of humor yet serious about the intention to give you what you are looking for: new concepts and techniques to help your clients. The 3-D concept of positioning with more advanced massage techniques combined with stretching, will expand your virtual tool bag of options to help clients that you may have had difficulty with attaining an optimal response and outcomes in the past. It will also provide an even better therapeutic experience with the rest.

Combining his years of education, training and experience of integrating his extensive background in engineering, personal training and specialization in Fascial Stretch Therapy™, Rob McCarthy has given you a practical manual of new techniques and routines that will work as soon as you implement with your clients.

I hope that this book will also serve to inspire you to seek training directly with Rob when offered, as his 'pearls of wisdom' and direct instruction are best passed kinesthetically - always the best way to obtain a new manual skill.

CHRIS FREDERICK

PT, Anatomy Trains® Structural Integration practitioner, co-author of *Stretch to Win* and *Fascial Stretch Therapy*, Co-Director of the Stretch to Win Institute

PREFACE

I CAME INTO MASSAGE by first becoming a personal trainer, then strength and conditioning specialist, then Fascial Stretch Therapist (FST)™.

I received stretch training from Ann and Chris Frederick who created Fascial Stretch Therapy™. Chris and Ann had gotten the "science right" and developed a very effective and therapeutic technique, so much so, professional athletes and a couple of NFL teams were using it. About the same time I took my first FST™ course, someone gave me a copy of Thomas W. Myers' book, *Anatomy Trains: Myofascial Meridians for Manual and Movement Therapists*. Serendipitously, it turned out FST™ uses Myers' concepts.

What I have since dubbed "the muscle and gristle highways that run through the body," Myers more precisely calls "myofascial meridians" – about 12 organizing networks that generate and transmit force and move us.

When I saw Myers' concept of muscle and connective tissue, I felt like I had just seen the anatomical equivalent of the "grand unified field theory" of physics. It was a brilliant organizing concept, and it fundamentally altered my approach to training – and now bodywork.

By the time I got to massage school, I had several thousand hours of stretch therapy under my belt and embraced Myers' work. I immediately began incorporating the theoretical concepts of stretch therapy into the classes. Whether the class was Swedish, Deep Tissue, Thai, Shiatsu, Reflexology, you name it; I always sought linkages to integrate these various techniques.

An FST™ background provided confidence to experiment with positioning the body for maximum therapeutic outcome - the body is three dimensional, so why not put the body in optimal positions in three-dimensional space for manual manipulation?

I base the technique in this book, in part, on the underlying concepts of Thomas Myers myofascial meridians. I do not intend this book to be a rigorous scientific text, although it is based on laboratory observations; especially those of Myers whose penchant for dissecting numerous cadavers over the decades has helped open a new paradigm of viewing myofascia, expanding the concepts of traditional muscle origins and insertions.

Myers' concepts of fascial connections are clear to me in every client I train, and every client I stretch or massage. You don't need to know his Anatomy Trains®, but you will be a better massage therapist or trainer if you study his concepts. The body of knowledge regarding fascia is rapidly evolving. Myers' work gives us a starting point and a "vocabulary" of how myofascia connects through the body.

My fundamental approach to myofascial release is mechanical based on torsion and shear of fascial sacks of muscle, and selective compression. These strokes are done in optimal positioning of the body to achieve tissue tension or slack. I don't purport to present a new paradigm of bodywork, just a practical and repeatable sequence that hopefully works, and keeps clients coming back.

This book is intended for massage school students, and those certified massage therapists who want to freshen up their routines. You will notice I repeatedly reference Mosby's *Fundamentals of Therapeutic Massage*, a wonderful text chock full of information, but rarely mastered in a 500-hour massage school curriculum.

The Mosby references are meant to help the massage school student in a practical setting when a more difficult client case is encountered. The practitioner must attempt to discern if this therapy would be appropriate, and if the technique worked ex post facto.

Most massage school students need help with muscle anatomy and kinesiology, so I attempted to use proper anatomical terms to help the student learn and navigate a human body.

I would like to thank Margaret Hines, Somatherapy Institute School of Massage, Rancho Mirage, California for her edits and helping set the tone of the book.

I would also like to thank Sallie Thurman who provided clarifications and insights from cadaver dissection, and furthermore forwarded several pages of the book to Dr. Gil Hedley for his information and review. Gratitude also goes to Professor Holly Clemens, Ph.D., for her review of the book.

I also owe a special debt of gratitude to Chris and Ann Frederick, whose Fascial Stretch Therapy™ training opened the world of therapy to me. I would also like to thank Chris for his review of the book and suggested changes. I especially thank Chris for his agreement to write the book's foreword.

A thanks also goes to my talent and film crew; production assistant Katja, and models Tama and Jolene. Tama is the main character in this book; I thank her for allowing me to use pictures of her when she was a bodybuilder and now a Pilates instructor. Jolene collaborated with me most Wednesdays over a two-year period to experiment and refine the routine. I also thank Tammy who is the model for the bolstering section.

The routine presented in this book is based on constant iteration and practice. I wish to thank all of my wonderful clients who have served as "guinea pigs" as I experimented on what worked - and what didn't. Their feedback, not to mention their return visits, were priceless.

Expand on this routine, deviate from this routine, and make it your own.

R.W.M.

TABLE OF CONTENTS

FOREWORD
by Chris Frederick

PREFACE
by Robert W. McCarthy 1

CHAPTER 1: INTRODUCTION 6
Anatomy Trains®–Myofascial Meridians 6
Myofascia 8
Bones 12
Nerves 14
Respect the Dermis 15
Fascial Restrictions 18
Clearing Fascial Restrictions 19
Massage Therapy as a Business 19
Condition Management vs. Therapeutic Change 20

CHAPTER 2: WHAT IS THE 3-DIMENSIONAL BODYWORK APPROACH? 22
Mechanical and Anatomical 23

CHAPTER 3: HALLMARKS OF THE ROUTINE 25
Hallmarks of the Routine 26
Tango 28

CARTOON FEATURING CLIENT TYPES 29

CHAPTER 4: TYPES OF CLIENTS
Types of Clients 31

CHAPTER 5: EQUIPMENT AND ROUTINE POSITIONS
Draping 33
Glide 33
Optional Running Shorts 33
Bolsters and Routine Positions 34

CHAPTER 6: CASE STUDIES: WHEN IS THIS TECHNIQUE APPLICABLE?

Case Study 1 – Functional (Soft Tissue) Deviations 37
Case Study 2 – Structural Deviations 37
Case Study 3 – Fascial Network-based Movement 38
Case Study 4 – Assessments May Fool You 39
Case Study 5 – Transitional Deviation 41
Primum Non Nocere, "First, Do No Harm" 42

CHAPTER 7: 3-DIMENSIONAL BODYWORK ROUTINE AND TECHNIQUE

Lower Supine (LS) – Turquoise-colored 45
Upper Supine (US) – Salmon-colored 64
Side Lying (SL) – Sage-colored 76
Sims' Lateral Recumbent (SLR) – Lavender-colored 83
Prone (P) – Blue-colored 91

APPENDICES 102

APPENDIX A (TRX® Movement Preparation Routine) 103
APPENDIX B (ViPR® Movement Preparation Routine) 105
APPENDIX C (3DB Expectations) 107
APPENDIX D (Waiver and Release) 108
APPENDIX E (Informed Consent) 109
APPENDIX F (Permissions, Boundaries, and Consent) 110
APPENDIX G (Course Syllabus) 111
APPENDIX H (Recommended Class Materials) 116
REFERENCES 117

3-D Bodywork

CHAPTER ONE
INTRODUCTION

"Ontogeny recapitulates phylogeny"

Dr. McGill, Marine Science Professor, USCGA

When my professor articulated Ernst Haeckel's axiomatic phrase, "ontogeny recapitulates phylogeny," I was immediately seized with an interest in fascial development similarities among different phyla to ascertain if there were any embryologic "fascial parallelism," especially from a histological perspective.

Nah, just joking with you.

This is a straightforward myofascial bodywork "how to" manual, not necessarily a scientific discussion of myofascia. We will go into a little bit of science, but not much.

If you are a massage therapist, you are theoretically taught massage and stretch, but many aren't comfortable straying from a standard Swedish routine - oh, "would you like light, medium, or hard pressure?"

Swedish massage is relaxing and generally feels good. But does applying lotion onto a two-dimensional planar surface, supine and prone, cross the threshold of being truly "therapeutic"? Sometimes you come across an exceptional therapist who can make a Swedish massage therapeutic, but this seems to be the exception, not the rule.

Wouldn't it feel better (and be more therapeutic) if a client were stretched and massaged at the same time, especially if limbs and body were three-dimensionally and optimally positioned?

Let's call this stretch-massage combination the "Peanut Butter Cup Effect": combine chocolate (massage) with peanut butter (stretch) and the resulting outcome is something better than the two individual components. It also called synergy.

This 3-Dimensional Bodywork technique (3DB), therefore, is a synergistic approach that not only feels good; it will give you a method to ensure your client receives a repeatable, positive therapeutic outcome.

ANATOMY TRAINS® – MYOFASCIAL MERIDIANS

Thomas W. Myers' book, *Anatomy Trains: Myofascial Meridians for Manual and Movement Therapists* provides the underlying anatomical organization from which this myofascial routine is based. Instead of focusing on muscle, the connective tissue, ***fascia***, will be our focus.

Through decades of cadaver dissection, Myers has identified about 12 continuous fascial and muscle networks, which generate and transmit force and move us.

Anatomy and kinesiology courses teach muscle origins, insertions, and actions; an individual muscle "starts here, ends here, and does that." Myers has found continuous linkages between these individual muscles when viewed from their fascial or connective tissue perspective. For example, his "Superficial Back Line" literally runs from head to toe.

You can see a photograph of this "continuous sheath of gristle and meat" running from the forehead, down the erector spinae group, through the sacrotuberous ligament, into the hamstrings, down the calves, into the Achilles tendon, finishing with the fascial trampolines of the foot and into the toes – no breaks, a continuous linkage from head to toe[1].

Myers' concepts, therefore, give us a "global" road map and diagnostic tool. For example, tightness in the foot or hamstring might cause lower back or neck pain.

You don't need to know Myers's myofascial meridians (although it would help), just know his concepts inform this step-by-step approach to massage and stretch.

If you have been taught Swedish massage and have a rudimentary knowledge of anatomy and kinesiology, you should be able to learn and apply this routine.

If you are also trained as a stretch therapist, learned stretch techniques presented in Mosby's *Fundamentals of Therapeutic Massage, 6th Edition*[2], learned any Thai stretch techniques, or have had any experience with sports assisted stretching, you will have a greater intuitive grasp of the technique. For those with prior stretch therapy experience, you should be able to integrate your knowledge with this myofascial release routine.

MYOFASCIA

Let's first simplistically define myofascia: ***Myo*** means muscle and ***fascia*** means band or connective tissue.

Fascia also includes tendons, covering around bones, ligaments, joint capsules, and tissue that hold organs and your brain in place - it's everywhere. It is also around every cell in the body and can even penetrate the cell wall through cell-adhesion receptors.

We should not view muscle and fascia as separate entities. Quite the opposite, muscle and fascia are *inseparable*. Your muscles would look like hamburger without an organizing fascia from the cell through the various muscle structures to the tendon. Most anatomy and physiology books show the structure of a muscle: sarcomere (actin and myosin) to myofibril to muscle fiber (cell) to fascicle to muscle to tendon (see following diagram).

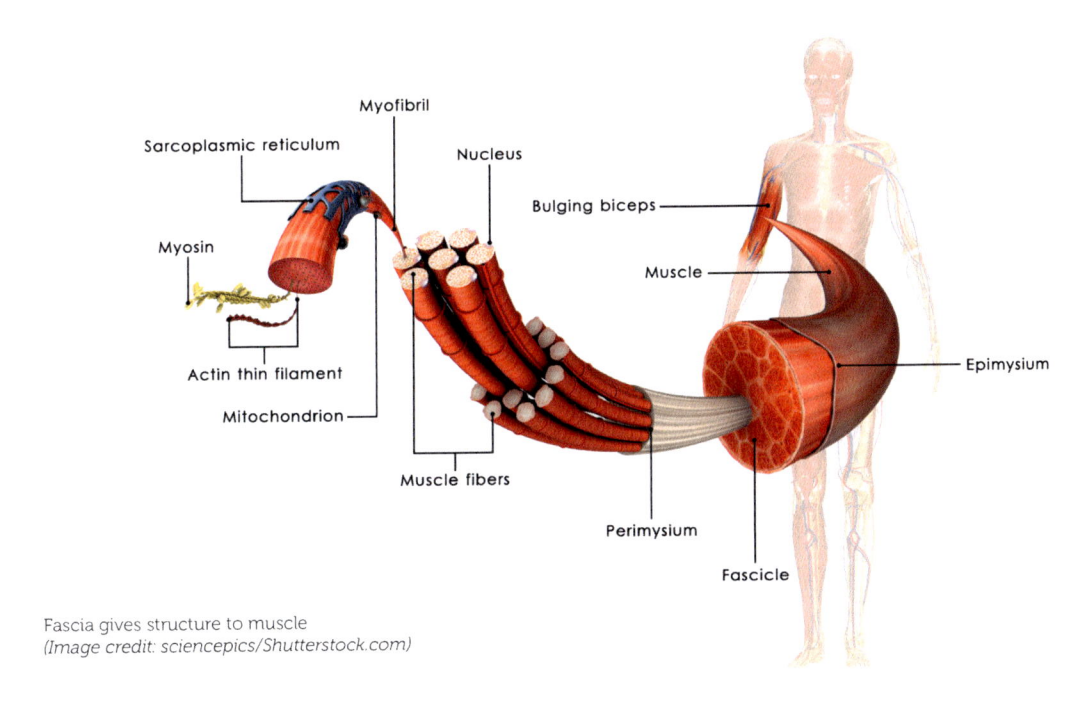

Fascia gives structure to muscle
(Image credit: sciencepics/Shutterstock.com)

In Dr. Vizniak's *Muscle Manual*[3], his description of the organizing structure of muscle includes an emphasis on fascia, which is *italicized* as follows,

> "Individual muscle fibers are surrounded by **endomysium** (fascia). Muscle fibers are bound together by **perimysium** (fascia) into bundles called **fascicles**; the bundles are then grouped together to form muscle, which is enclosed in a sheath of **epimysium** (deep fascia). Nerve tissue is distributed throughout the muscles & fascia to provide motor control & sensory feedback."

Understanding the importance fascia has to muscle organization, calling the biceps brachii simply a "muscle" falls short of a deeper appreciation that muscle is **an inseparable myofascial structure.** Mosby states,

> "...the myofascial system is a three-dimensional continuum; this means that we cannot truly separate muscle or any other type of tissue from the surrounding fascia or the body as a whole **(i.e., there is no such thing as an individual muscle)**[4]."

What are these fascial organizing structures and coverings made of? Without going into too much detail, fascia is a "stretchy mesh" made of collagen and elastin fibers[5]; and "glue," more properly called ground substance, which is an extracellular matrix around all cells that is viscous and gel-like.

Fascia can be remodeled and is constantly changing – in either good or bad ways. Your body - fascia, bones, and muscle respond to the loads, forces, and direction of those forces placed upon them. *We are changing all the time.*

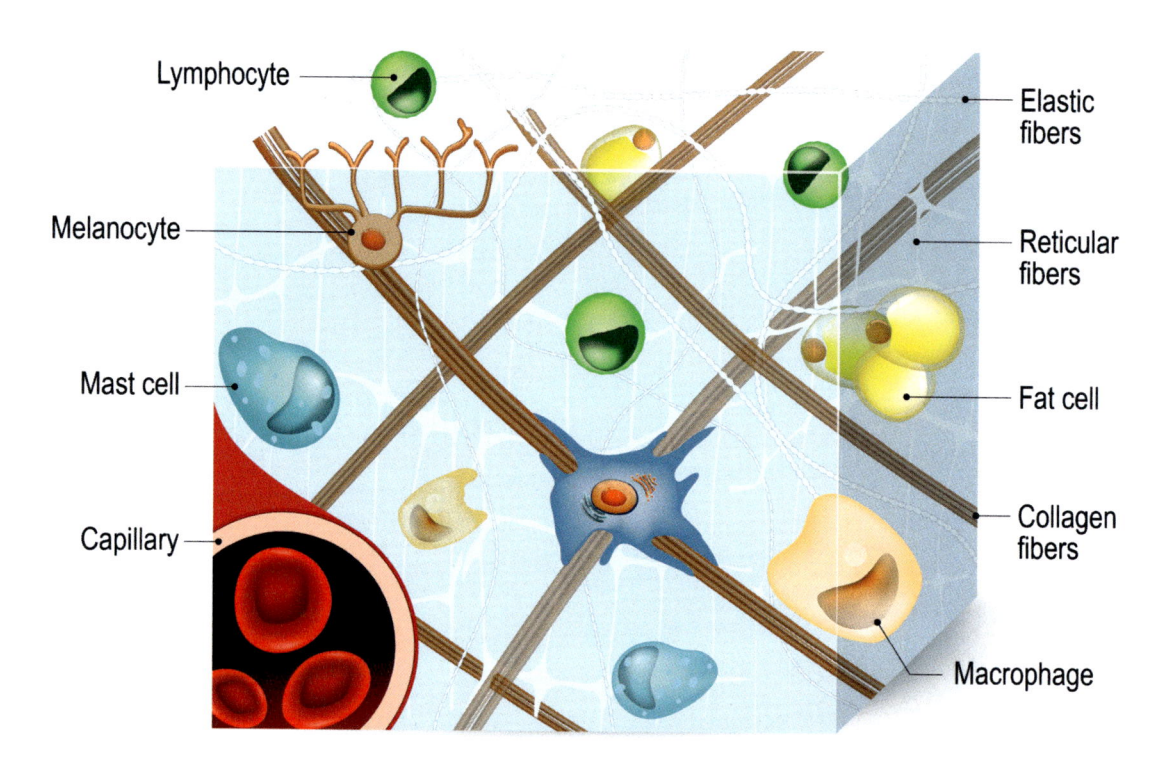

Collagen, reticular (a type of collagen fiber), and elastin fibers make up a "stretchy mesh" of connective tissue. Extracellular matrix, or ground substance (blue coloring) can be viewed as a viscous gel-like "glue."
Image credit: Designua/Shutterstock

Myofascia and bones restructure and change given the loads placed upon them.
(Photo courtesy of Tama Starczack)

Fascia Research Congress℠

Aside from the simplistic definition of myofascia, and the generalized explanation of fascia presented in this section, you should be aware of the more precise definition of fascia and the fascial system.

The following was extracted from the Fascia Research Congress' website (**fasciacongress.org**):

"**FASCIA** is a term which continues to carry different meanings for various professions and perspectives. Based on the connecting nature of this tissue and the interdisciplinary range of related professionals working with it, the Fascia Nomenclature Committee (FNS) of the Fascia Research Society recommends the following two major usages:

A **FASCIA** is a sheath, a sheet, or any other dissectible aggregations of connective tissue that forms beneath the skin to attach, enclose, and separate muscles and other internal organs.

The **FASCIAL SYSTEM** consists of the three-dimensional continuum of soft, collagen containing, loose and dense fibrous connective tissues that permeate the body. It incorporates elements such as adipose tissue, adventitiae and neurovascular sheaths, aponeuroses, deep and superficial fasciae, epineurium, joint capsules, ligaments, membranes, meninges, myofascial expansions, periostea, retinacula, septa, tendons, visceral fasciae, and all the intramuscular and intermuscular connective tissues including endo-/peri-/epimysium. The fascial system surrounds, interweaves between, and interpenetrates all organs, muscles, bones and nerve fibers, endowing the body with a functional structure, and providing an environment that enables all body systems to operate in an integrated manner."

BONES

Most anatomy or kinesiology classes have a skeleton in the classroom's corner. Is it standing or hanging?

In these front and back views, the skeleton appears to be standing, but the one in your classroom is hanging. From the skull all the way to the distant metatarsals and phalanges, all the bones are pinned and hanging.

So, in one sense, **bones are passive structures.**

This statement should make you say, "hold it, you just told us bones respond to forces and direction of loads – they are changing all the time." Aren't bones dynamic? Yes.

In fact, bones are amazingly *dynamic*. They change shape and thickness depending on how they are loaded. There is even a name for this dynamic process, Wolff's Law. Named after Julius Wolff, a German anatomist and surgeon (1836-1901); his law says bones adapt to the loads placed upon them. Remember, "Wolfs chew bones," and you will never forget his law.

Bones have connective tissue such as articular joint capsules and ligaments, but even if we bound the bones together, the skeleton could not stand on its own. It is the force of gravity, fascia, and myofascia that load and pull on bones making them change shape and density. And it takes this muscle and connective tissue to make our skeleton stand, and move the body in three-dimensional space.

So, it is in this context we state bones are passive structures, they require muscles and connective tissue to move them. Think of a cable moving a crane arm. Bones are in constant

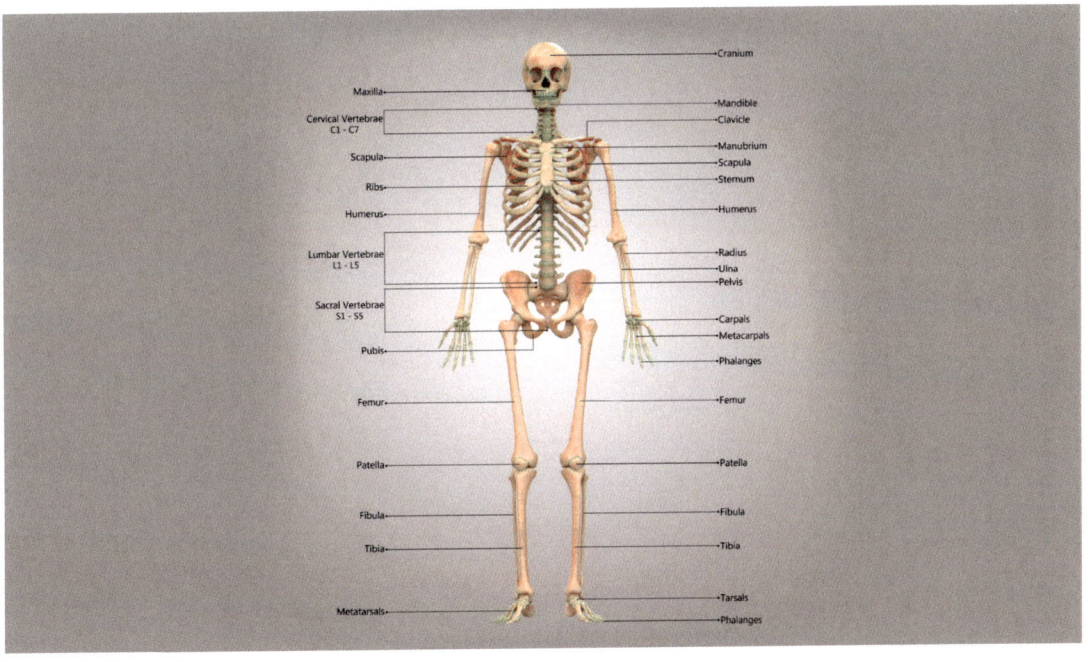

Does the classroom skeleton stand or hang?
(Image credit: Magic mine/Shuttertock.com)

myofascial interplay of tension or compression. You may have heard of the word **tensegrity**, which describes this compression - tension dynamic[6].

Your focus in using the 3-Dimensional Bodywork routine is to free up fascial adhesions, and release all or part of the myofascial meridians. If a bone "adjusts" because you released myofascial tissue that should be viewed as an added secondary benefit, but it's not our primary goal.

You are not a Chiropractor. Leave bone adjustments to them. And if a Chiropractor doesn't address the myofascial forces on a bone, and only adjusts the bone, they may not be addressing the root cause of a client's issue.

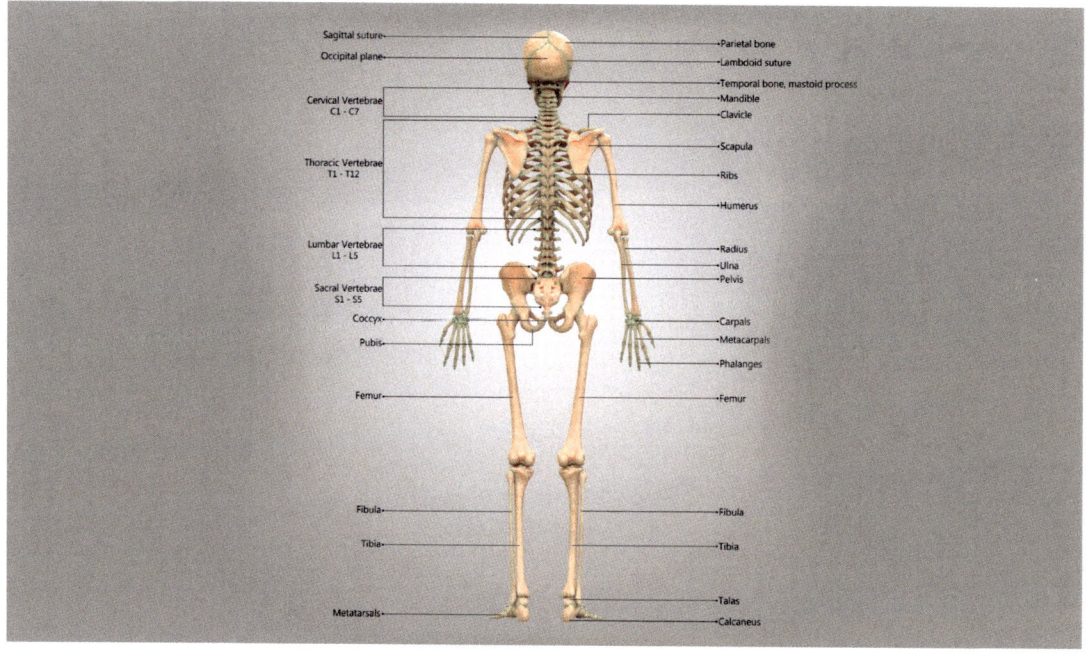

All bones are "passively" pinned and hanging in a classroom skeleton
(Image credit: Magic mine/Shutterstock.com)

NERVES

Fascia is full of nerve receptors. Some sources say fascia has about 10 times the amount of sensory nerve receptors than muscle[7]. The list of sensory receptors sounds like a cast of an Italian opera with brothers Ruffini and Pacinian, or a German opera with brothers Meissner, Merkel, and Krause.

The human body has an extraordinary ability to signal and communicate with its myriad sensory receptors[8]. Consider the incredible conduction velocity of the proprioceptors and Golgi Tendon Organ (GTO), the rapid action of the muscle spindles and cutaneous mechanoreceptors, the somewhat slower nociceptors and thermoreceptors - it is as if an incredible sensory intelligence, or "fascial intelligence" resides within the body.

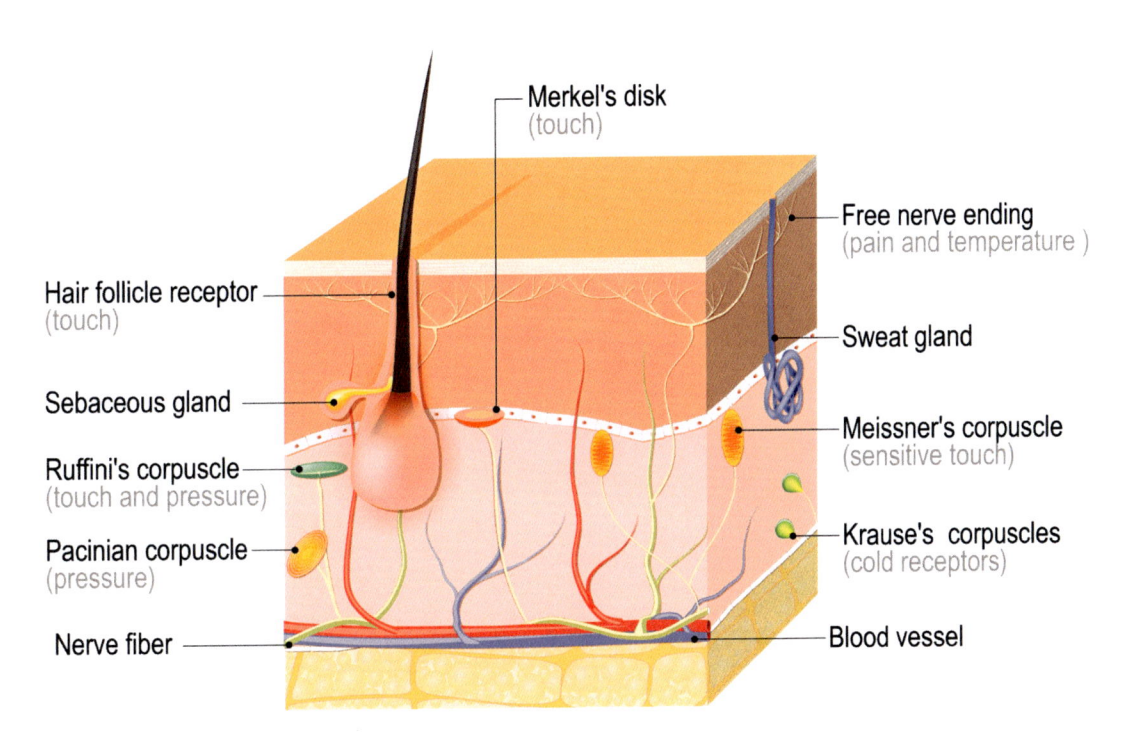

Sensory Receptors in the Skin
An "Italian and German opera cast" of various cutaneous sensory receptors
(Image credit: Designua/Shutterstock.com)

RESPECT THE DERMIS (AND EPIDERMIS AND HYPODERMIS)

Before we leave the topic of sensory receptors, especially in the skin, let's gain a deeper appreciation of this largest organ in the body. In embryologic development, the outer layer of skin forms with, and can be viewed as a *sensory extension of the brain.*

Brain, spinal cord, eyes, peripheral nervous system, and the outside layer of the skin all form in the same part of the embryo (ectoderm) to help you look for, touch, and pick up your smart phone. So let's respect the epidermis, dermis, and hypodermis.

Here is an illustration of skin layers.

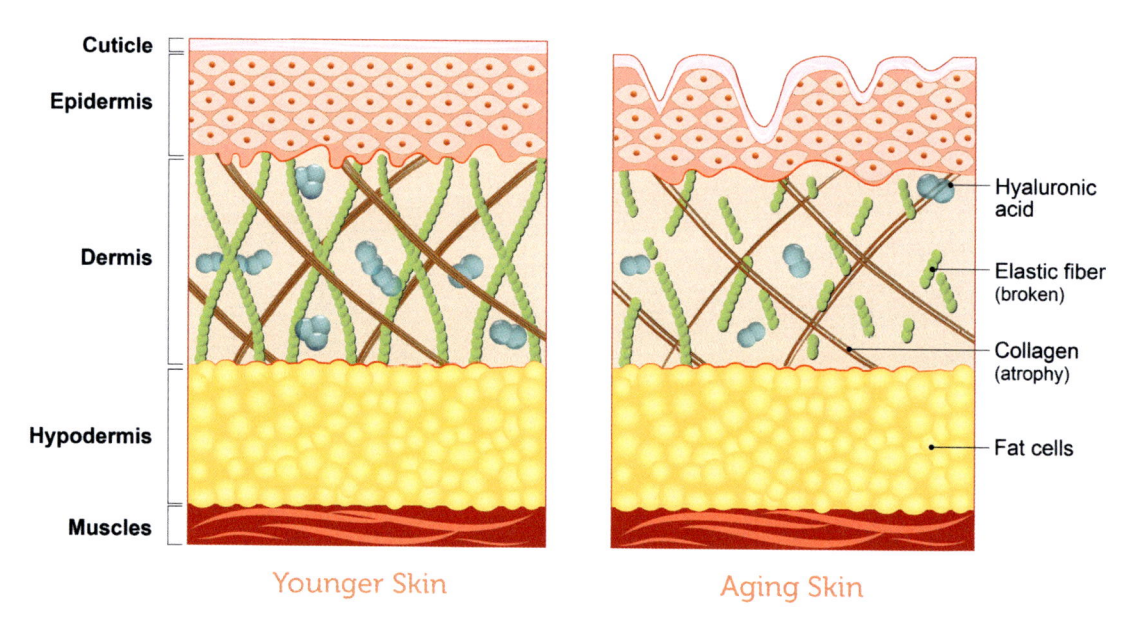

Three layers of skin: epidermis, dermis, and hypodermis; the dermis loses elasticity with age
How is the hypodermis or fat, connected to the muscle beneath it?
(Image credit: Designua/Shutterstock.com)

Aging skin shows why your aunt just got a face-lift. The figure also helps explain why working on an older adult will feel different than working on a younger adult. Aside from your aunt's vanity, let's look at the structure of skin, young or old.

Some people's skin slides and moves easily over underlying muscle. On other people it feels stuck. Right now, move and slide just the skin and fat over your forearm muscles. How did it feel? Dense, stuck, and rigid? Or slack, slick, and almost watery?

Skin, or dermis, is *tightly connected* to the looser fat beneath it, called **hypodermis**. It's also called **superficial fascia.** Depending on the text or reference it is additionally referred to as subcutaneous, subcutaneous adipose, adipose, subdermis, or tela subcutanea.

Superficial fascia or hypodermis, fat, is usually more loosely connected to the muscle layer beneath it. Hence, why it feels like you can "slide" the dermis and hypodermis over the muscle in our forearm experiment.

If you could cut away just the top dermis off of the hypodermis, which is hard to do, and cut the hypodermis away from the underlying muscle, which is easy to do, it would look like a one-piece yellow snowsuit covering the whole body (slender people have a thin snowsuit, obese people have a thick snowsuit).

Skin (epidermis and dermis) and fat (hypodermis) together create a **sensory snowsuit**. The sensory snowsuit slides over yet another wetsuit that wraps the whole body, all the muscles, like a one-piece transparent shiny unitard. This unitard covers the muscles and connective tissue of the deep fascia.

So, when you slide the skin and fat over your muscles, you are "sliding" the skin-hypodermis sensory snowsuit over the transparent, slippery unitard covering the muscles, or deep fascia.

Hypodermis or superficial fascia looks like a yellow snowsuit
(Image credit: Natalia Rapoport/Shutterstock.com)

Hypodermis or superficial fascia connects to a thin, one-piece, transparent "unitard" covering the body. The unitard covers the deep fascia muscle.
(Image credit: Jeff Holcombe/Shutterstock.com)

A Systematic Approach to Myofascial Network Release

The Fuzz Speech

A pioneer in cadaver fascial dissection is Gil Hedley, Ph.D. His website, **gilhedley.com,** shows a complete dissection of the superficial fascia "snowsuit." Dr. Hedley refers to the "unitard" beneath the superficial fascia snowsuit the "perifascia" (his word), also known as "fuzz" (his word). His The Fuzz Speech video is humorous and is a fun place to start if you wish to gain a greater understanding of fascia; it's complexity, layers, and beauty.

Why do we go into such detail about our sensory snowsuit?

- You must appreciate how the skin and its underlying fat layer provide a *global sensory network* covering the body, providing communication and instruction to deeper fascial layers, as well as communication to distant fascia.
- Understanding the function and feel of superficial fascia will make you a better therapist as you penetrate and manipulate deeper layers of fascia.

"Interstitium" – A New Organ?

Researchers at Mount Sinai-Beth Israel Medical Center in New York City used a new laser sensor to unveil fluid-filled spaces between cells, previously viewed as tightly packed connective tissue (go back and look at the blue-colored "glue" in the previous Connective Tissue graphic). Fluid between cells was known. The human body is about 60% water, one-third of which is outside cells known as interstitial fluid. What was not known was the idea of a larger connected "interstitium," fluid-filled spaces between tissue – to include below the skin's surface and surrounding muscles. Some refer to this fluid-filled highway as a new organ system. The findings have implications for cancer research and lymphatic drainage. As you massage and manipulate your client's tissue, be aware of the amazing three-dimensional structure and fluid flow beneath your hands.

Reference Scientific American, March 27, 2018, *Meet Your Interstitium, a Newfound "Organ"*

FASCIAL RESTRICTIONS

If you are healthy without disease, move properly, exercise properly, and stretch regularly – congratulations - you are probably relatively free of pain and issues.

If you are a sedentary couch potato, you are remodeling your body and will function as a sedentary couch potato. Most likely, your fascial sacks are getting glued and adhered to one another, not to mention muscle atrophy and muscle imbalance.

And if you are an athlete that engages in a repetitive activity like ultra-marathons, you are altering your fascia and creating fascial restrictions, too.

So, fascial restrictions caused by being an undercooked couch potato, or an overcooked athlete, you should know that restrictions are multi-causal. Colloquially let's call them "kinks and adhesions." A partial list may include,

- trauma
- injury
- surgery
- scar tissue
- poor posture
- improper gait
- falls
- cuts
- burns
- inflammation
- knee and hip replacements
- breast augmentation
- inactivity
- improperly loaded repetitive activity
- too much overload
- sitting all day looking at your smart phone in cervical flexion

In Ruth Duncan's book *Myofascial Release*, she describes a myofascial restriction as,

> "Each layer (sac of muscle) should glide over its neighbor; however, when a restriction is present, the gliding process is hindered and in some cases the layers become completely glued together where fascia's ground substance has solidified and the collagen and elastin fibers have become stuck together, rather like Velcro[9]."

When these restrictions occur, myofascial release can help clear them.

CLEARING FASCIAL RESTRICTIONS

There are many excellent techniques to help clear myofascial restrictions, ranging for example, from a "microscopic" manipulation of a deep spinal rotator trigger point to globally addressing fascial networks through stretch therapy.

Not all techniques work on all people and on all restrictions. Sometimes you need to apply different techniques. Sometimes stretch therapy is best; sometimes manual manipulation is best.

How is the massage school student or practicing therapist to know which technique is appropriate?

Those of you with a solid understanding of gait, postural, neural, structural, and movement assessments to identify the root cause of a fascial restriction should be commended and probably have an idea of what technique should be used for a situation.

Most likely, however, most massage therapists have yet to gain these skills; not to mention the cost, years of study, and years of practice it would take to refine such knowledge and experience.

In the meantime, for the rest of us massage therapists, the goals of this 3DB technique are to:

- give you a systematic routine that works the whole body,
- clear out fascial restrictions using a variety of techniques and optimal body positioning,
- manipulate myofascial meridians, and
- fill a typical 60- to 90-minute massage session.

If you follow the 3DB routine, you may be pleasantly surprised that you can resolve a good number of your client's issues. Not all, but a lot.

MASSAGE THERAPY AS A BUSINESS

Foremost, you need to monetize your practice. You need to have your clients appreciate the benefit of your work and say things like, "Amazing! That's the first *real* massage I've ever had."

That is feedback I have received more than once, and I want you to receive the same feedback. You can have all the social media, advertising, and websites you want; never forget "word of mouth is the best advertising[10]."

Once you get a client from whatever source, you need to keep them and have them come back for more. As they say in acting, you are only as good as your last performance. Your clients are paying a lot of money; you better give them good service and good results. You want regular clients who return week after week and become a word-of-mouth referral source.

Referrals and client retention happen when a technique *works*. Your client should have a **positive therapeutic outcome** after the session, that night, the next day, etc. Meaning, you resolved or lessened their issue or pain. Secondly, the technique needs to *feel good* and be *effective*. Remember, our goal is to build repeat clientele.

If your present technique, assuming it has some therapeutic validity, causes the client to flinch and withdraw from a painful stimulus - whether it's from your "iron" thumb on a trigger point, or your "howitzer" elbow in their back - most likely you'll eventually if not immediately drive the client away.

CONDITION MANAGEMENT VS. THERAPEUTIC CHANGE

I love golf. Not to play, but what it does to people. Golfers may play one or several rounds, only to come back the following week seeking relief for their painful lower back. That's okay, and it's not a bad business model.

So, in our golf player example, you are attempting to manage a recurring condition week after week. This is called **condition management**[11]. You won't solve their issue, but your client should feel a positive therapeutic effect one to three days after the session.

Let's take another example of a client who survived an unbelievable 18-inch blood clot, leaving her arm dysfunctional and edematous (swollen with lymph). Her doctors thought she would never regain full function of her arm. Neither did I.

It scared the heck out of me to work on her. At the time, I was developing the 3-Dimensional Bodywork routine. She agreed to be one of my experimental prototypes - or "guinea pigs." This was a case where I thought I would be doing, at best, condition management.

Not knowing how to approach her, I just started doing my routine, week after week. She came back week after week because she knew she was experiencing *positive therapeutic outcomes* - her condition was improving and discomfort was lessening.

After using the 3DB routine on her upper body, she regained more function in about six months, then started working out doing a suspension trainer routine I had developed that focused on stretching and activating fascial networks (Appendix A).

After more months of therapy and exercise - in less than 18 months - she had miraculously regained mostly full function of her arm. This case of condition management became a better case of **therapeutic change**. Therapeutic change does not happen quickly, it may take months or years.

Rule of Thumb, you will know therapeutic change is possible:

"If the client reports improvement immediately after the massage and at least 50% of the improvement remains 24 to 48 hours later, the compensation pattern is reversible[12]."

In the hierarchy of outcomes, therapeutic change is our preferred goal followed by condition management. If these two outcomes are not possible, then **palliative** care is generally a nice safe option.

A lot of Swedish massage sessions are palliative. They feel good; they reduce stress; they have some therapeutic value, and you may pay a lot of money for one at a fancy spa. The value of a Swedish massage in our industry is undisputed; it makes up most of the revenue in massage businesses.

The 3DB technique you will learn, however, is for a smaller subset of the population. This method and technique are *fundamentally therapeutic*, not necessarily palliative.

That said, one client stated, "I have to drive home under the influence of massage" because she was so relaxed. Feeling deeply relaxed is a nice side benefit of the routine.

> The routine you will learn is for clients seeking **condition management**, and/or **therapeutic change**. A palliative sense of relaxation and stress reduction is a nice side benefit.

In summary, 3DB is designed to work, feel good, and keep them coming back for more - maybe you can become that word-of-mouth referral therapist known for resolving pain and discomfort.

Myofascia in action
(Image courtesy of Tama Starczak)

CHAPTER 2

WHAT IS THE 3-DIMENSIONAL BODYWORK APPROACH?

The 3DB technique is a type of myofascial "release," MFR. (See discussion at end of this chapter regarding "release.")

You might ask, "why is this 3DB fascia technique better than the dog's breakfast?" Especially when there is a ton of fascia techniques and devices in the market today – Self Myofascial Release (SMR), fascial stretch, Fascial Stretch Therapy™, Fascial Distortion Model®, Myofascial Trigger Points, Active Release Technique, Myofascial Release Technique, etc. There are even complete catalogs on fascial release devices you can buy.

You can spend a lifetime learning these techniques and acquiring all the certifications, many with real benefit and validity.

The primary goal of this book and course is simply to give you a repeatable, effective routine for the massage school student, or a practicing massage therapist who wants to freshen up their skills to include a more three-dimensional massage experience for their client. And maybe become the referral "go-to" massage therapist because you deliver an efficacious form of therapy that eliminates or reduces most pain most of the time.

Let's take the title of this book and dissect it. ***3-Dimensional Bodywork: A Systematic Approach to Myofascial Network Release for Massage Therapists.***

- **3-Dimensional** means you will place the body and limbs in optimal positions for massage and stretch.
- **Bodywork** means more than just the typical effleurage-petrissage-focused massage; it implies stretch, high friction, cross-fiber, length of fiber, shearing, and torsional tissue manipulation discussed later.
- **A Systematic Approach** is self-defining. The goal here is to give you a "system," meaning a step-by-step, repeatable routine that's color-coded for ease of learning different positions (lower supine, upper supine, side lying, etc.).
- **Myofascial** refers to muscle and connective tissue, which as discussed earlier, should be viewed as inseparable.
- **Network** refers to Tom Myers' Anatomy Trains®, the 12 or so organizing myofascial meridians. His meridians give us a diagnostic tool to look for distant or referred discomfort. This technique does not require you to know or memorize these myofascial meridians, but it will help if you take the time to familiarize yourself with them.
- **Release** means we want to anatomically (neurologically and mechanically) relax and/ or attempt to break up fascial restrictions.

- **For Massage Therapists**, the technique is a massage; best experienced using draping only in a typical 60- to 90-minute session. Use of this technique implies you are studying to become certified, or already are certified by your state to legally perform massage. After all, you will be placing draped clients in various three-dimensional positions for optimal manipulation. A high degree of trust is implicit between client and therapist. If you are personal trainer and stretch therapist, you should go to massage school first to use this technique.

MECHANICAL AND ANATOMICAL

On the Therapeutic Massage Tree[13], showing branches of different massage techniques, this technique is on the Connective Tissue Branch. This branch is mechanical; you are physically breaking up adhesions or releasing fascial sacks from one another. Other techniques on the connective tissue branch include Rolfing, Structural Integration, and Myofascial Release.

Mechanical techniques also include friction, credited to Dr. James Cyriax[14], which provides shear force to the tissue, usually applied transverse to the muscle, or cross-fiber.

The 3-Dimensional Bodywork technique is anatomical. Know your muscle origins and insertions and brush up on kinesiology to know muscle actions, too.

Knowledge of kinesiology will help you understand how individual muscles connect into the myofascial meridians. You can blindly follow the 3DB routine and be okay without this knowledge, but you will be a much better therapist with a solid knowledge of muscles, bones, and bony landmarks.

To re-emphasize, the Connective Tissue Branch and the 3DB technique are mechanical.

The Connective Tissue Branch is separate from the Energy Branch, a branch that often focuses on psycho-biological states of vibration, harmony, or resonance. Acknowledge the emotional and psychological state of a client, but a client's "energy" is not the primary focus of the technique. Depending on a client's neurological state, they may feel varying sensitivity to depth of pressure, or frictional glide.

Also, you are not seeking extended multi-minute holds in this technique, nor are you attempting to achieve or focus on "vibrational resonance" with your client (although some clients may feel this as a byproduct of your work).

Remember, your goal is to *free up fascial sacks and break up adhesions* like a good body mechanic.

Image credit: Ivan Kulikov/Shutterstock.com

Myofascial "Release"

We mentioned Myofascial Release (MFR) is a type of massage that belongs on the connective tissue branch, where we are **MECHANICALLY** breaking up restrictions or adhesions and, thus, "releasing" them.

Are we really? Talk to anyone after a palmar fibromatosis Dupuytren's Contracture operation (which truly does release a clawed hand). And ask if any manual therapist's myofascial release work could ever break up, free up, or release post-operative scar tissue. Maybe, if the forces exerted were great enough and held long enough – so much so the application of force would most likely be intolerable. Manual therapies on such scar fascial restrictions usually have limited effect. So, when we say we are freeing up a fascial adhesion or restriction, we may not be mechanically breaking up anything.

"Hold it," you say, we often can feel muscle or tissue relax and "melt" under our manipulation – maybe not tough scar tissue, but other muscle and connective tissue. What's happening with all that myofascial plasticity going on under our hands?

I prefer to use the term "release" loosely, not in its literal sense to "set free," but rather a **NEURAL-REFLEXIVE RESPONSE** to our manipulation - which turns our hypertonic myofascia back to normal tone.

We are mechanically applying forces of tension (stretch), torsion, shear, and compression. We may to some degree free up one fascial sack from another; but we are often not breaking up adhesions mechanically; rather, we are causing mechanoreceptors and nerves – and, hence, myofascia - to reflexively relax.

Because "release" is so ingrained in massage school vernacular, and is embodied in the phrase "Myofascial Release," I will continue to use that phrase instead of a more cumbersome, "Myofascial Neural-Reflexive Response," which I believe is the more accurate description of the effect of our bodywork.

Schleip, R. (2003). *Fascial plasticity – a new neurobiological explanation, Part I, Journal of Bodywork and Movement Therapies*, 7(1), 11-19, January 2003

Schleip, R. (2003). *Fascial plasticity – a new neurobiological explanation, Part II, Journal of Bodywork and Movement Therapies*, 7(2), 104-116, April 2003

CHAPTER 3
HALLMARKS OF THE ROUTINE

In the Myofascia section, we discussed the concept of a muscle being an integrated, inseparable myofascial structure, with the epimysium as the outer fascial covering. For our purposes, let's refer to muscles and their fascial covering as **_myofascial sack_**, or simply a **_fascial sack_**. Myers says, "there really is only one muscle; it just hangs around in 600 or more fascial pockets[15]."

Let's take the quadriceps thigh muscles as an example. The fascial sack of the vastus lateralis is next to the fascial sack of the vastus intermedius, that is next to the fascial sack of the rectus femoris; and as the vastus lateralis wraps around the back of the leg, it is also next to the fascial sack of the biceps femoris. The iliotibial band slides on top of various parts of these fascial sacks, with the whole lot inside a bigger fascial sack that raps the whole body like a wet suit, the unitard discussed earlier.

Simply, muscles can be viewed as fascial sacks next to other fascial sacks all wrapped in a bigger sack (see the photos below.)

You will have a greater intuitive grasp of the 3DB routine if you first view the body as one big sack divided up into smaller sacks, and then view these sacks as being connected to other sacks and fascia, which makes up various myofascial meridians running through the body.

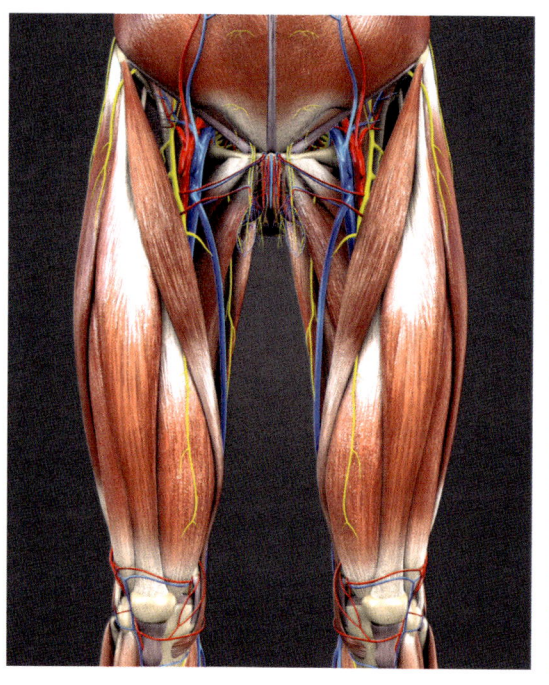

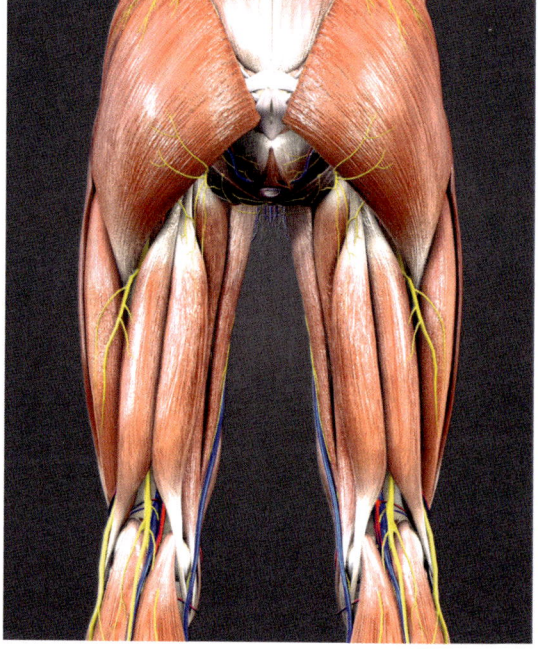

Right: posterior view of "fascial sacks" of the thigh - left: anterior view of quadriceps "fascial sacks"

The technique and routine, therefore, needs to:

- free up an individual sack
- free up one fascial sack from another
- free up and relax sacks along myofascial meridians
- free up adhesions and restrictions wherever they may be

HALLMARKS OF THE 3DB METHOD AND ROUTINE:

- **Three Dimensions** - Place limbs and position the body for optimal manipulation. Sometimes you want the fascial sacks in slack; sometimes you want fascial sacks in tension.
- **Slack** – Position the fascial sacks to make them soft and pliable. Slack muscles allow you to more deeply penetrate tissue to break up adhesions; and allow greater twisting and torsion of multiple fascial sacks.
- **Tension** - Stretching muscles puts the muscle in tension, which helps the muscle regain its proper extensibility, and is another way to help release fascial sacks.
- **Multiple Positions** - Manipulate a given fascial sack from various positions, some causing slack, and some causing tension. Each position will feel different to the client and have a different therapeutic effect.
- **Torsion** – Release fascial sacks from one another by torsion or twisting. Always think, work tissue "deeply" without using deep tissue massage techniques.
- **Shear** – Release adhesions by using transverse cross-fiber friction strokes on long fascial sack groups, for example, the erector spinae group.
- **Compression** – Also release adhesions and relax muscle by using longitudinal friction strokes along fascial sack fibers; again, the erector spinae group is a good example. This stroke is also good as you separate "valleys" between fascial sacks. Also, remember that compression with passive joint movement creates a friction stroke[16].
- **Petrissage** – a combination of vertical "lift and twist," petrissage is one of the great massage manipulations; when in doubt, petrissage or knead tissue like dough, especially if you are marking time tying to remember where you are in the routine.
- **Peaks** - In general, stay off peaks (ridges), which are usually muscle and tendon over bone. It doesn't feel good and hurts to compress peaks.
- **Valleys** - In general, seek valleys (visual or palpable grooves), which are usually separations between fascial sacks. It feels good to separate these sacks.
- **Gravity** –Pull and manipulate slack tissue against the force of gravity, typically by reaching on the opposite side of the body; for example, from the "sleepy" or side lying positions, vertically pull and shear hip muscles that tie into the greater trochanter.
- **Golgi Tendon Organ (GTO)** – GTOs are usually found in the muscle-tendon interface, often near where the tendon connects to bone. Using firm but gentle compression or shearing of the GTO can have an effect of relaxing and releasing the entire muscle.

- **High Friction Glide** – skin on skin contact is essential for shearing one sack of fascia off another. Use a high friction glide to reduce excessive skin burning sensation. The more lubricant, the more the session shifts from myofascial release to feeling like a traditional Swedish massage.
- **Slow** – Take your time when performing any of the above strokes or movements. Fascial sacks soften with a slow application of force. They harden with a rapid application of force. Allow the tissue to "invite you in" (see following discussion on Tango).
- **Four-to-8 Count** - About 4-8 seconds is the perfect tempo for massage strokes, about two bars of spa music or soft rock. Allow time for the slowest afferent neurons to signal the brain. So, find some old school 1970's Barry White and you and your client can get into a nice parasympathetic groove. Mosby tells us, "Generally, a compressive force need not be sustained for longer than 15 seconds to achieve results[17]." That said, sometimes a very slow 30- to 60-second high-friction stroke is optimal for fascial release.

Bottom line: don't be in a hurry.

TANGO

Earlier we mentioned 3DB is mechanical and anatomical, and that you should view yourself as a good body mechanic. We also mentioned the incredible number of sensory receptors in the body and the concept of the skin and superficial fascia being a sensory snowsuit, or "global sensory network."

As you allow the tissue to "invite you in," as you feel the resistant end-point of tissue and joints, as you work superficial fascia, as you work more deeply into the layers and separations within deep fascia, you will do an **Intuitive Tango Dance** with your client.

Feel and honor the unique resistance of your client's tissue. Just like Tango, suggest the next move to your partner, don't force it. So if you wish to call this achieving harmonic resonance with your client or feeling your client's energy, feel free to do so. Just because you are a good body mechanic doesn't mean you can't "dance" with your client. You can learn technique, but you have to develop your own intuition. You will develop intuition and perfect this technique through practice.

Develop an intuitive feel of your client's tissue. Like the Tango, suggest the next move, don't force it; let the tissue invite you in
(Image credit: Tutti Frutti/Shutterstock.com)

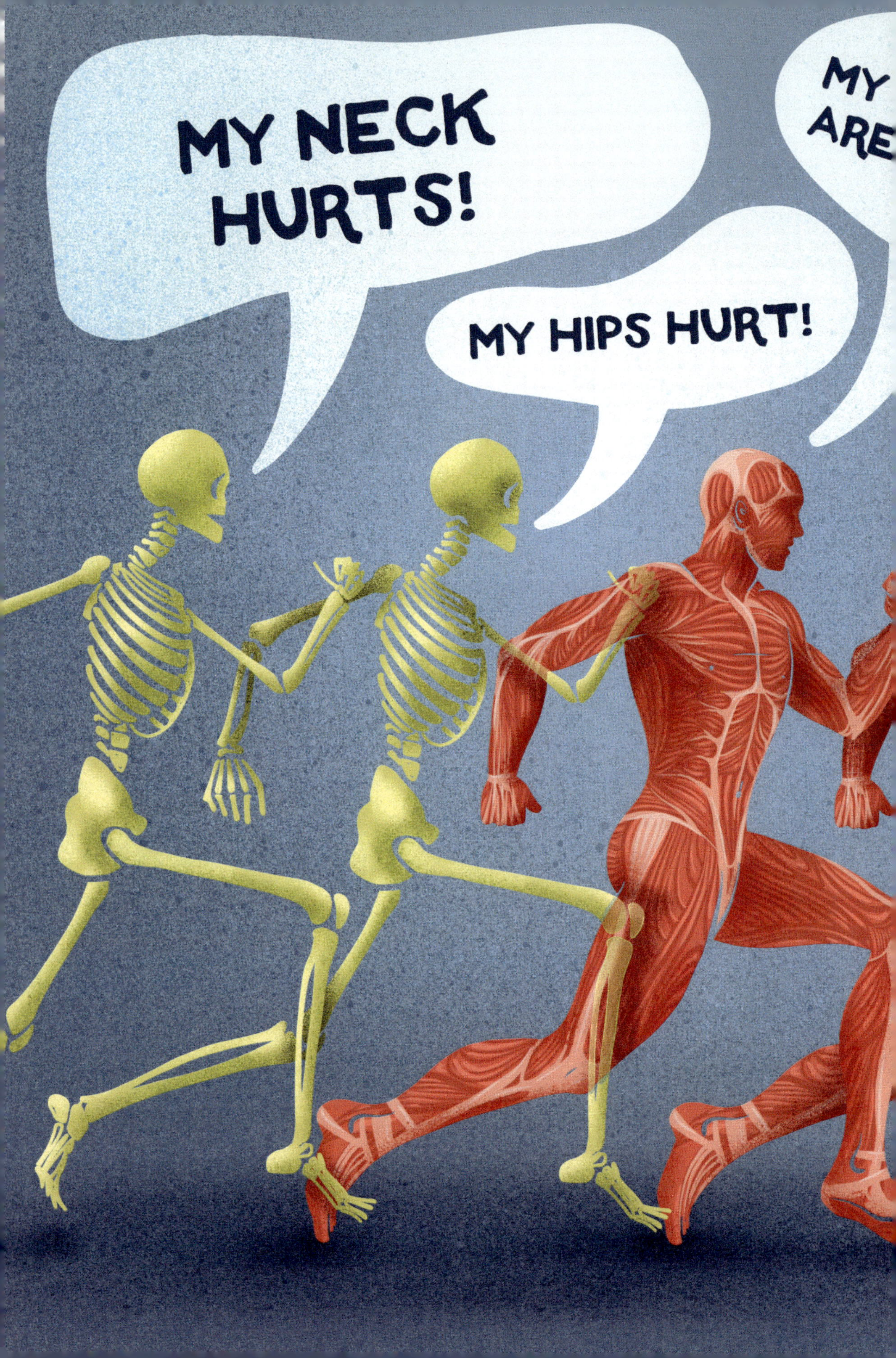
MY NECK HURTS!
MY HIPS HURT!

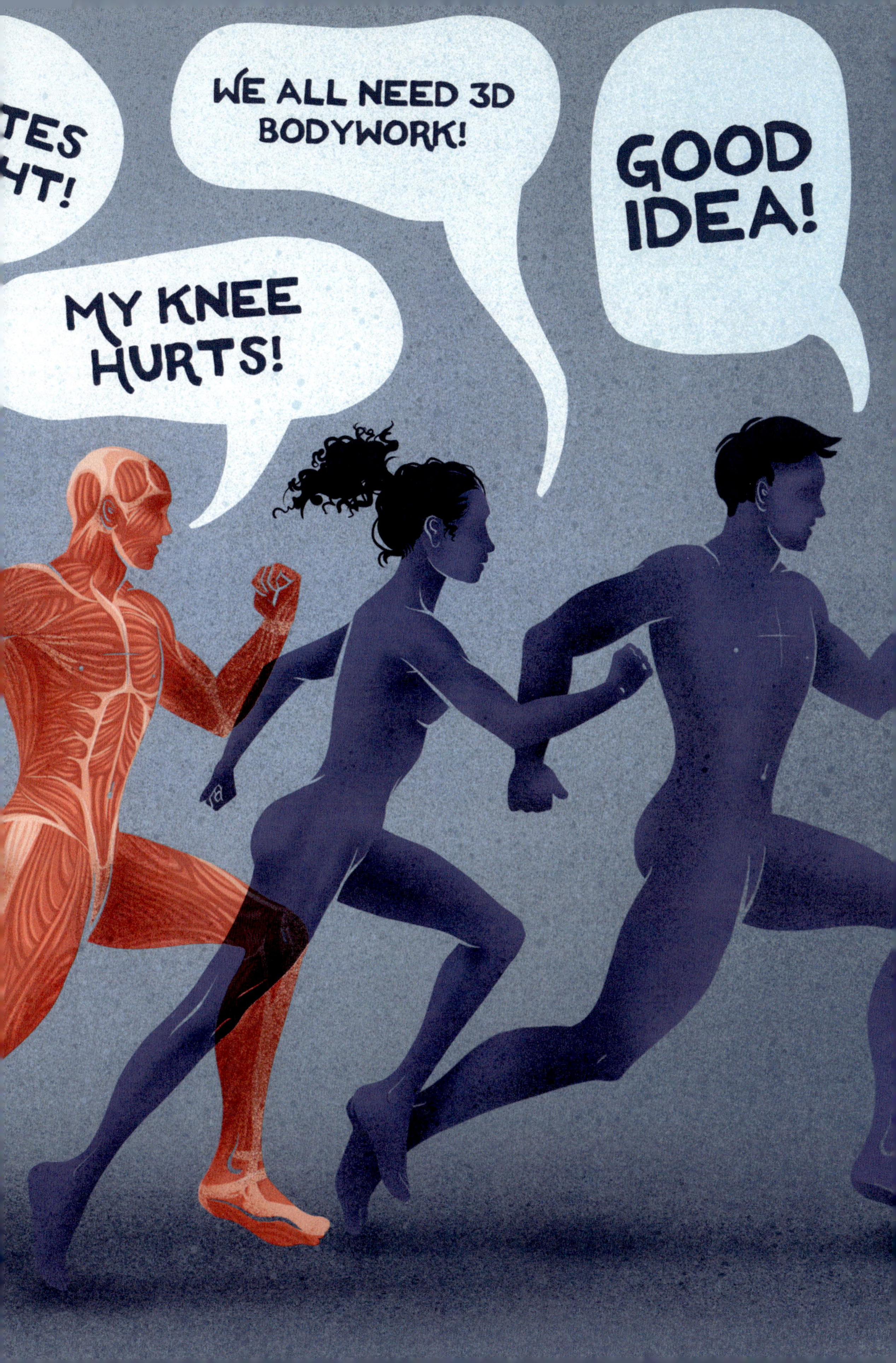
MY KNEE HURTS!
WE ALL NEED 3D BODYWORK!
GOOD IDEA!

CHAPTER 4
TYPES OF CLIENTS

Where would you use this technique? Consider that you are placing body and limbs in optimal three-dimensional positions. You will most likely be using draping since the client is there for a 60- to 90-minute massage. Put those two facts together and the client may have his or her leg splayed out while draped.

This technique is **not appropriate at a spa**, for example, when "first-time, only-time" clients are seeking a nice traditional, palliative Swedish massage.

This technique is appropriate for:

- Clients who are comfortable with bodywork and massage,
- Regular clients where trust and rapport are already established,
- Clients who need a more therapeutic massage,
- Clients who are coming to you with specific pain or discomfort.

Since you may be working near sensitive areas with the body optimally three-dimensionally positioned, **always have the client disrobe to the level of their comfort.**

To protect yourself and the client, use the following forms upon a client's first visit:

- **First, take SOAP notes** (Subjective, Objective, Assessment, Plan), focusing on what the client tells you about their "Subjective" issue or health history, and what you "Objectively" observe. This is a good way to establish rapport as you LISTEN.
- **Explain the routine's focus** on myofascial meridians and myofascial release, and tell clients what to expect from the technique. To help you **manage expectations**, use the **3DB Expectations sheet** (Appendix C) to discuss and explain the technique; the sheet can also be used as a marketing tool to describe 3DB.
- **Have clients sign a Waiver and Release** (Appendix D), which should be standard industry practice. It's a bit tongue-in-cheek but tell clients they can expect one of three outcomes: "you will make them better, there will be no change, or you will make them worse." That's a way of emphasizing the client's **assumption of risk** when they undertake any form of therapy or bodywork.
- **Have clients sign an Informed Consent** (Appendix E). Read each paragraph to the client to make sure they completely understand the routine works best when only draping is used, but it can be done at any level of draping, underwear, sports attire, or even clothed depending on the client's comfort and modesty level. It is imperative the client feels **secure and relaxed** for the technique to work. Also emphasize the client can **stop the massage at any time** if they feel uncomfortable – and make clear they should **immediately verbalize this request** to adjust the level of clothing or draping and continue with the session or stop the session entirely.

- **Have the client sign a separate checklist** (Appendix F) - Depending on the client's issue and therapeutic need, especially if the therapeutic need implies working near sensitive areas such as the groin or breast tissue, you and the client should mutually agree to specific therapy, discussing permissions, boundaries, and consent.

Feel free to edit these forms to suit your practice. When in doubt, have a lawyer review them for proper wording.

CHAPTER 5

EQUIPMENT AND ROUTINE POSITIONS

The 3-Dimensional Bodywork routine is self-defining; it works tissue in three dimensions.

You will place the body and limbs in optimal positions for stretch and massage. You will need proper draping and bolsters. Here are some ideas of what works well. Use any comparable product you prefer.

DRAPING

Any sheet will work, but sheets with some stretch like those made from bamboo or beech (pictured) work best. Draping with stretch allows you or the client to hold a tighter drape around sensitive areas, for example the inguinal crease where the top of the thigh meets the torso. You will also need a bath towel and several smaller hand towels to cover sensitive areas.

GLIDE

Some of the routine (and even all the routine) can be done skin on skin with no lubricant. In some cases, high-friction glide makes skin on skin contact more pleasant and effective. Massage oil will not work. Use minimum amounts of a good high-quality lotion to get optimal high-friction glide. You can also use a specific high-friction glide like Rock Rub® for certain local applications.

OPTIONAL RUNNING SHORTS

It is extremely important to have the client feel safe, comfortable, relaxed, and secure. The routine is best done with draping only, but for first-time clients, suggest they keep underwear on, or use a pair of running shorts. Running shorts that open at the side with built-in liners work best. You may wish to keep a pair of medium, large, and extra-large on hand just in case.

BOLSTERS

You will need a standard pillow for the client's head in the supine position, especially for those with head forward posture. If it's comfortable for the client, encourage him or her to not use a pillow to keep spine and head in alignment. You will need a pillow, however, for the client's head in the side lying position. You will also need a larger bolster for the side lying position, where the client is on their side, bottom leg straight, and top leg over the bolster. The bolster should be long enough to support the bent top leg and help cover breast tissue. A king-size extra-firm pillow works well.

Lastly, you will need a smaller bolster or small firm pillow to support the hip in the Sims' position (lateral recumbent position, named after the gynecologist J. Marion Sims[18]). Since some people fall asleep with one arm behind or under them and one leg bent in this position, we can use "sleepy" position as an apt shorthand descriptor. For clarity, colored-coded pictures of each of the five positions used in the routine with bolstering are shown. Also shown are common bolsters for knees or ankles. Half bolsters and three-quarter bolsters work well; these bolsters are shown on top of draping for illustrative purposes only.

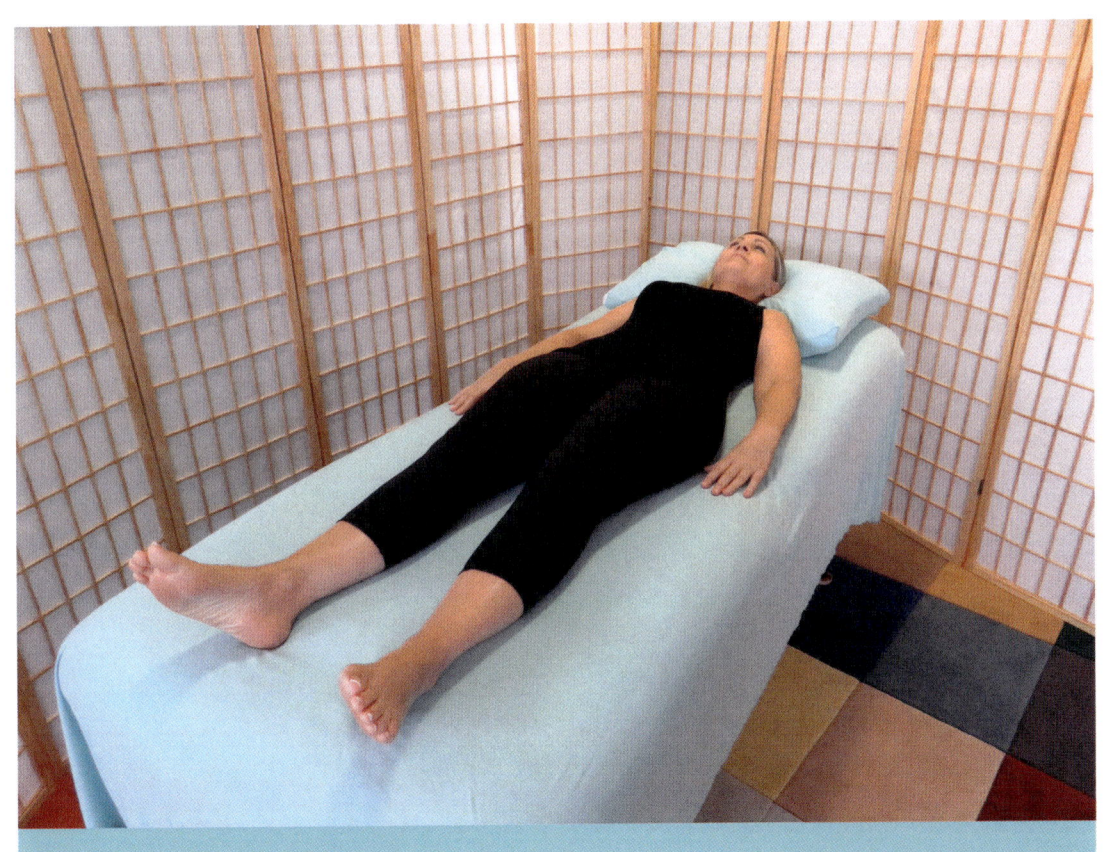

1. Lower Supine (LS) | TURQUOISE-COLORED ROUTINE
Note: use of pillow is optional.

2. Upper Supine (US) | SALMON-COLORED ROUTINE
Note: use bolster under knees to relieve lower back pressure. Use of pillow is optional.

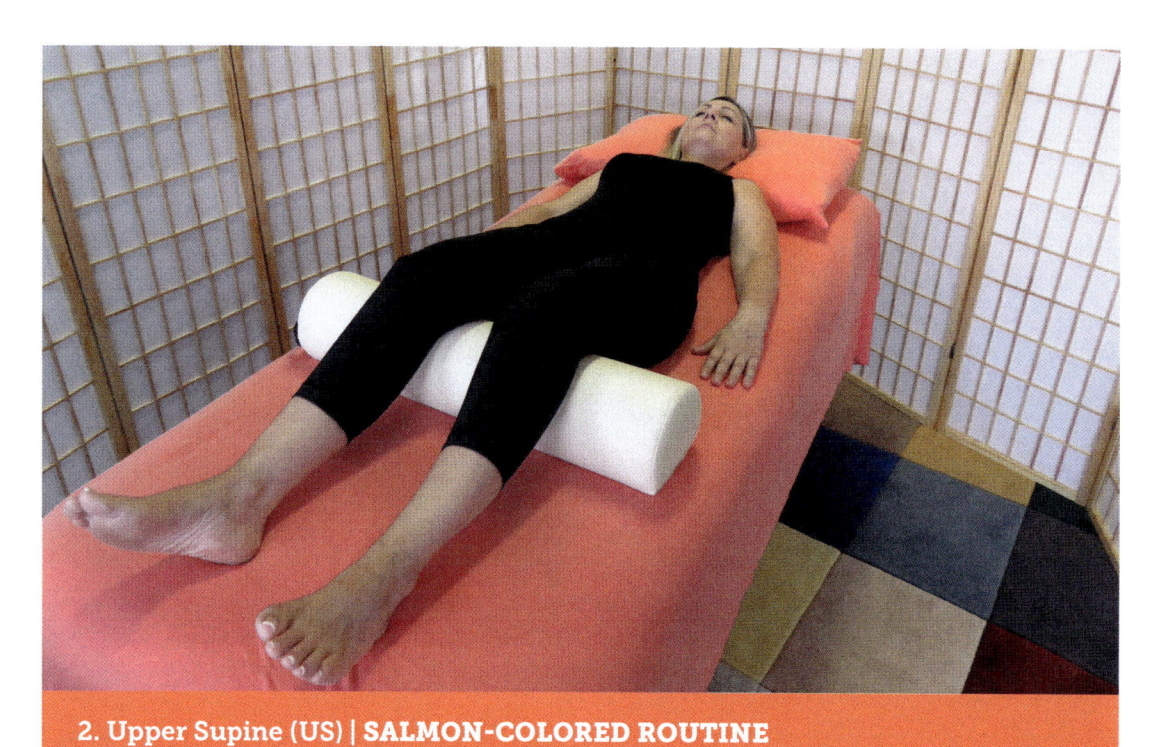

3. Side Lying (SL) | SAGE-COLORED ROUTINE
Note: keep torso stacked on its side, not rotated forward.

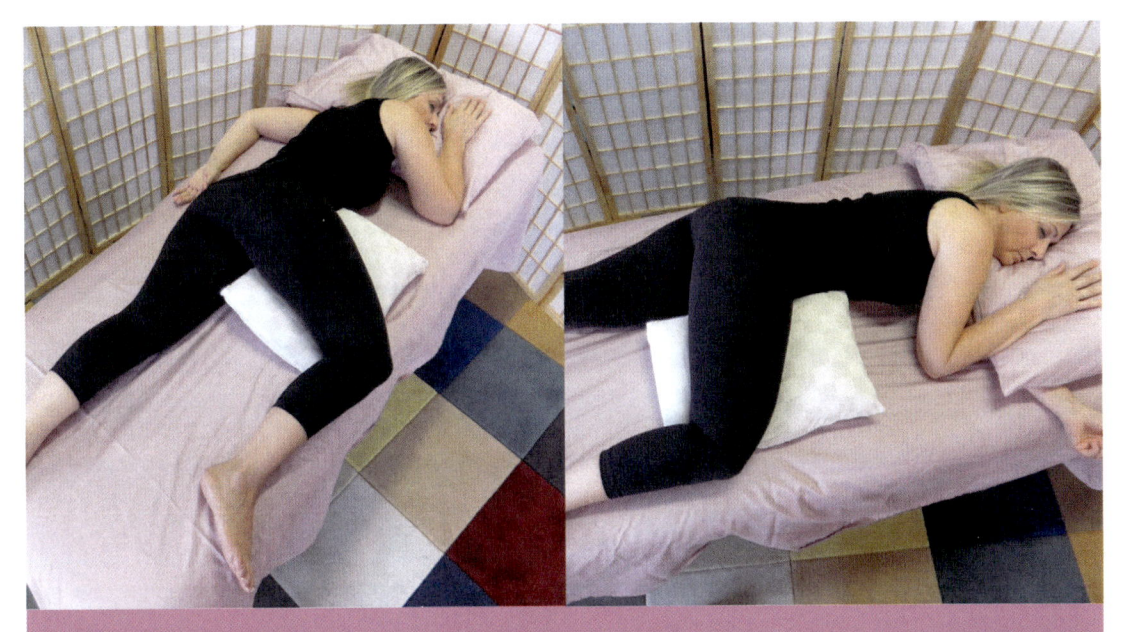

4. Sims' Lateral Recumbent (SLR) | **LAVENDER-COLORED ROUTINE**
Note: the head is rotated relative to the spine. If a cervical "kink" develops, you may have the client put their arm under them (see the right-hand image) not behind them (as in the left-hand image). In both positions, the body is rotated forward, not stacked as in the Side Lying position.

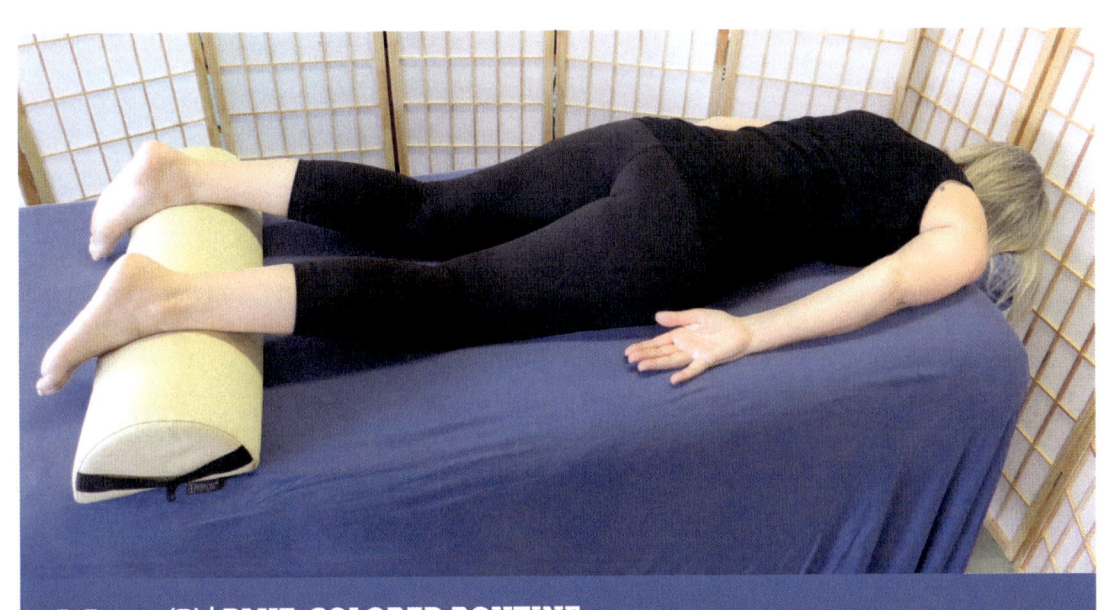

5. Prone (P) | **BLUE-COLORED ROUTINE**
Note: use a bolster under the ankles for leg comfort and to relieve pressure. Also use a multi-positional face cradle if possible, to accommodate cervical comfort for a variety of clients.

A Systematic Approach to Myofascial Network Release

CHAPTER 6
CASE STUDIES: WHEN IS THIS TECHNIQUE APPLICABLE?

Whenever I learned a technique, or read a book on bodywork, or came across some new device, I came away with a sense the inventors, creators, or proponents were trying to promote their "latest and greatest snake oil that will cure all ills." But can they really?

This routine can't cure all ills either. The following case studies will help guide you in your decision-making process on when to apply this technique.

CASE STUDY 1 – FUNCTIONAL (SOFT TISSUE) DEVIATIONS

A very active, athletic client in his 70's who had been previously bow-legged with a lifelong externally rotated knee, like a cowboy who had ridden horse from Texas to Montana all his life, came in with a new knee replacement.

The surgeon had given him a wonderful new right knee that was now *perfectly aligned*, with his knee facing *perfectly forward*.

Guess what? The new orientation of his fascial nets and resulting tightness of his fascial sacks caused considerable pain in the right side of his body and pain in his hip joint. The client's new structurally deviated knee caused a **Functional Deviation**, or deviation in his soft tissue fascial sacks.

I spent about a 60-minute session doing the 3-Dimensional Bodywork routine, focusing just on his right leg, buttock and back, and the client felt immediate relief after the session. (Teaching point: 3DB can be applied to the whole body or just part of the body if the client's issue is localized and obvious.)

Did I completely solve his problem? No. He is a work in progress but given the Rule of Thumb presented earlier regarding Therapeutic Change, he is a good candidate. And he is also a good candidate for word of mouth referrals – the session felt good and provided immediate relief and benefit.

> Soft tissue functional deviations usually respond well to this routine and technique.

CASE STUDY 2 – STRUCTURAL DEVIATIONS

People with scoliosis typically have discomfort issues as the battle between short-tight muscles and long-taut muscles rages in their back. One client came to me with an extraordinary 60-degree scoliosis of her spine. She was athletic, active, played golf and, amazingly, came in with a relatively minor complaint of discomfort in her compressed waist side. We did a quick massage on her obliques along with a Fascial Stretch Therapy™ side-lying stretch, and she felt much better.

Was I ever going to correct her? No. She had a ***Structural Deviation***, meaning a deformity with permanent bony changes.

> Structural Deviations will probably not respond well to this routine and technique; although, at best, the technique might provide some temporary relief.

CASE STUDY 3 – MYOFASCIAL NETWORK-BASED MOVEMENT EXERCISES MAY WORK BETTER THAN THERAPY

As a trainer and strength and conditioning specialist, I've come across some interesting cases; for example, complications from heart surgery leaving a client's shoulder dysfunctional because of damage to the brachial nerve complex, coupled with previous injuries to include a full thickness supraspinatus tear, atrophy of the infraspinatus, full-thickness tear of the subscapularis, degenerative glenoid labrum, and cephalad migration of the humeral head - oh, and let's also include osteoarthritis and bursitis.

I had no idea how to rehabilitate this complex of a shoulder issue, so I simply applied basic principles of myofascial network-based movement preparation, two routines found in Appendix A and B (feel free to recommend these to clients and trainers you may know).

After a few months, the myriad connections of his fascial networks ***self-organized*** and it seemed as if his fascial nets wove themselves back together like the ***warp and weft of a fabric***. My client has regained so much shoulder function, he is now breaking personal bests, lifting more now at age 72 than at any other time in his lifelong pursuit of weightlifting.

Massage and stretch in this case might have helped relieve some discomfort, but it would not have helped my client regain function of his shoulder.

> Proper myofascial network-based movement and exercise is often required to regain function; massage therapy, while palliative, may not help certain cases.

The fields of therapy and training are very humbling. We would be remiss to take credit for all our client's success. Many times, all we can do is provide an evidence-informed formulaic input, or guess, and recognize that,

> The client's body is much more intelligent than the therapist.

Never forget, either in therapy or training,

> Provide the appropriate input, exercise or therapy, and observe how the client's body intelligently self-organizes and begins to heal (or correct) itself.

CASE STUDY 4 – ASSESSMENTS MAY FOOL YOU

Look at the following pictures of a Pilates instructor. Let's call her "Miss Symmetric."

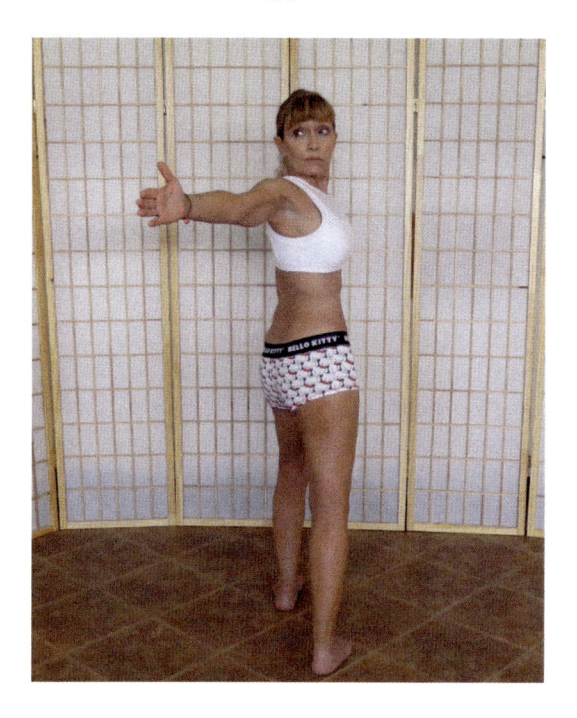

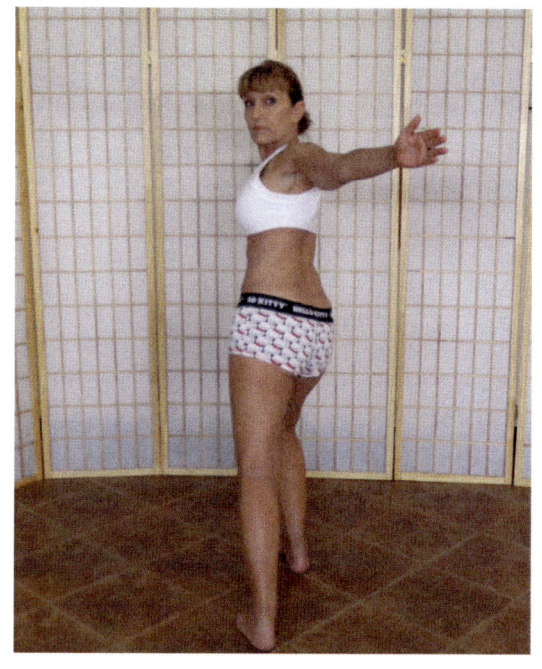

Now look at the next set of pictures I call "Mr. Joke of a Human Being." This guy is so asymmetrical it is embarrassing to look at him. He is me.

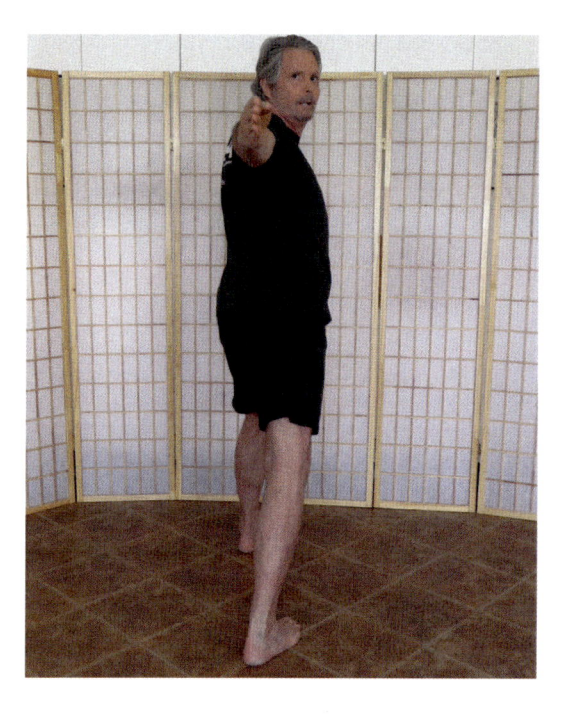

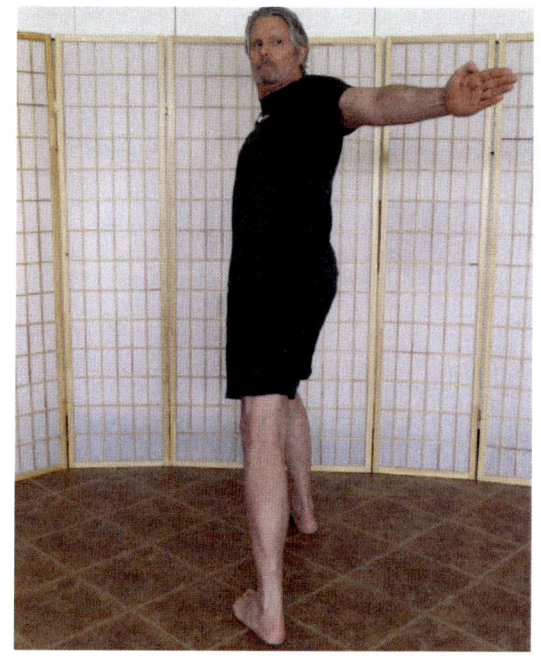

So from an assessment test, if you were a massage therapist, and I came in as a first time client, you may immediately assume I need about a year's worth of your best skills as a therapist to correct this one transverse asymmetry issue, and I'm sure you can find many more asymmetries. Whereby I should become a multi-year regular client to correct this "joke of an asymmetrical human being," probably enough years to put your kids through college.

But the truth is, I am relatively free of any issue. I was, however, a starboard oarsman in college on a competitive team, and between the ages of 18- to 22-years-old I baked into my body an asymmetry of always pulling very hard on an oar from my left. (Rowing starboard always felt comfortable to me, even as a freshman, so maybe I was "genetically asymmetric" before I started.)

Therefore, if you take me to my *limits* of my transverse fascial networks and structure, I have some definite asymmetries. However, *within a normal range of motion of my fascial networks* - at least for me - I am very functional and symmetric, with no pain or perceived range of motion limitations.

Like the scoliosis case that was mostly free of pain and issues, her body was very smart and self-organized as she adapted to her structural deviation through life.

Similarly, my body adapted to whatever structural deviation was baked into it genetically or was baked into it through habituation or activity.

The human body is an infinitely complex, marvelously designed miracle. Take a cadaver dissection course, preferably with a fresh, not preserved, cadaver and see for yourself. One stunning observation of the eight cadavers I saw being dissected was the variation of structural and fascial differences *among the different cadavers, and* **between each side** of each cadaver.

So, don't assume the results of any postural assessment, gait assessment, or symmetry assessment will always yield a correct road map to a treatment plan. The body **resourcefully compensates** to adapt to trauma or habituated repetitive use pattern[19].

Please don't misunderstand, of course it is important to do assessments and analyze asymmetries. Just be careful of what I crudely call *picking fly poop out of the pepper*. For example, "Holy geez! Your right shoulder is slightly elevated, and one leg is ¼ of an inch longer than the other!" Balance your assessments with the intelligence and resourceful compensation patterns that reside within your client's body.

> Attempt to free up fascial networks, ameliorate pain or discomfort, and give clients as much range of motion and function as possible, given their unique structural state, or resourceful compensation.

Look again at Miss Symmetric. Look closely at her eye gaze. You will notice there is subtle, but observable deviation in her cervical spine to her shoulder. Her right shoulder and neck are an issue. She also has issues in her hip rotators, erector spinae group and hamstrings. So, Miss Symmetric is a case where traditional postural and symmetry assessments may *fail* you. After several sessions with *dialogue and feedback* we were able to begin to address her deeper issues.

Another point, you cannot diagnose and prescribe, because as a massage therapist this is out of your scope of practice. You are, however, a downright, certified *suspectition*. You can suspect what is wrong, and with your client's feedback, help them address their issues.

Be realistic of your knowledge and experience level. Know whom you can help and whom you can't.

You are not attempting to structurally change your client. Your goal is to help free up what they've got.

Be a suspectition; work together with your client and through dialogue and feedback, attempt to find the root cause of an issue.

When in doubt, apply the routine in this book and you may be pleasantly surprised with the positive results.

CASE STUDY 5 – TRANSITIONAL DEVIATION, TRAINING AND THERAPY

Recall earlier when we mentioned muscle, bones, and fascia constantly change because of the loads placed on them.

A 74-year-old Tai Chi instructor client was diagnosed with a bunion on the medial side of her right great toe 14 months earlier. The bunion made her toe rigid, caused toe angle valgus at the distal joint, which in turn caused her to walk with an externally rotated, pronated foot like she was "skating." The gait deviation caused painful knee joint misalignment and valgus. Further up her kinetic chain, her upper outside buttock "seized, and tightened up with every step" causing pain and discomfort.

This is a case where she was in the process of eventually building in permanent structural changes in her body, known as a ***Transitional Deviation***. Her functions of everyday life, like walking, became increasingly compromised, so much so, walking to the store was an effort causing her to stop and stretch out her buttock and lower back every few steps. Her surgeon at first refused to operate, so she was becoming increasingly resigned to her new reduced function.

If she had come to me for relief of her tight back and sore knee, I would have seen her week after week performing *condition management,* discussed earlier. I might have temporarily relieved her symptoms, but the next week she would come back with an ever-increasing level of pain and discomfort.

When the surgeon advised her that she should now have surgery, she showed me she could ever so slightly bend her toe.

We immediately started doing corrective exercises to realign and strengthen her fascial networks. Simple exercises, like demanding she plantar flex a straight foot bending the great toe as much as possible and strengthening and stretching her under activated gluteus maximus and medius. Proper alignment biomechanics brought relief to her tight buttock and lower back.

Within three weeks, I received a glowing email stating how she regained significant function and had relieved significant discomfort and tightness.

We had not done any therapy up until this point, but I asked her how she felt about beginning therapy now, versus if we had done therapy before the correction?

She said,

> "Therapy before the correction only would have temporarily helped. At some point I would have stopped coming. Therapy after the correction, you now have a client for life. The exercise helped the cause, and the therapy will now help further correct my back and alleviate residual discomfort."

She just described a perfect case of changing from condition management to ***therapeutic change***, discussed earlier.

Most of you reading this book are massage therapists, not corrective exercise specialists. Just be aware that you will come across difficult cases. Be careful of taking money week after week doing condition management, when therapeutic change may be possible.

You are a "suspectition." Work as a team with your client to ascertain root causes of issues and refer out when needed. Try to form your own referral network of colleagues who may have other skills to help your client.

When in doubt, refer out.

PRIMUM NON NOCERE, "FIRST, DO NO HARM"

I would like to say (but can't) that my routine and technique are the elixir of life, it will cure all ills, and can apply to anyone. I mentioned earlier the technique is applicable for people with soft tissue issues and fascial adhesions. I have had success with athletes, former athletes, active seniors, seniors with new hardware like a knee replacement, etc.

Clients usually provide positive feedback: "gee, I feel *amazing*," they say.

"Wow," I say to myself, "isn't my technique just the cat's pajamas!"

In general, I get positive feedback and results from about 80 percent of my clients and referrals. "Hold it," you should ask. "What about the other 20 percent?"

Now let's talk about that hip replacement done 24 years ago, that horse accident where the pony fell and crushed a guy's pelvis decades earlier, that competitive former college gymnast now in her 50's with overly lax and diseased joints, that peripatetic office worker with a structural foot problem cascading issues up her kinetic chain, etc.

This technique is for fascial adhesions. If the underlying causes are related to underlying pathologies, especially diseased bones and joints, overuse injuries such as painful tendinitis, and compression of bony structures on nerves, the technique might not work well. And be careful. Do you want to stretch and three-dimensionally manipulate the pinned hip and pinned sacroiliac joint of an octogenarian? Maybe, but *most likely probably not.*

And what if you can't penetrate deeply enough to reach the fascial adhesions; for example, a fibromyalgia client who had very dense fascia? The slightest pressure would cause pain - I couldn't penetrate the tissue enough to break up any adhesions. The technique presented did not work well, and I was relegated to doing a light palliative Swedish massage with some gentle FST™ stretching.

Yet another client had Von Willebrand's disease, a hereditary blood clotting disorder. Again, extreme caution was warranted not to cause bruising so again, a light palliative Swedish massage was used with some gentle FST™ stretching. You will encounter difficult cases, especially if you do bodywork on older populations. Use your judgment and use caution.

When stretching may be contraindicated, notice where an "*" is shown in the following routine. You can use this technique to ameliorate discomfort in difficult cases where you are not sure (and the client is not sure) if it is a good idea to stretch and manipulate a joint and limb.

So, don't worry, you can still apply many elements of this myofascial release technique, just do it conservatively. Always, remember, "First, do no harm."

One last didactic point: be relentlessly critical of yourself and your technique. Bodywork is an art form. View yourself as an artist: practice-practice-practice.

Iterate your skill sets to improve them. Enjoy and accept those times when you can help a client improve, manage their condition, or lessen discomfort. After all, it's why most of us do massage and bodywork in the first place.

Always seek honest feedback from your clients. If this technique is not helping a client, don't keep taking their money. Have the courage to look your client in the eye and tell them, "if you aren't experiencing positive therapeutic outcomes from our session(s), try something else, this approach is not working for you."

Have fun. Help others. And do no harm.

A Systematic Approach to Myofascial Network Release

CHAPTER 7

3-DIMENSIONAL BODYWORK ROUTINE AND TECHNIQUE

Lower Supine (LS) | **TURQUOISE-COLORED**

Just like the subway trains in Manhattan, all trains run through midtown, whether they go uptown or downtown. If you observe the Myers' myofascial meridian Anatomy Trains®, most run through the hips, or "midtown." So, if you start with releasing the hips, you can sometimes address issues uptown, the upper body; and downtown, the lower body, legs and feet. We start with the lower supine part of the routine, which is hip focused. Also, the client starts face up to help facilitate dialogue and feedback.

See discussion on the preceding page regarding (*).

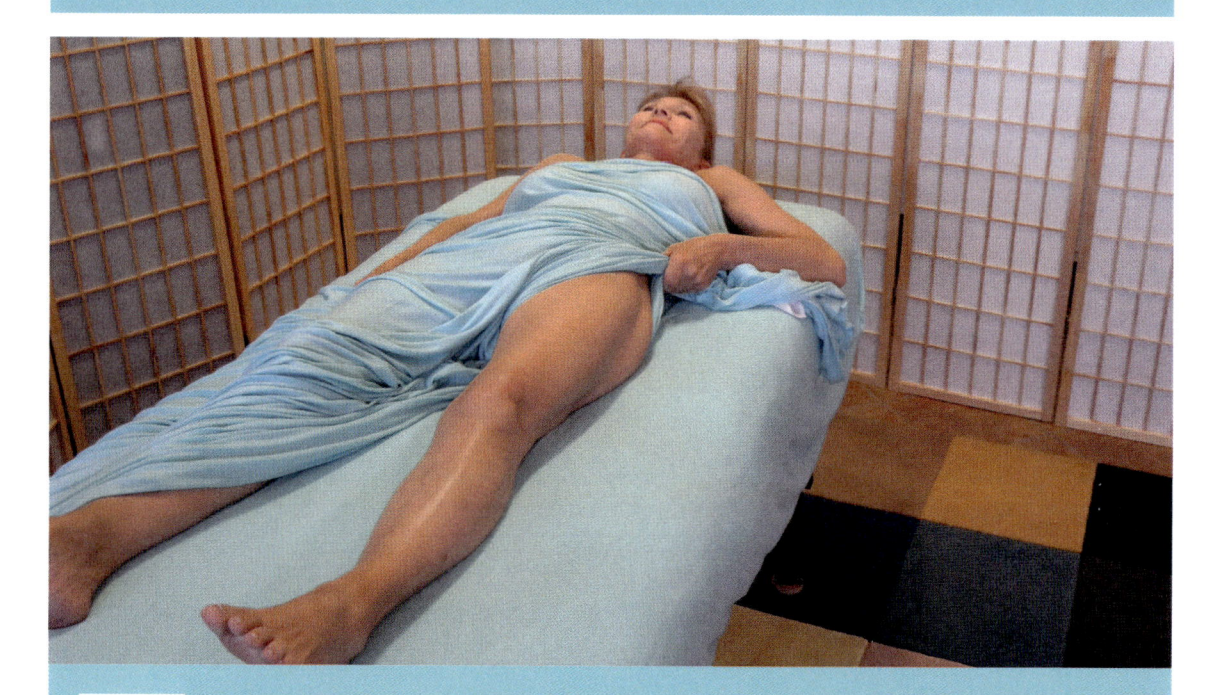

LS 1

Secure Draping

Make sure the client feels relaxed, secure, and comfortable. Use a "diaper" drape. Notice how the bottom of the drape and top of the drape can be controlled and held by the client. This ensures a tight fit around the leg to protect and cover the groin area.

LS 2

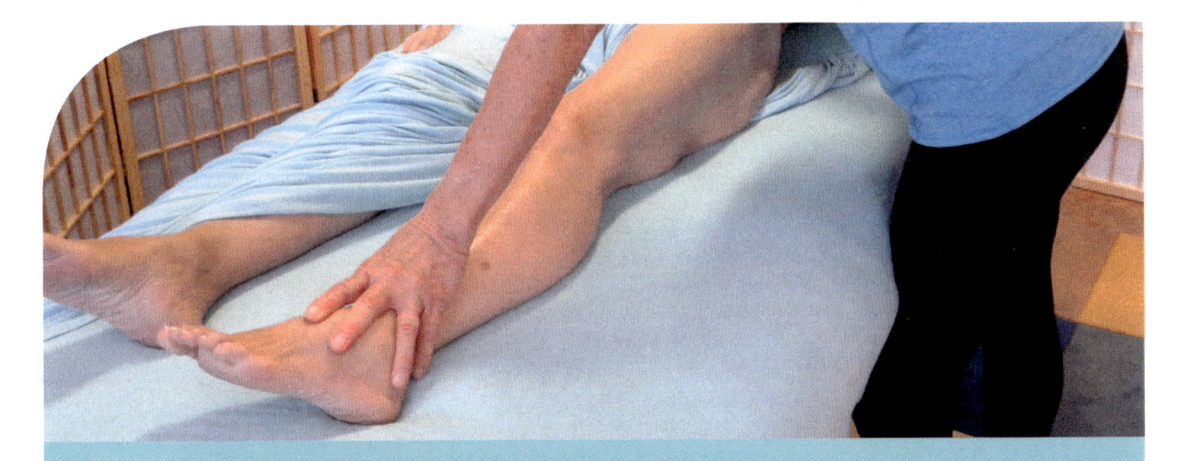

Assess Lower Back and Outside Hips

Feel the erector spinae group for tension and hyper-tonicity. Palpate, by cross-fiber friction strokes pulling lateral, from the erector spinae down along the posterior iliac crest and gluteus medius. Continue palpating down along the biceps femoris to the knee. The client may feel an immediate release sensation especially in the gluteus medius and sacroiliac joint area. (*)

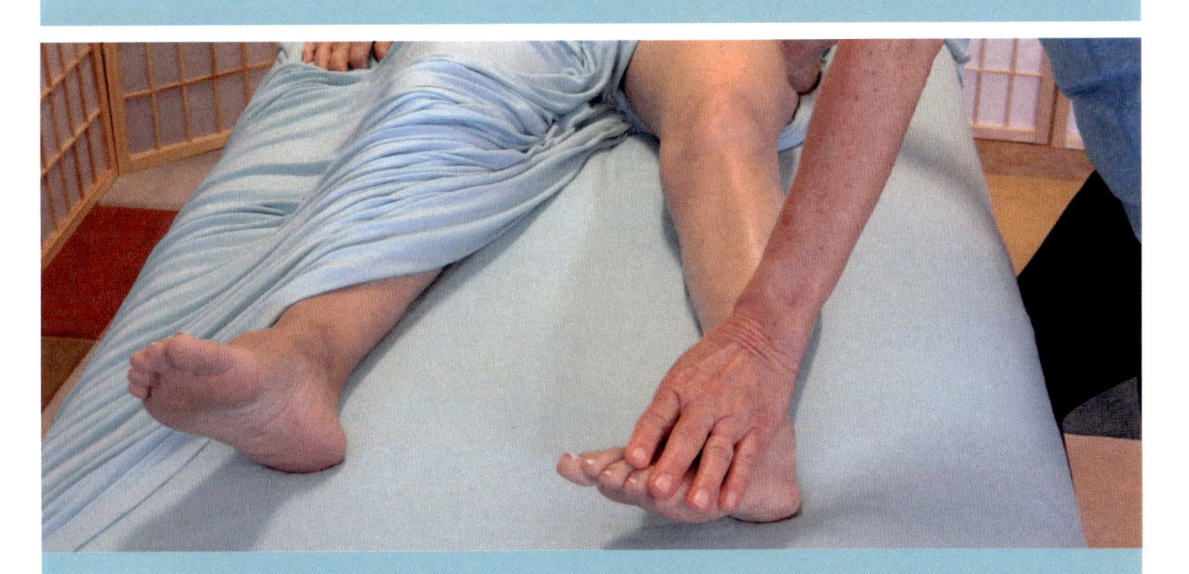

LS 3

Iliotibial Band Shear

Medially rotate the foot and ankle as you shear the tensor fascia latae and iliotibial band downward, working distal toward the knee. (*)

LS 4

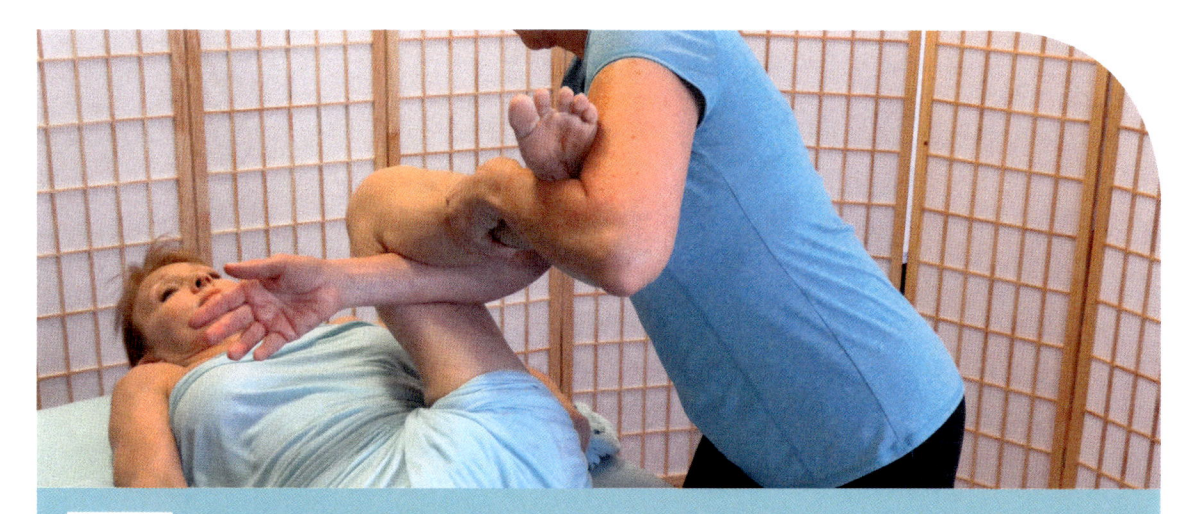

Lower Back Stretch

Cradle the leg and calf with the down-table arm, as you use your up-table forearm to press into the lateral hamstring distal just below the knee, working down proximal close to the hamstring insertion at the ischial tuberosity.

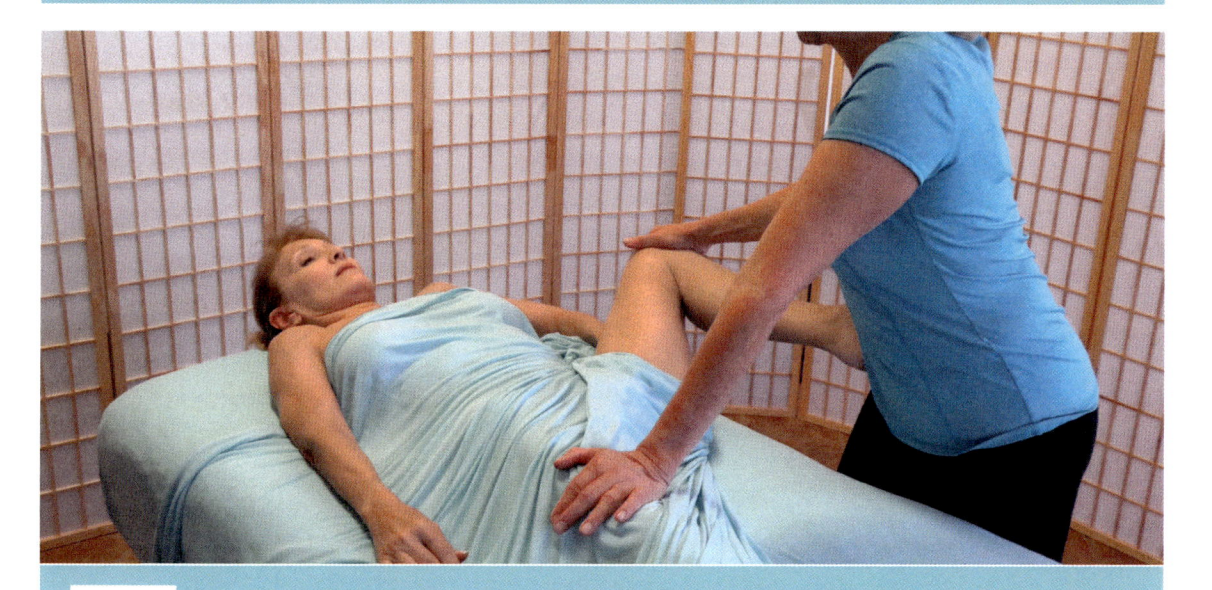

LS 5

Adductor Stretch

Place the client's foot on your hip as you move forward and gently stretch the adductors. Ask for feedback of any hip joint pain or impingement.

LS 6

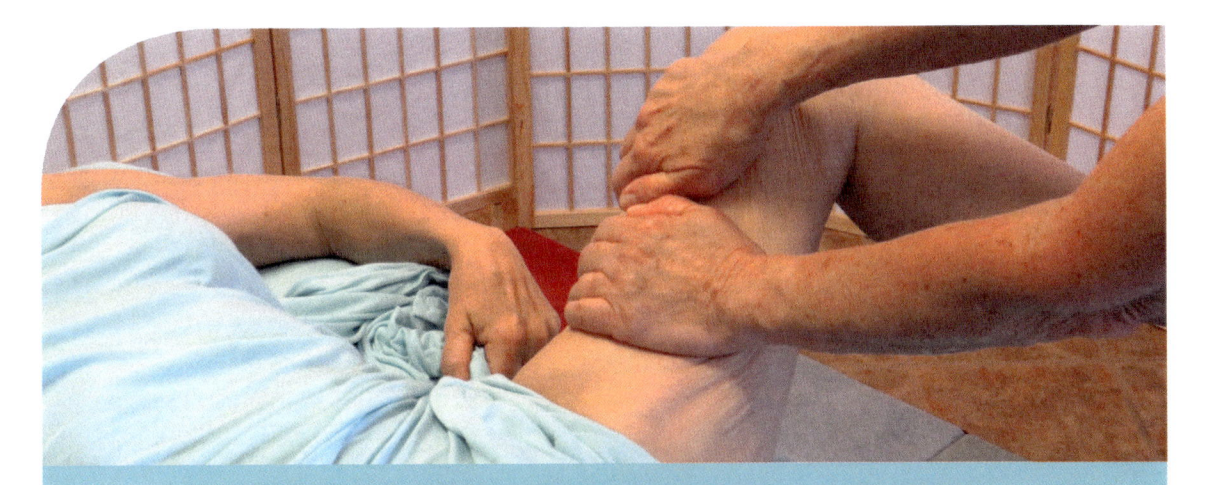

Quadriceps Shear
With thigh 90 degrees to the torso, place both hands on top of the quadriceps and pull the quadriceps and the tensor fascia latae toward you, shearing fascial sacks off one another.

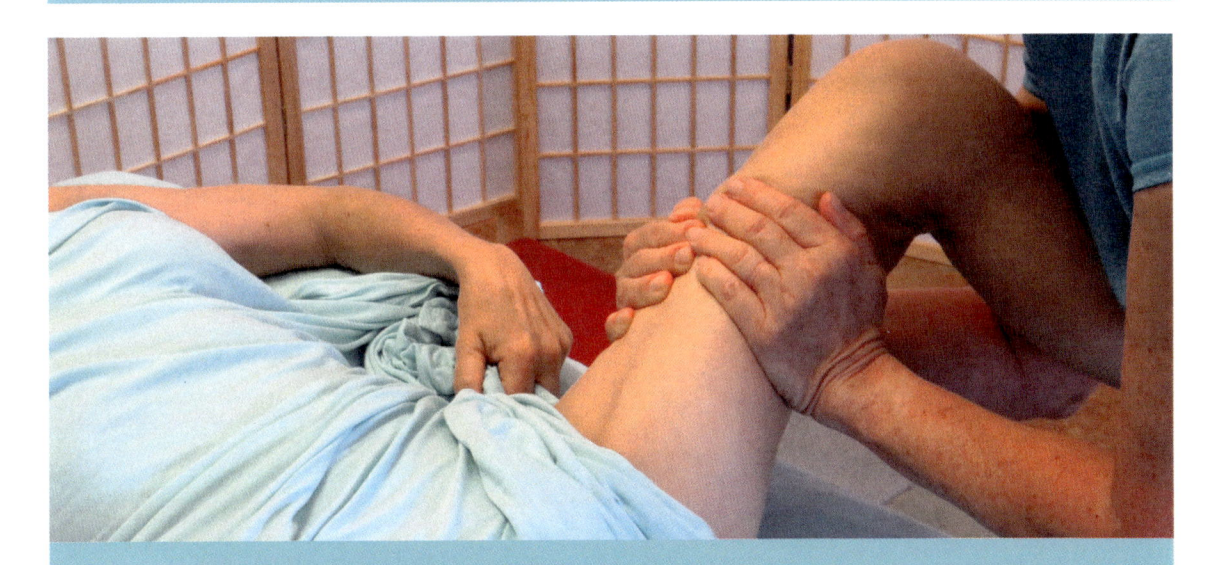

LS 7

Adductor Shear
Use both hands, one on top of the leg, and the other on the bottom, apply an upward torsional shear force distal from the knee, working proximal toward the adductor origins, stopping at the drape.

LS 8

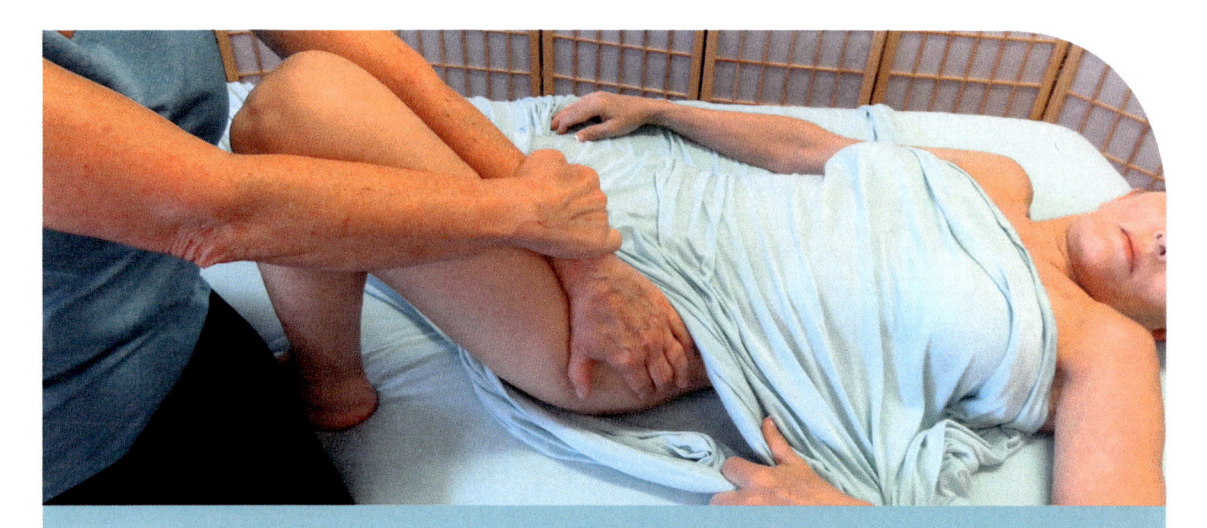

Thigh Pull Lower Back Traction

Sit on the table facing the client. Place the client's heel close to the buttock, use both arms as you grab the client's thigh, in three positions, proximal to distal, leaning back with your body as you traction the hip joint and lower back. The low proximal position usually provides the greatest therapeutic effect.

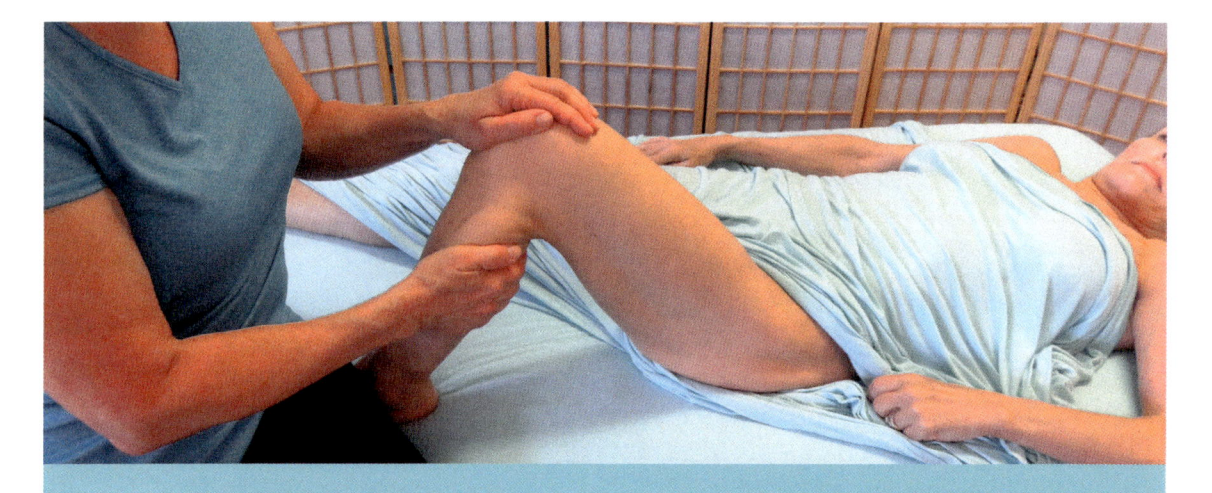

LS 9

Calf Shear

Secure foot under your thigh, and shear calf from medial to lateral, and then lateral to medial, starting from the knee and working distal toward the ankle. Next grab calf with both hands and shear clockwise and counterclockwise.

LS 10

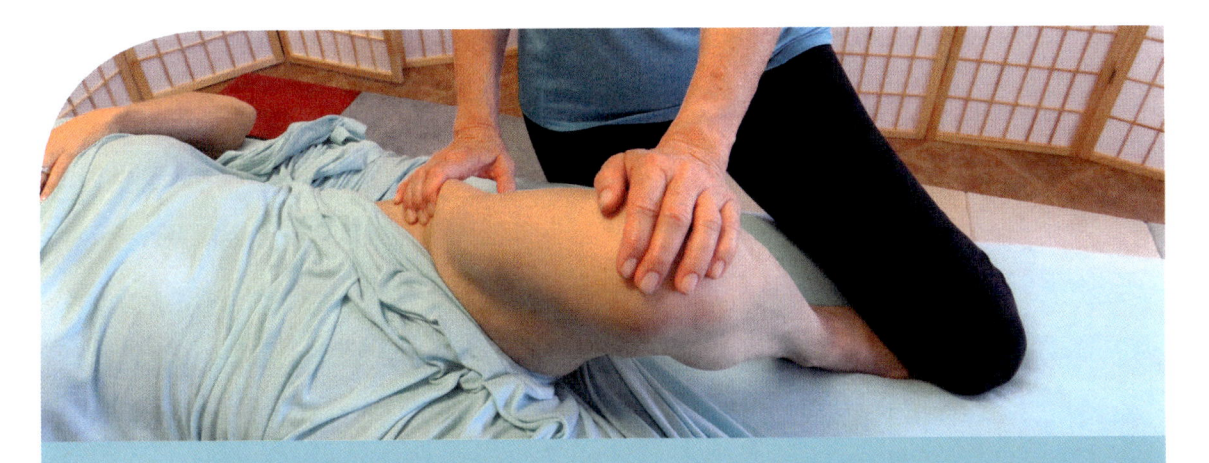

TFL Cross Fiber

Standing facing the client, secure foot with your knee, with a cross fiber friction stroke using the pads of your fingers, pull the tensor fascia latae from medial to lateral as you push knee medially in.

Then grab adductor group with a flat hand and shear the inner thigh toward you with no hand slippage as you push knee medially in.

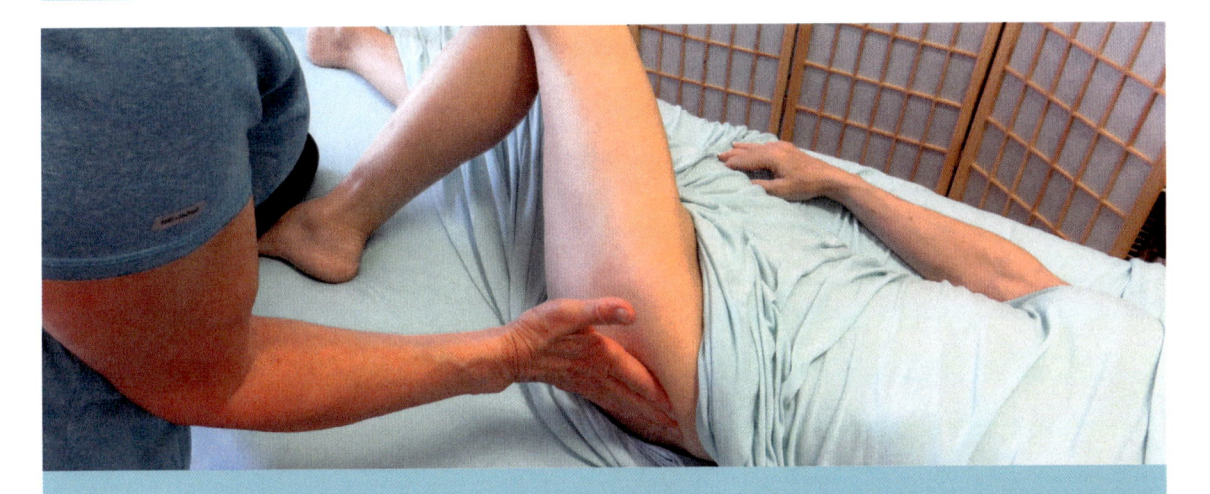

LS 11

Gluteus Medius Compression

Secure foot with your knee, press fingers into outside of hip above the greater trochanter, working superior and medially as you apply compression to gluteus medius, while simultaneously pushing knee in with each compression.

A Systematic Approach to Myofascial Network Release

LS 13

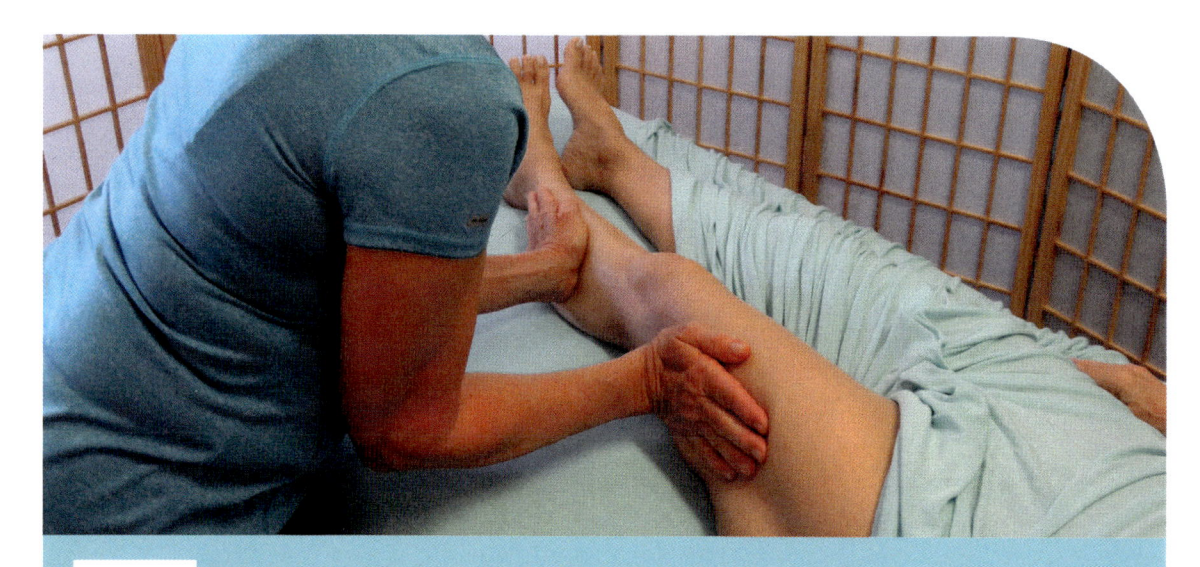

Side Leg Fascial Spread and Retinaculum

With some glide, start at knee pointing hands inferiorly and superiorly; simultaneously spread tissue toward ankle, and iliac crest. Finish with an opposite hand torsional shear of the ankle retinaculum like you are twisting a rag. (*)

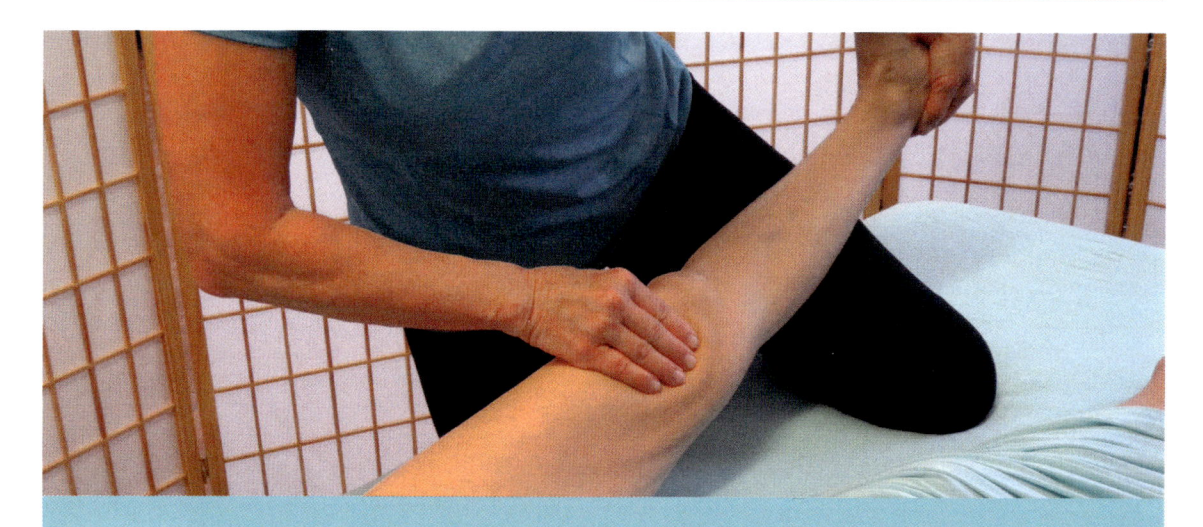

LS 12

Calf Stretch

Support the leg with knee, grab the heel and use your forearm as you lean and apply bodyweight towards client's head, stretching gastrocnemius and soleus. (*)

LS 14

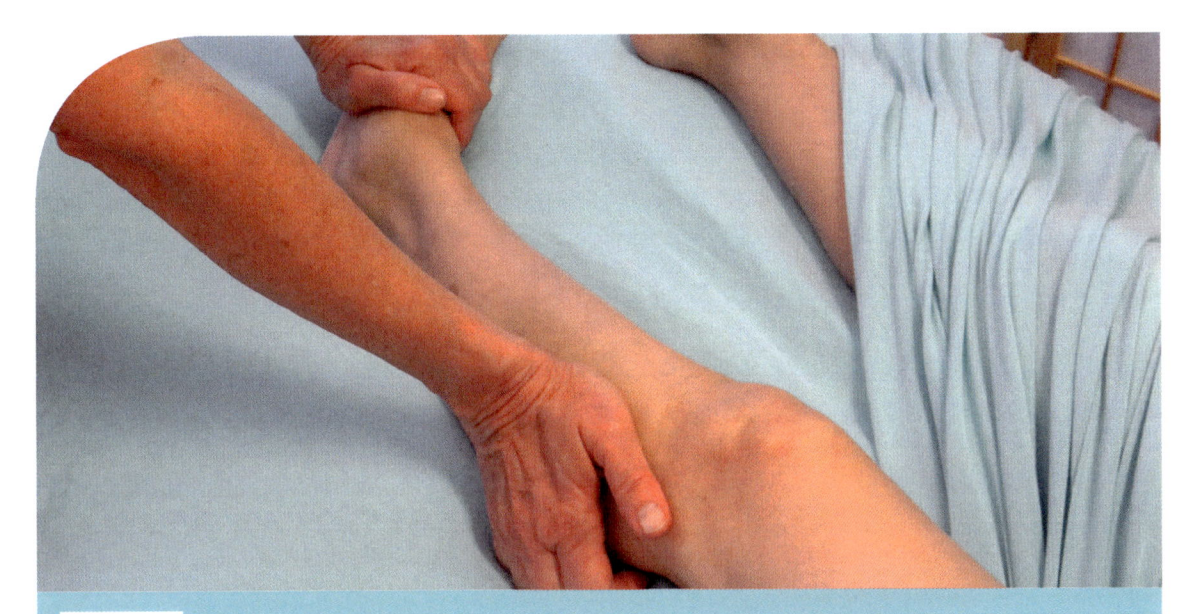

Tibialis Anterior Shin Shear

Use palm of hand as you press and shear tibialis anterior from medial to lateral, as you simultaneously rotate ankle and foot medially, working from knee distal toward ankle. You are creating friction with compression and movement. (*)

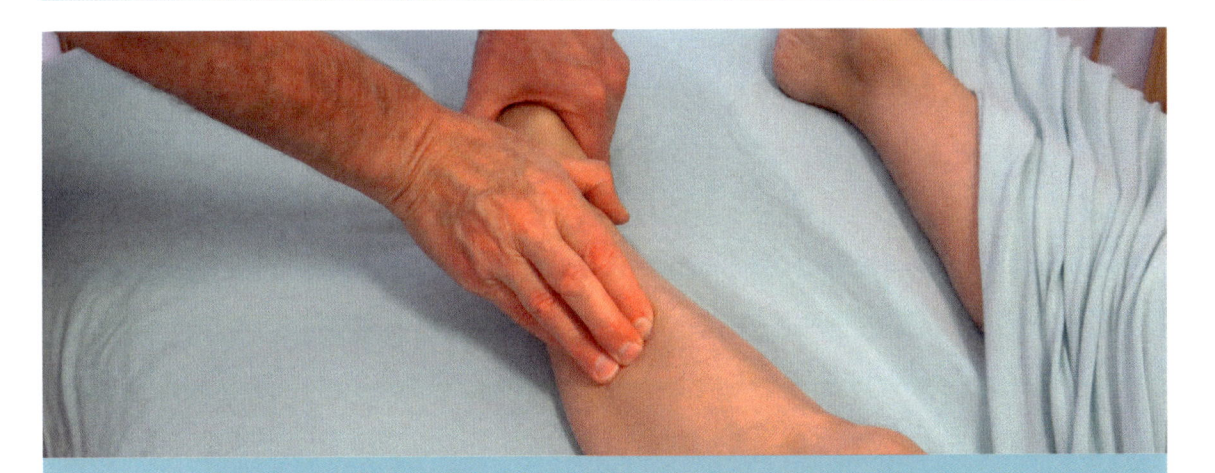

LS 15

Tibialis Anterior Compression

With foot and ankle medially rotated, use fingers to apply longitudinal compressive friction strokes to the tibialis anterior. (*)

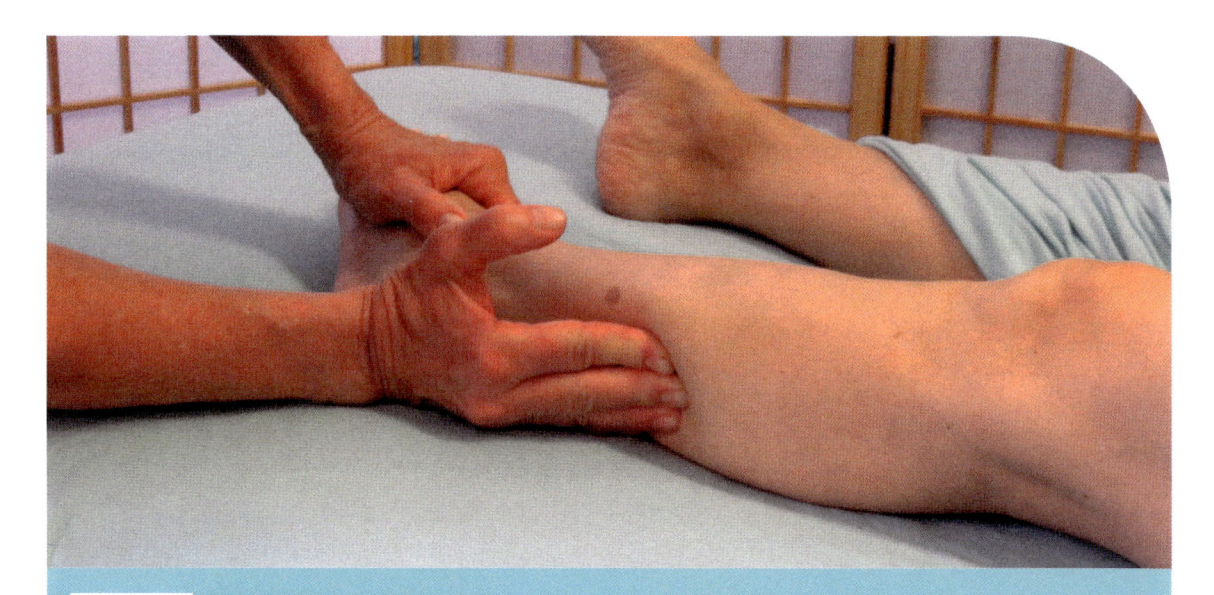

LS 16

Fibularis Separation

With foot and ankle medially rotated, use fingers to apply longitudinal compressive friction strokes to the valleys of the fibularis muscles. (*)

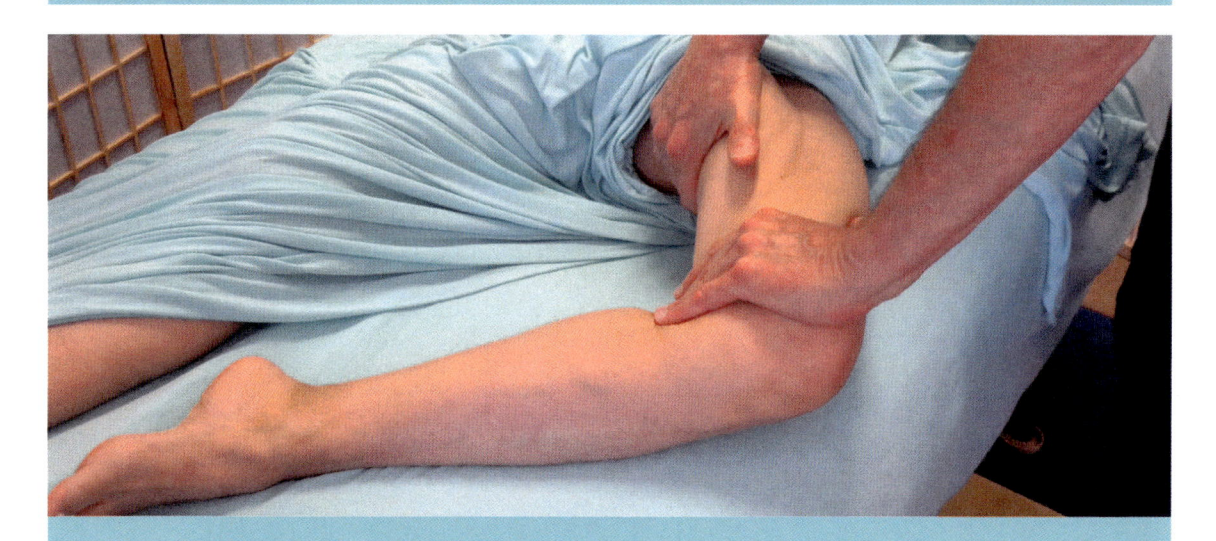

LS 17

Posterior Thigh Shear

With leg bent, secure the knee, grab the back of the thigh and pull up towards you with no glide and minimal slippage shearing the fascial sacks of the posterior thigh.

LS 18

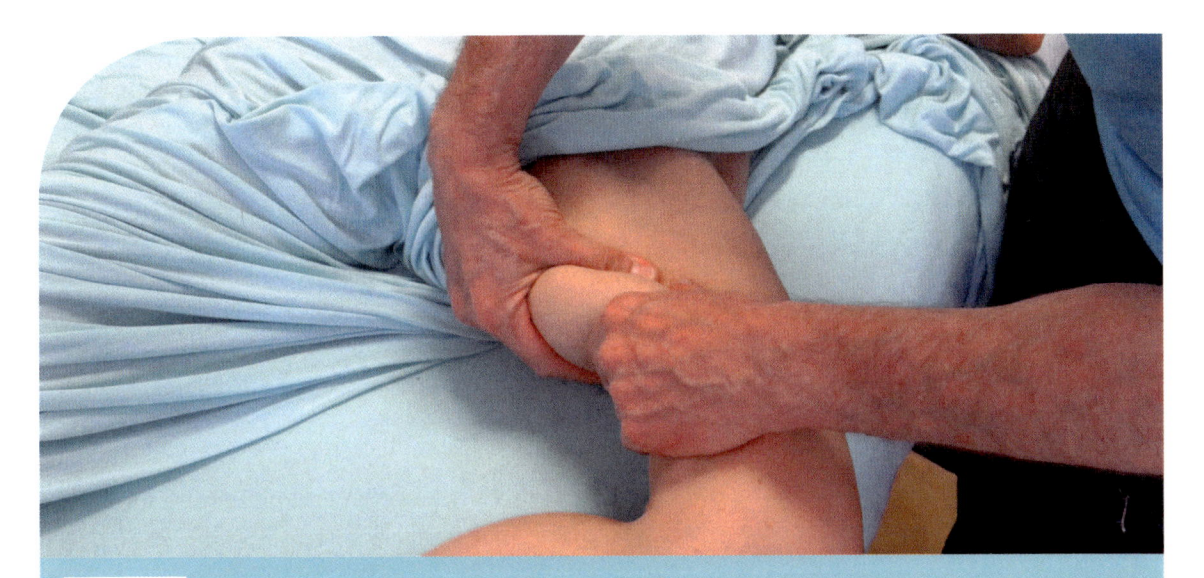

Thigh Petrissage
Apply minimal glide to entire thigh and petrissage.

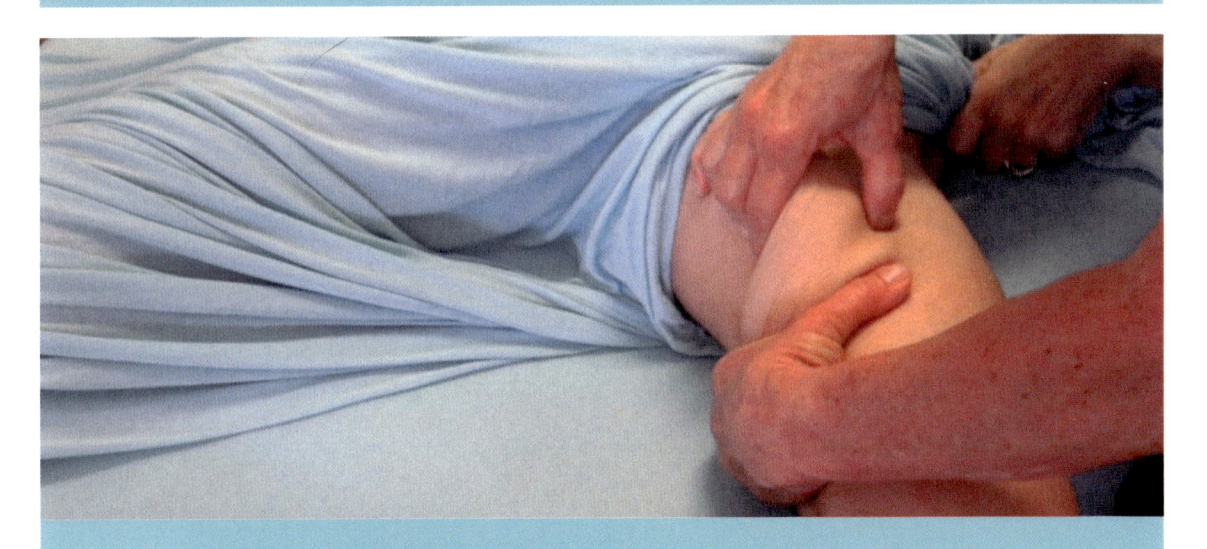

LS 19

Thigh Torsion
With minimal glide, apply torsional strokes with hands twisting in opposite directions from knee to drape.

LS 20

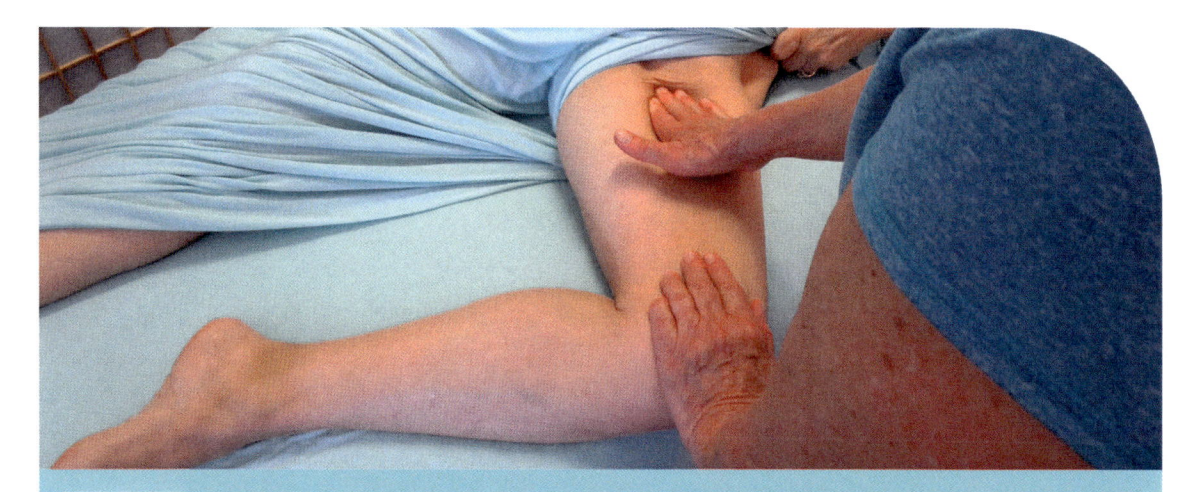

Adductor Separation

Use some glide; longitudinally separate valleys on the anterior and posterior sides of the short adductor group.

Use some glide, then wrap hands around the back of the thigh, find the valleys on the back of the leg as you lift vertically against gravity, gliding your fingers distally toward knee.

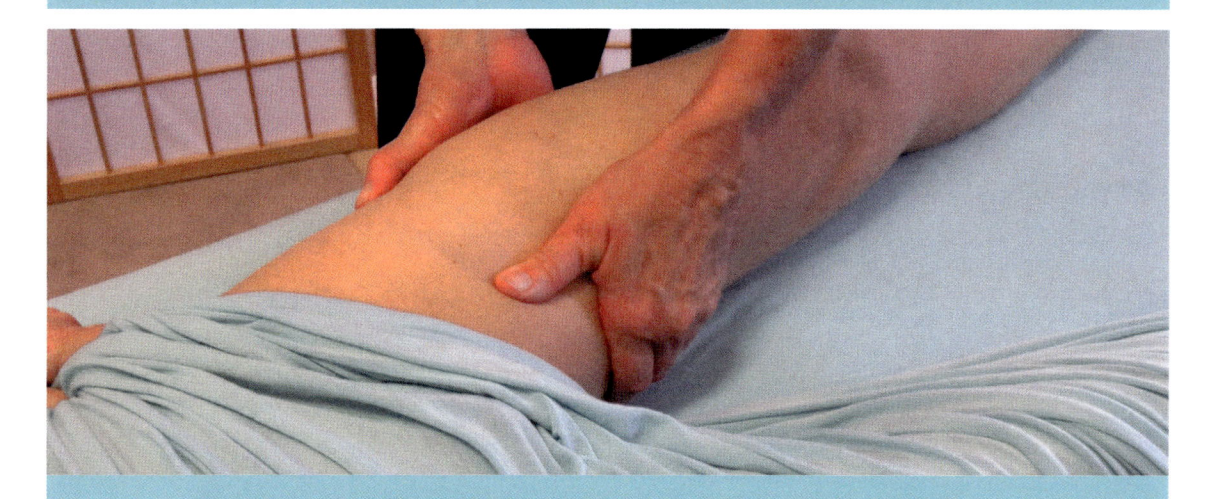

LS 21

Posterior Thigh Valley Separation

Use some glide; wrap your hands around the back of the thigh, find the valleys on the back of the leg as you lift vertically against gravity gliding your fingers distally toward knee. (*)

LS 22

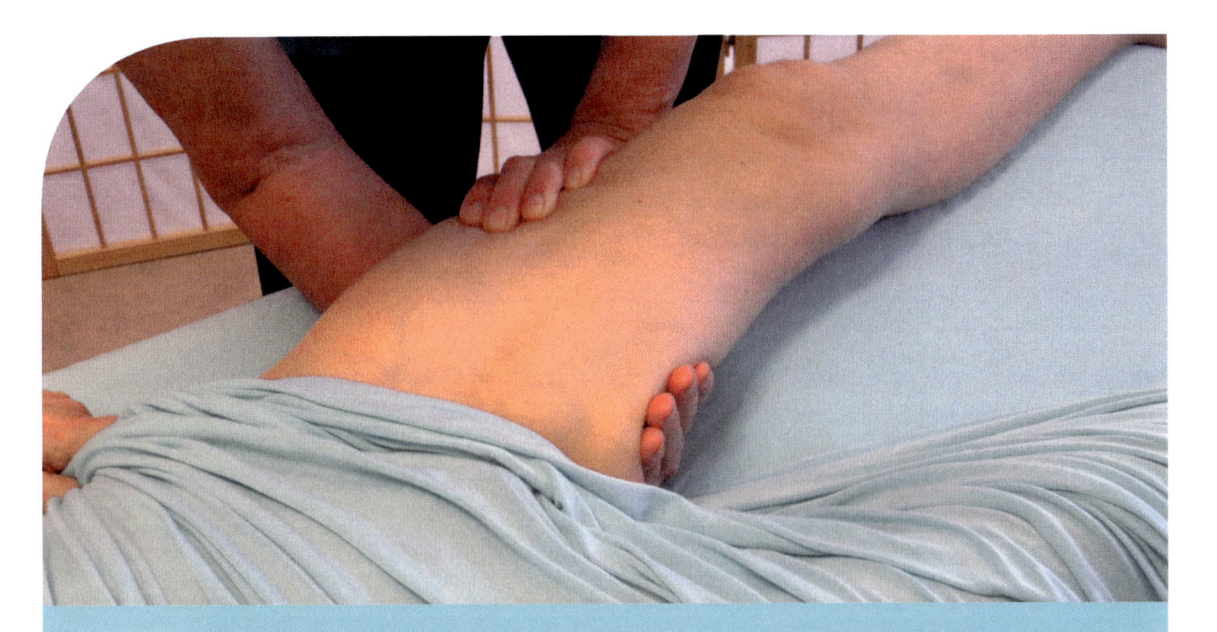

Thigh Fascial Sack Twist

Grab thigh with both hands and twist fascial sacks around the femur clockwise and counterclockwise. (*)

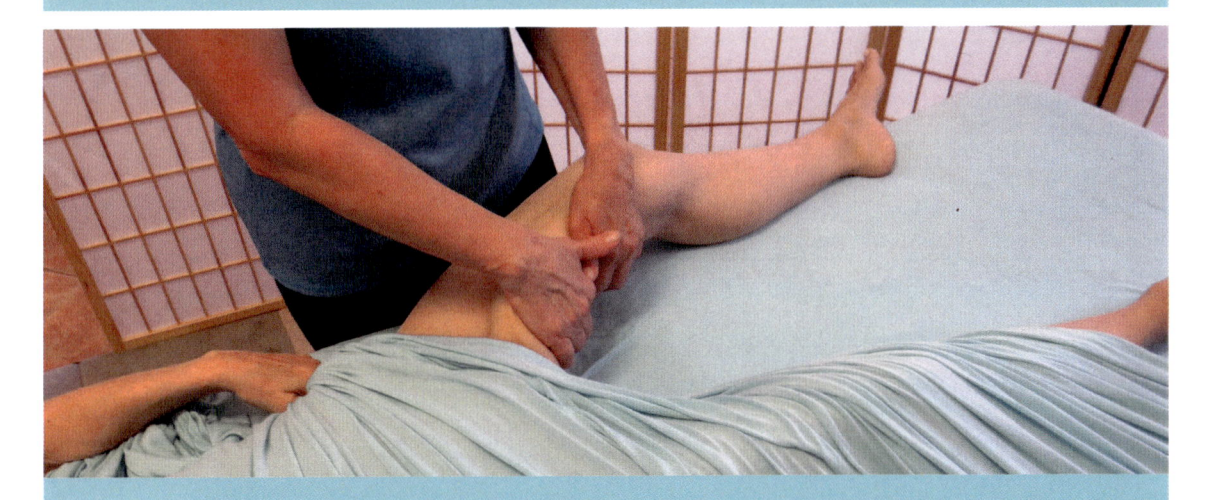

LS 23

Long Adductor Shear

Support client's leg, grab and pull long adductors and medial hamstrings vertically against gravity shearing the fascial sacks. (*)

LS 24

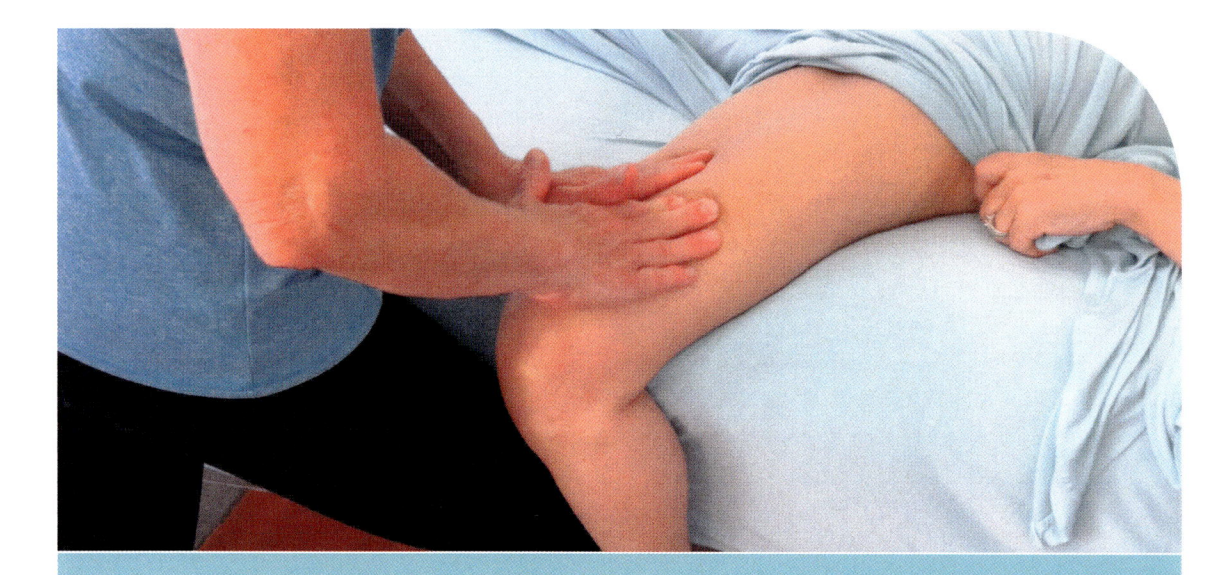

Quadriceps Stretch
Angle thigh so lower leg hangs off table. Push ankle in with your leg to stretch quadriceps. Using longitudinal compression strokes with glide, separate peaks and valleys of anterior thigh fascial sacks.

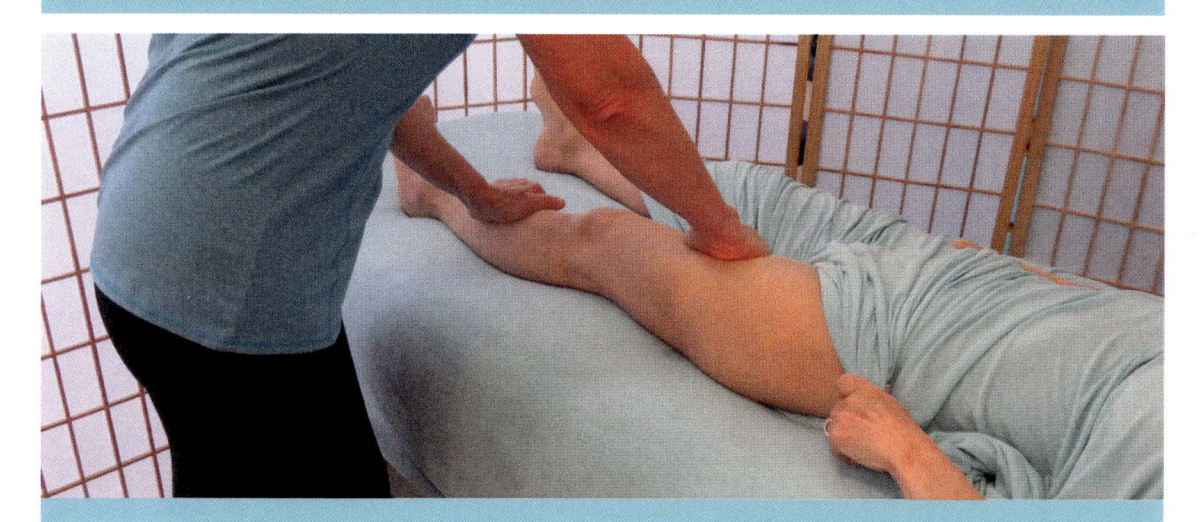

LS 25

Rock Hip Joint
Rhythmically rock leg back and forth, moving the head of the femur in the acetabulum. (*)

LS 26

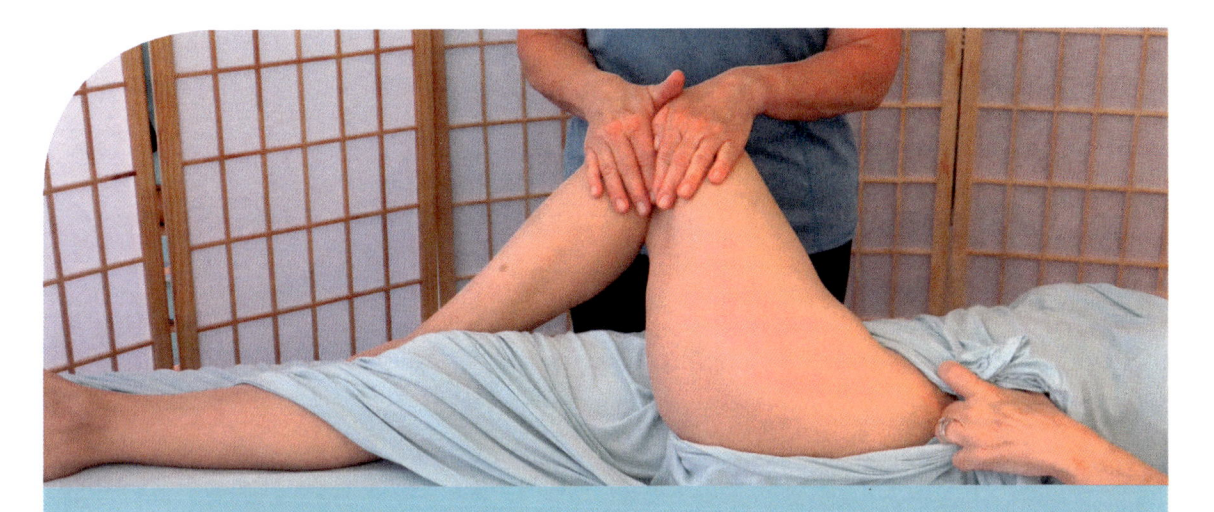

Hip Rotator Stretch

Place foot on outside of opposite thigh. Be careful of hip joint binding or impingement, which will be felt as a pain in the client's groin. Gently pull outside of knee toward you.

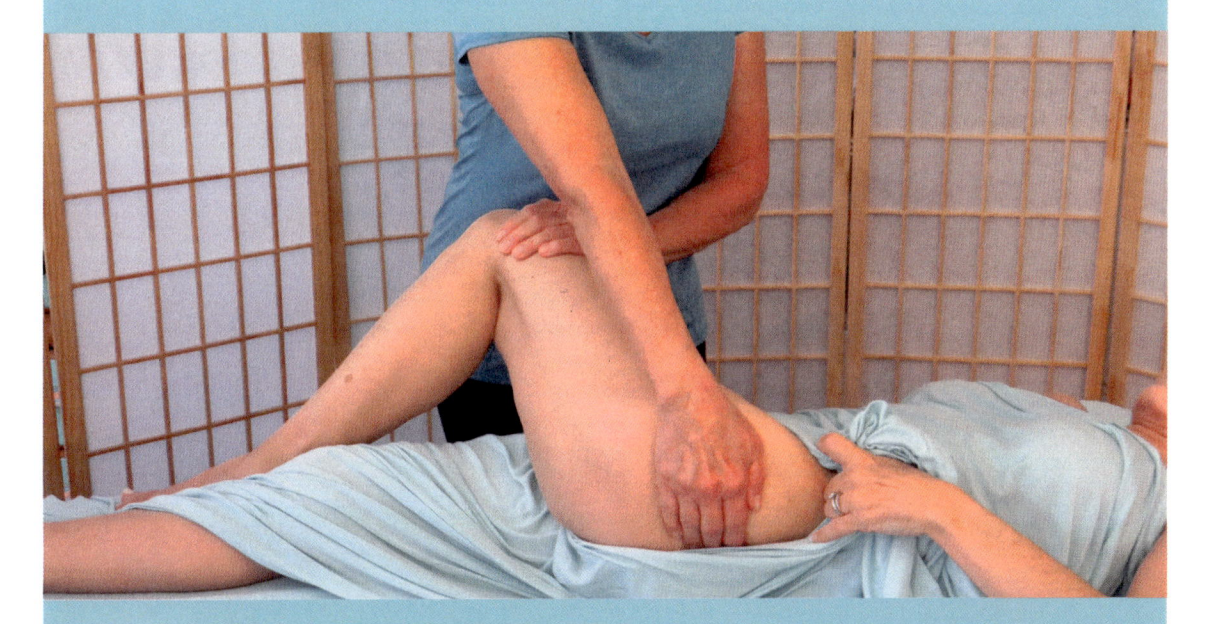

LS 27

Gluteus Cross Fiber

Grab the outside of the hip, cross-fiber shear the gluteus and hip rotators from the iliac crest, moving inferiorly to the ischial tuberosity.

LS 28

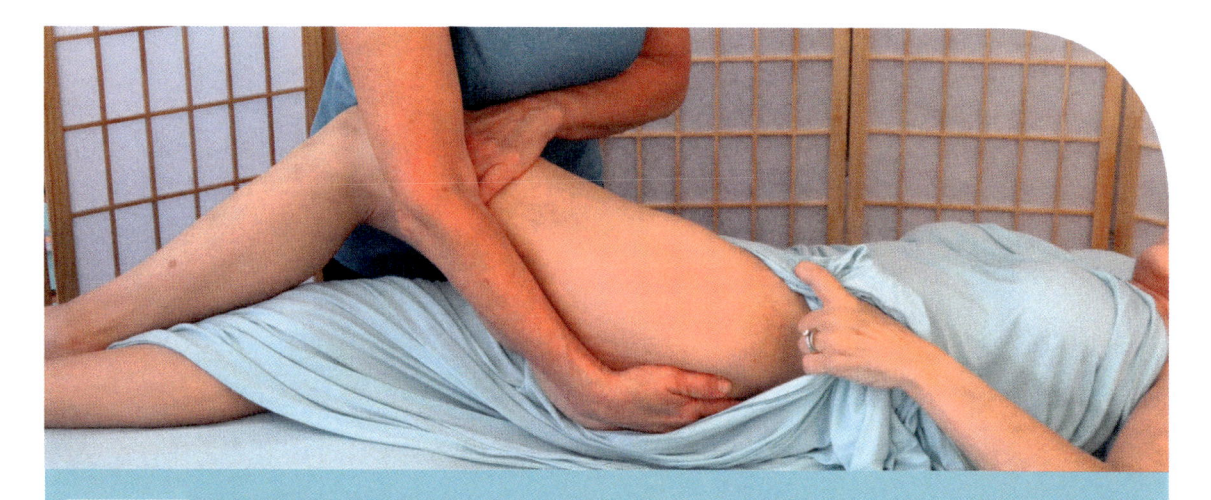

Sacral Traction to Longitudinal Glut Rake
Pull the client's thigh toward you, prying the opposite hip up; place your hand on the client's sacrum, applying traction. Use some glide, then rake from the sacrum to the ischial tuberosity keeping lateral to the anal cleft.

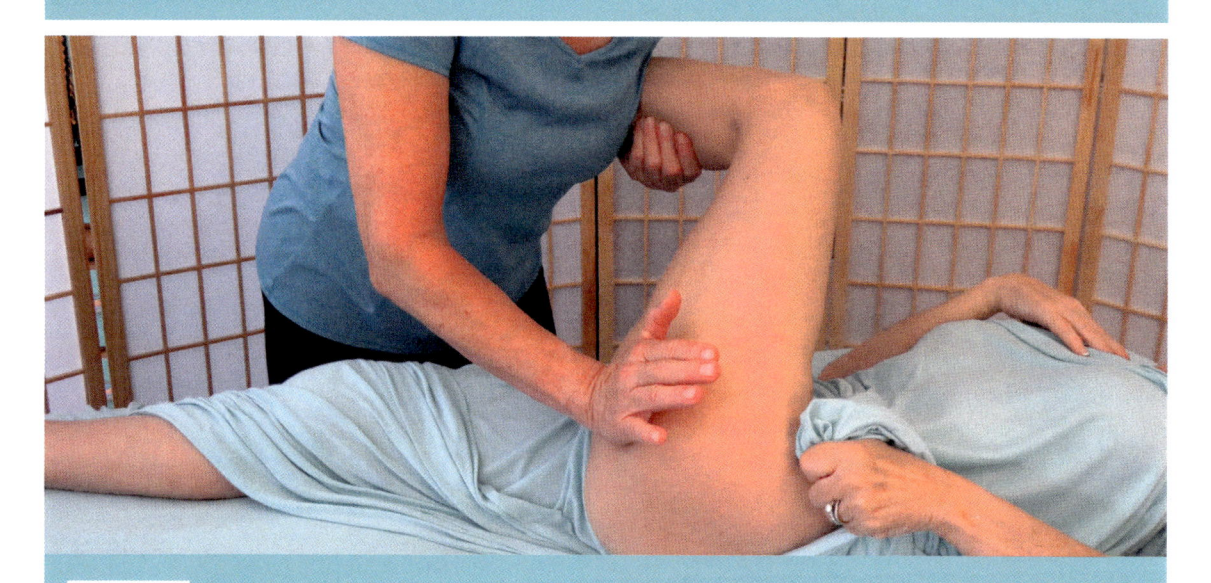

LS 29

Gluteus Maximus and Medius Stretch
Secure the client's ankle above your hip with your up-table arm; gently fan the glut back and forth; use your palm to compress and twist down the posterior groove of the femur into the linea aspera continuing into the ischial tuberosity.

LS 30

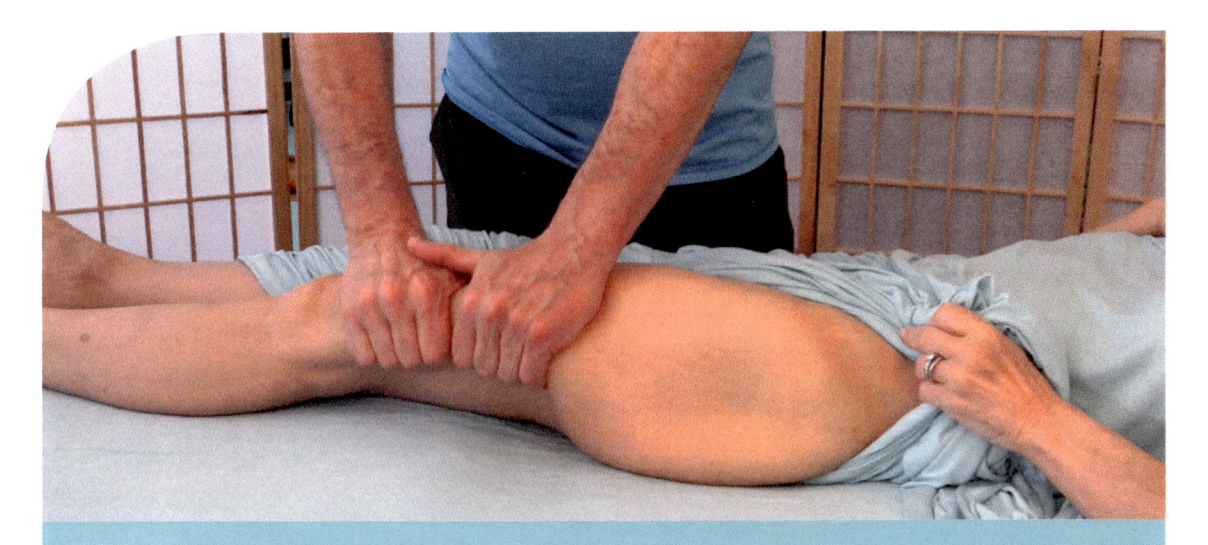

Lateral Line Shear

Reach across and grab the upper outside gluteus medius as you pull up against gravity working your way inferiorly to the knee; on the femur, lift tissue away trying to free Iliotibial band from the vastus lateralis and the biceps femoris. (*)

Then with minimal or no glide, place fingertips on the medial border of the TFL and gently push laterally.

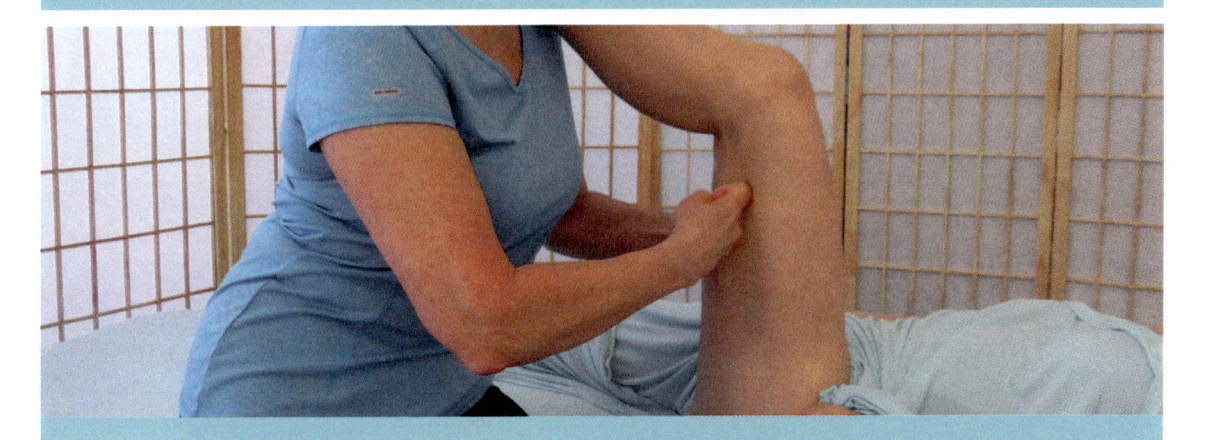

LS 31

Hamstring Separation

Sit facing client with the client's ankle resting on your inside shoulder, use supported thumbs or knuckles to free up all three hamstrings one at a time from the knee toward the ischial tuberosity.

A Systematic Approach to Myofascial Network Release

LS 32

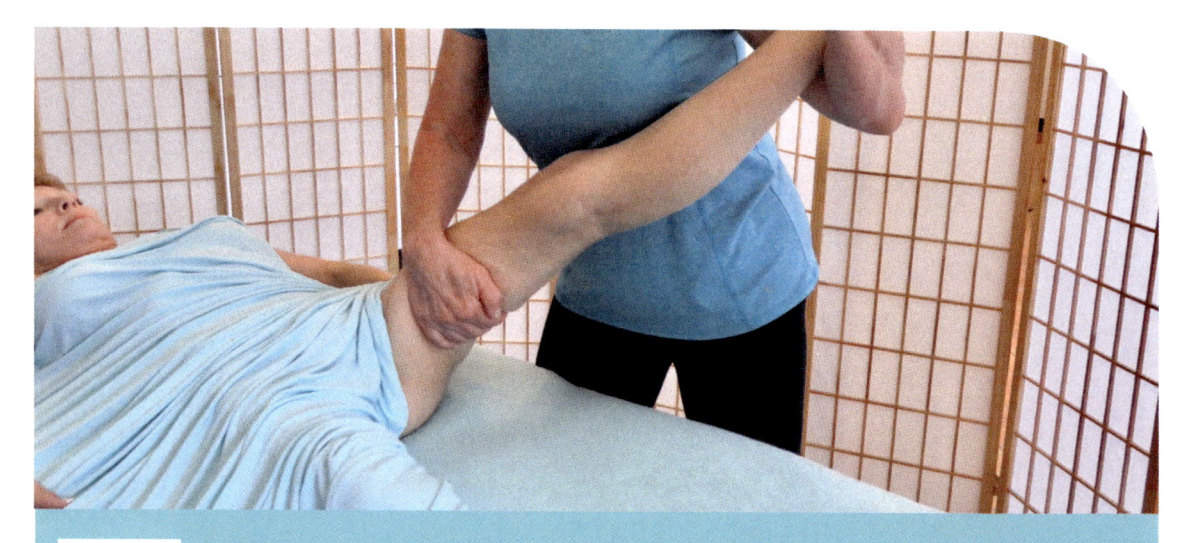

Long Adductor Torsion

Hold the client's ankle in the "V" of your down-table arm, as you use your up-table arm and hand to torsion the adductor muscles from knee proximal to the drape, then back distal to knee.

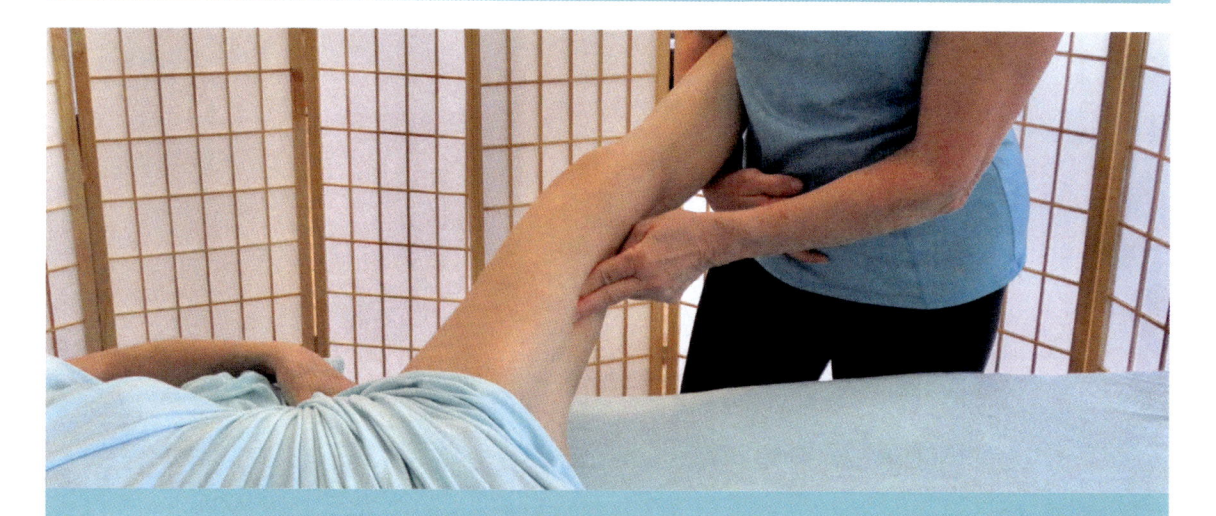

LS 33

Long Adductor Separation

Using some glide, secure the client's ankle above your hip with your up-table arm, then use the down-table arm to longitudinally separate the valleys of the medial hamstrings and gracilis from knee gliding proximal to drape.

LS 34

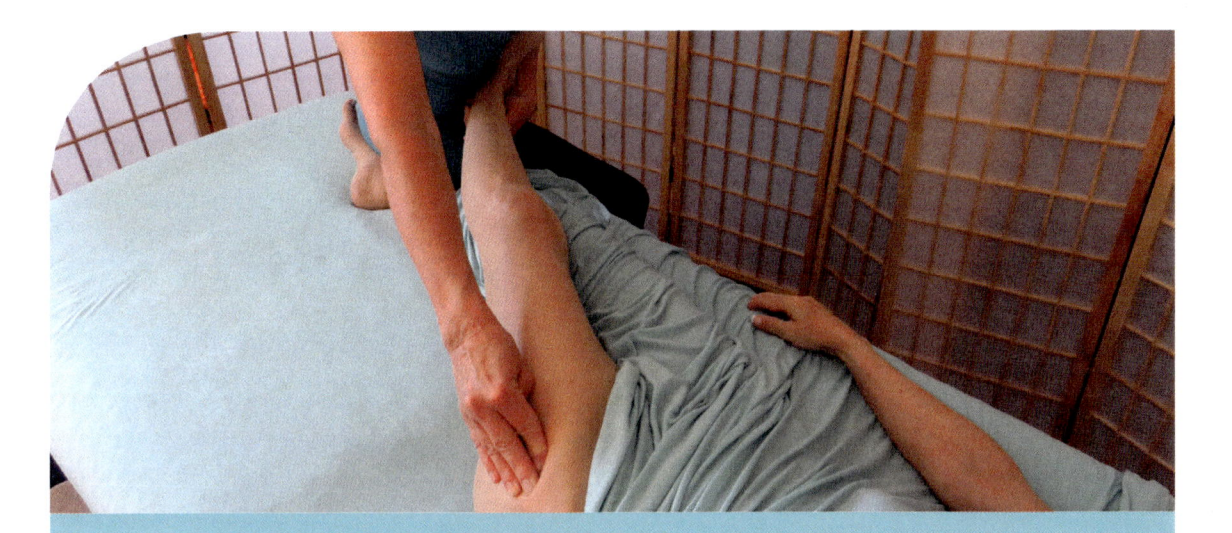

IT Band Tension and TFL Compression.

Hold client's ankle with your down-table arm, as you stretch the iliotibial band and tensor fascia latae, while using your up-table hand to compress tissue using a longitudinal friction stroke.

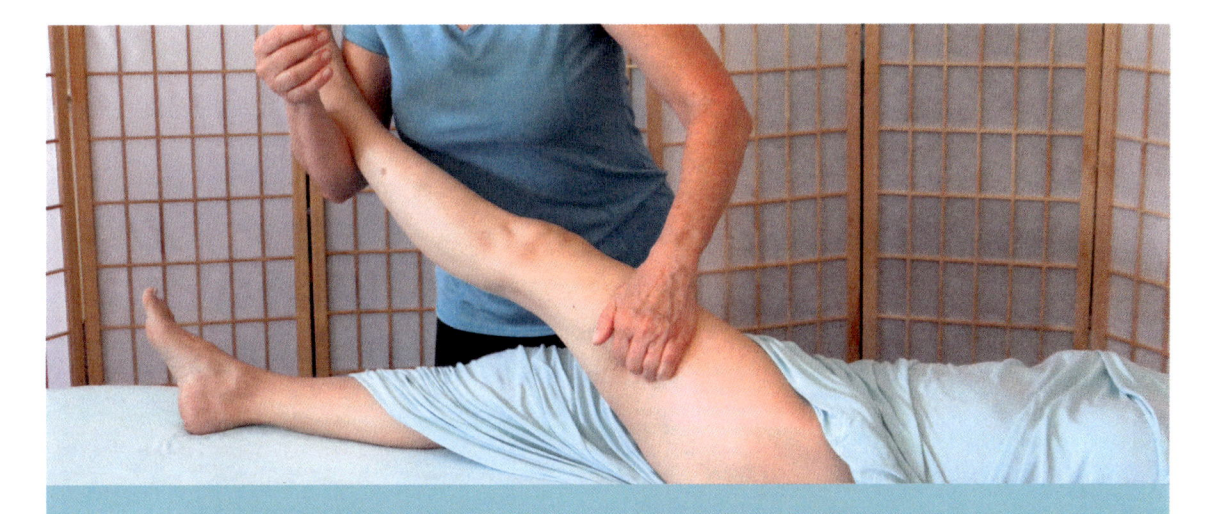

LS 35

Spiral Line Gluteus to Hamstring

Hold the client's ankle in the "V" of your down-table arm, while using your up-table arm to cross-fiber and then glide longitudinally to separate the valleys of the vastus lateralis and biceps femoris.

A Systematic Approach to Myofascial Network Release

LS 36

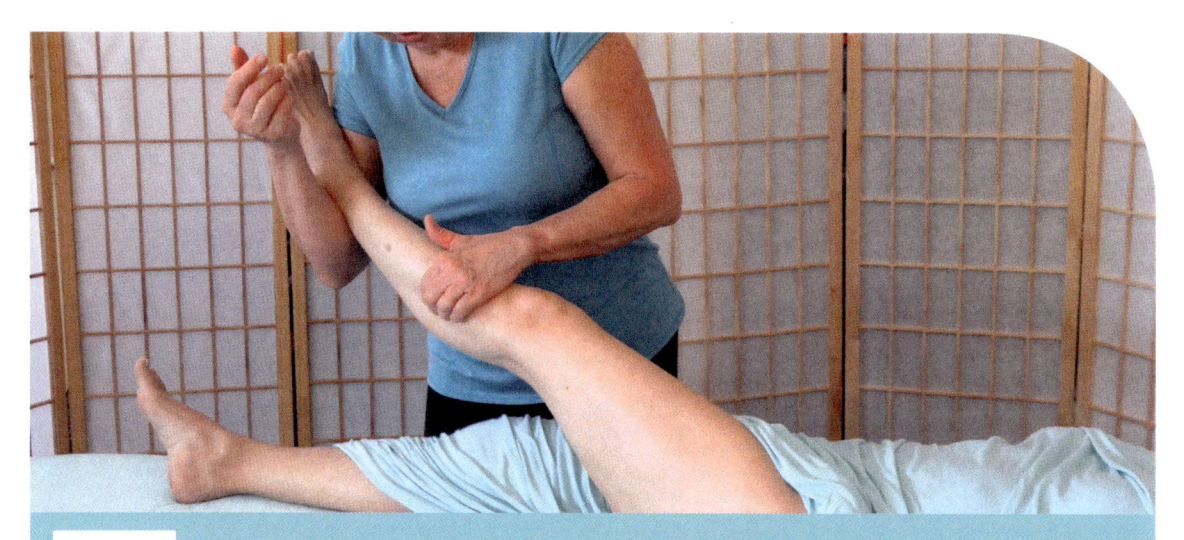

Spiral Line Hamstring to Fibularis
Hold the client's ankle in the "V" of your down-table arm, continuing raking using longitudinal stokes or cross fiber into the fibularis valleys to the back of the malleolus and then back to the knee.

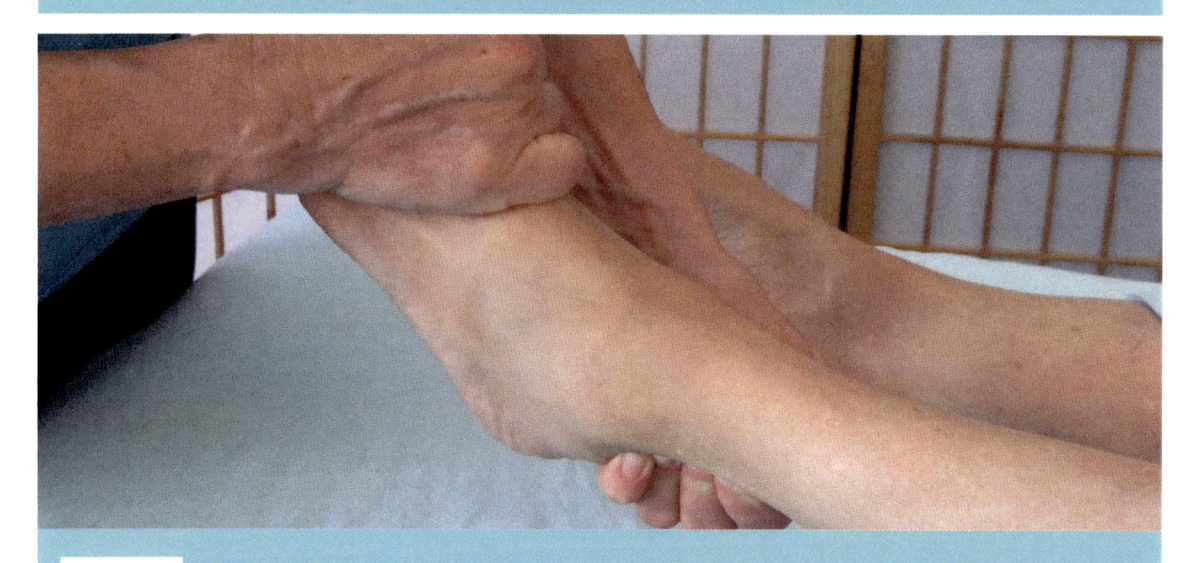

LS 37

Cross Achilles Twist
Pull the Achilles tendon from medial to lateral as you invert the foot; then pull the Achilles tendon from lateral to medial as you evert the foot. (Optional finish with a foot massage depending on time and client's need.) (*)

Upper Supine (US) | **SALMON-COLORED**

Continuing with our Manhattan subway train analogy, many of Myers' myofascial meridian Anatomy Trains® converge uptown at the neck and wrists. For you Chinese meridian enthusiasts, ever notice how many acupressure points reside in the head, neck, wrists, and hands? (The Chinese meridians, and Myers' meridians, also pass through the hips as they converge downtown at the ankles and feet, which we just addressed in the last sequence.) Since the client is already supine, now let's "take the trains uptown" to the upper body.

Entire section okay for (*).

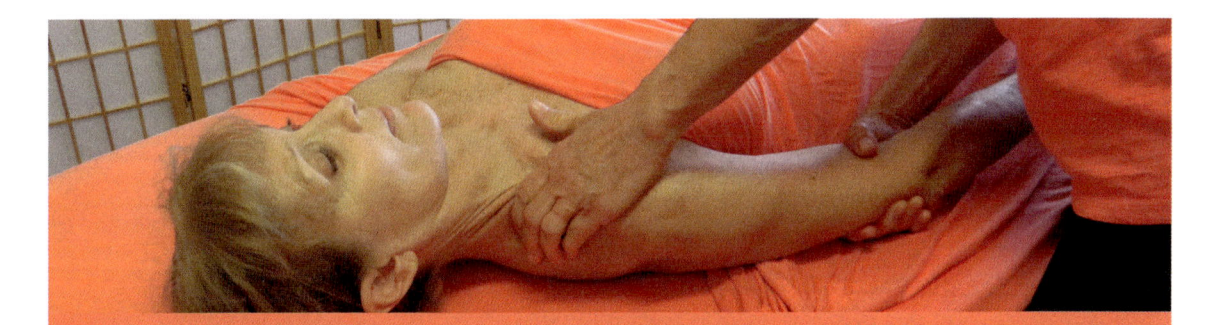

US 1

Upper Trapezius Shear

Traction the client's shoulder as you use your up-table hand to shear the upper trapezius muscle.

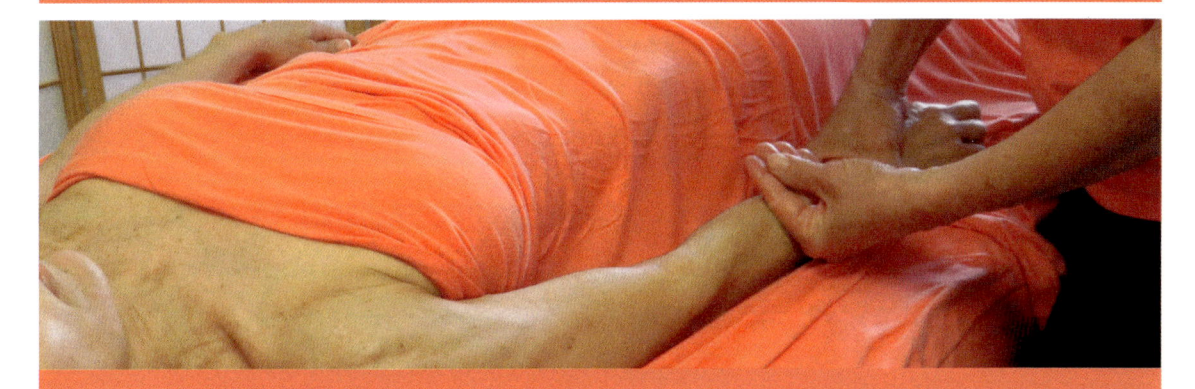

US 2

Arm Compression and Effleurage

Apply some glide to arm and shoulder, focusing on compressing wrist extensors and lateral triceps.

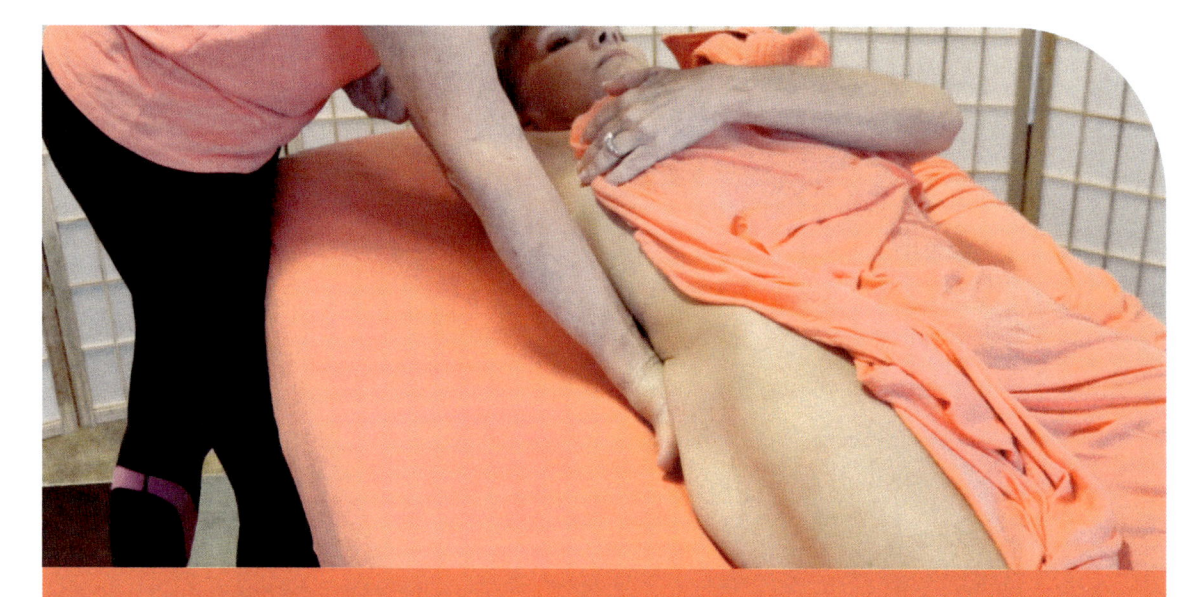

US 3

Functional Line Effleurage

Fold the drape back to expose the Lateral Line and side of the Functional Line from the lateral gluteus medius to axillary. Have the client hold breast tissue away if necessary, using drape or towel.

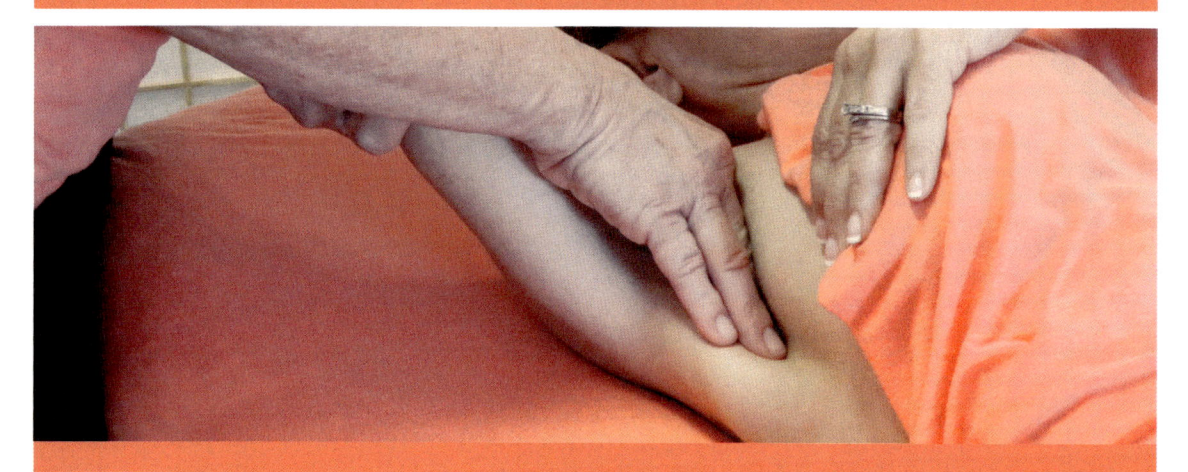

US 4

Subscapularis – Serratus Separation

Support the client's arm between your arm and torso. Then, using some glide, separate the subscapularis from the serratus anterior using your down table palm, then with your fingers as the tissue invites you in.

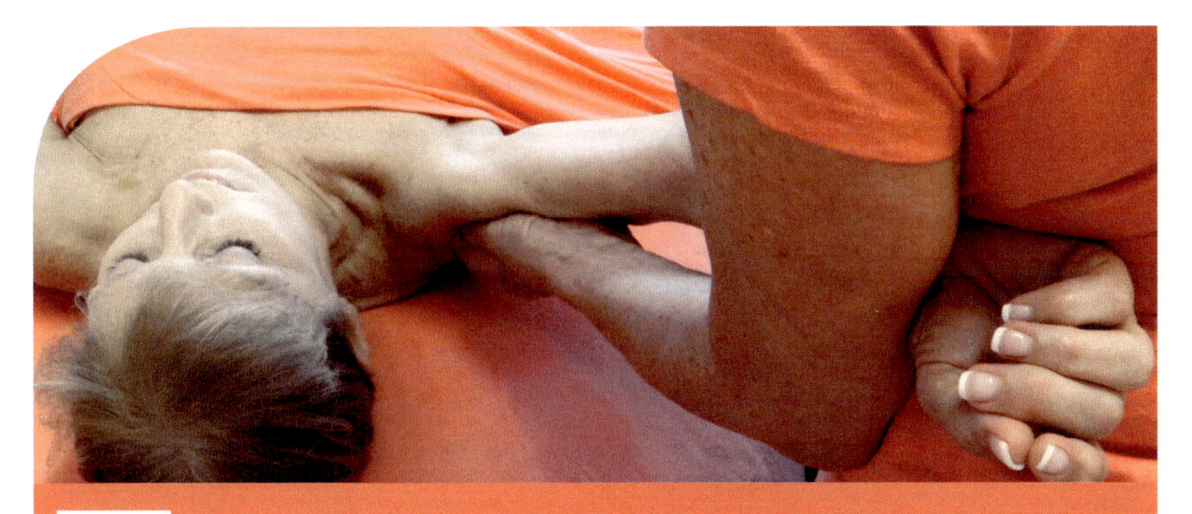

US 5

Deltoid Petrissage

With the client's arm still held secure between your torso and arm, use up-table hand to petrissage the deltoids.

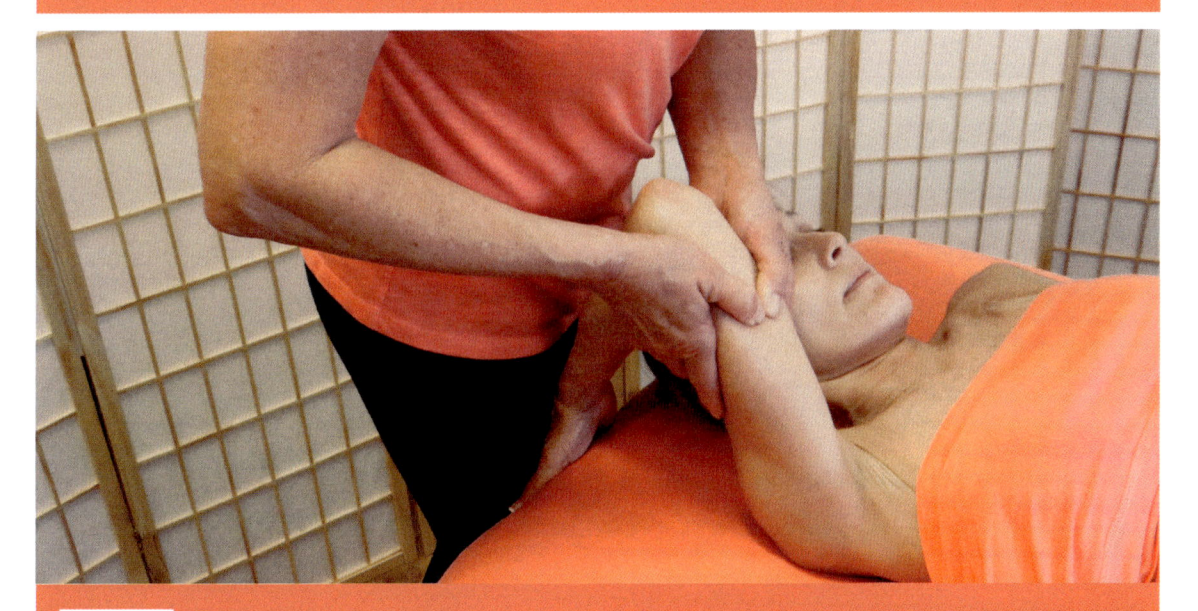

US 6

Tricep Shear

Secure the client's hand palm on table edge, between your thigh and the table. Use supported thumbs to compress triceps over the radial nerve groove shearing back and forth, and then longitudinally compress as you work from elbow proximal to axillary.

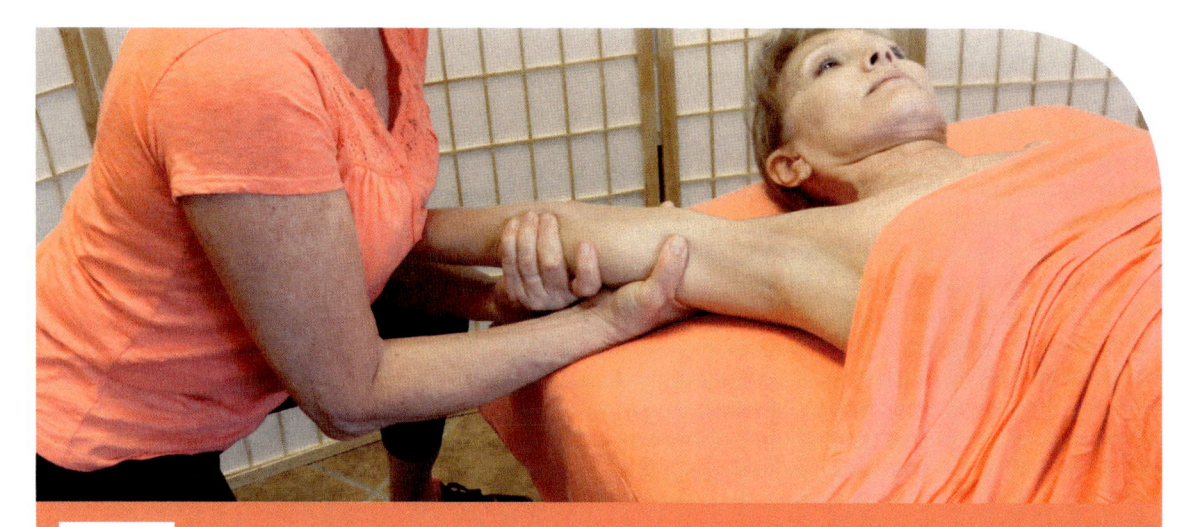

US 7

Pectoralis & Latissimus Stretch

Using glide, wrap both hands around client's arm at the axillary, then pull and rake arm from axillary to wrist. You can use opposite twisting motion, like wringing out a rag, repeatedly twisting proximal to distal, finishing at the wrist retinaculum.

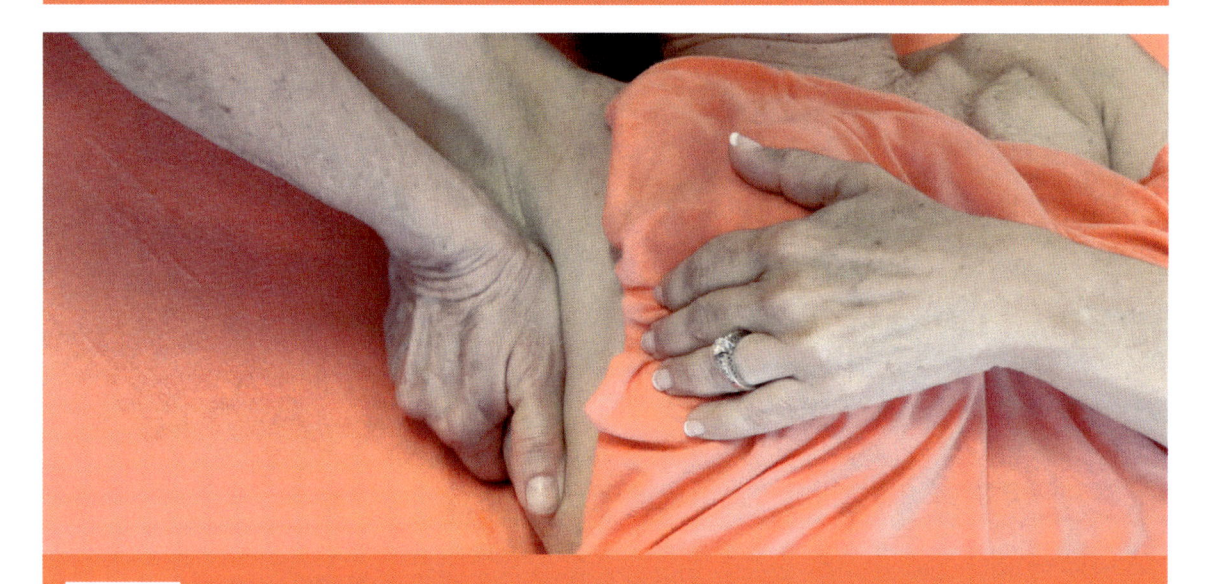

US 8

Teres Major Compression

With client's arm resting on table, elbow above the axillary, compress and shear the teres major with your palm.

US 9

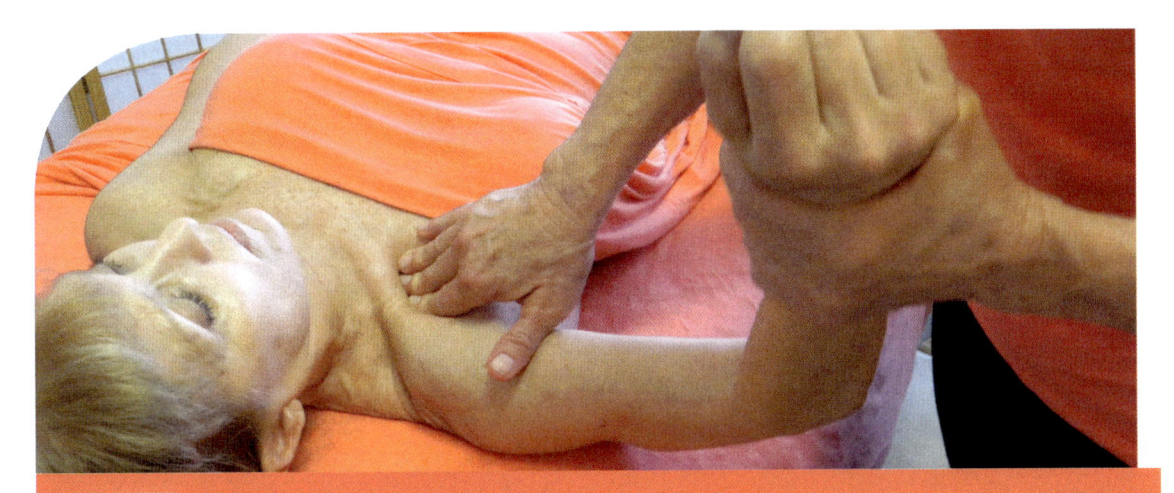

Subclavius Separation

Support the client's wrist with your up-table arm. Randomly move the client's arm as you work your fingertips into the pectoralis major clavicular head. As the tissue invites you in, work deeper into the subclavius as you continue to slowly move the arm in random motions to achieve more penetration.

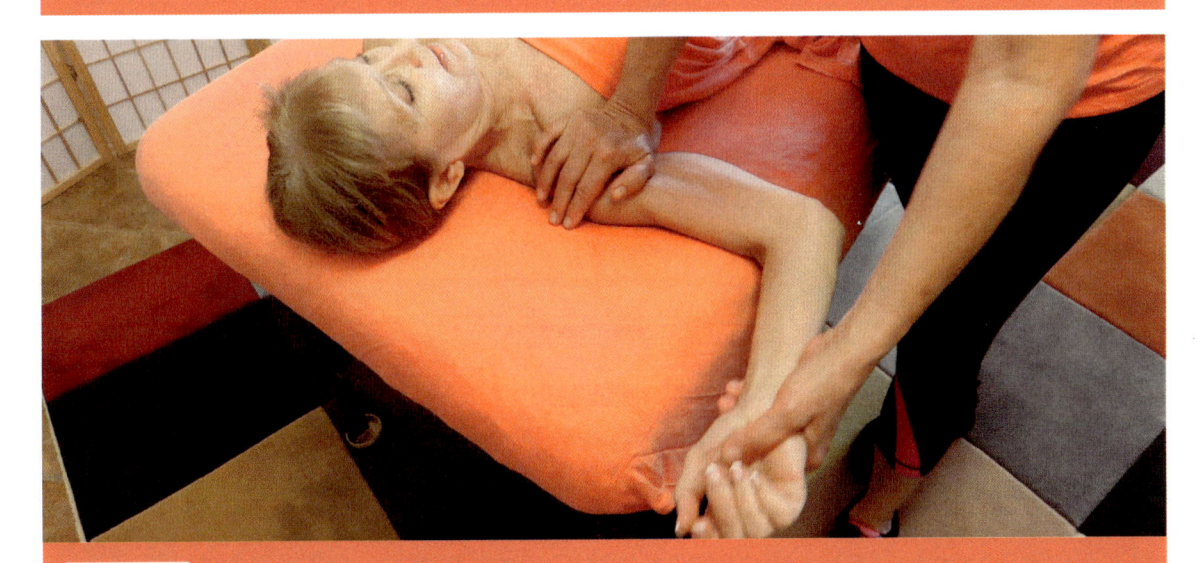

US 10

Pectoralis Minor Stretch

Use your palm to gently pin the hollow of the shoulder at the coracoid process, then gently externally rotate the arm.

US 11

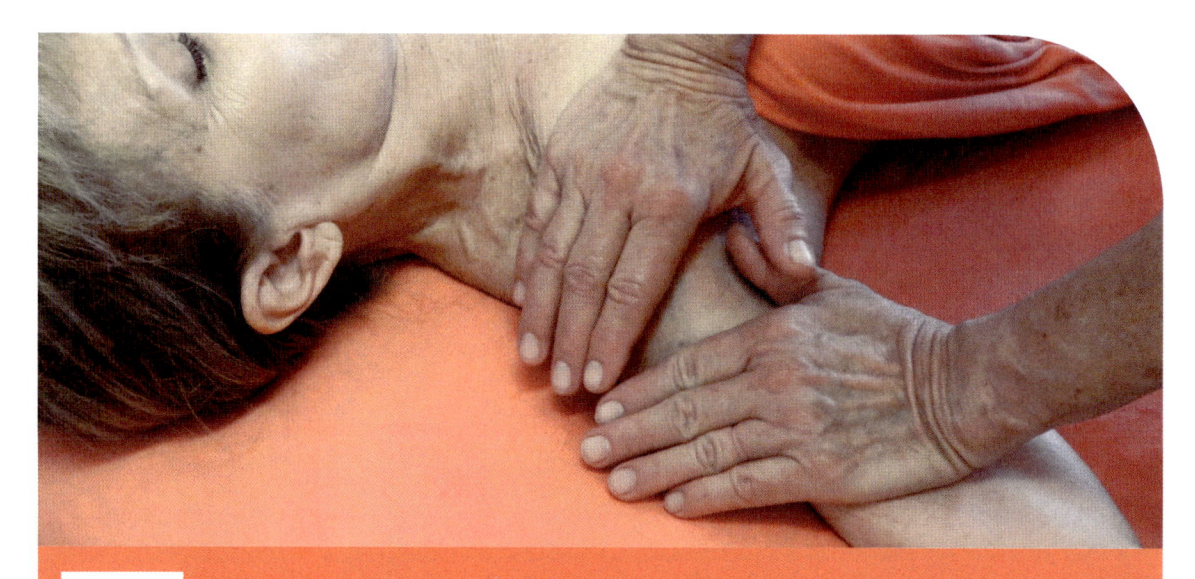

Pectoralis Major and Anterior Deltoid Shear

Use both palms of hands and simultaneously rotate outward and inward, providing a compressive shear force to the pectoralis major and the anterior deltoid.

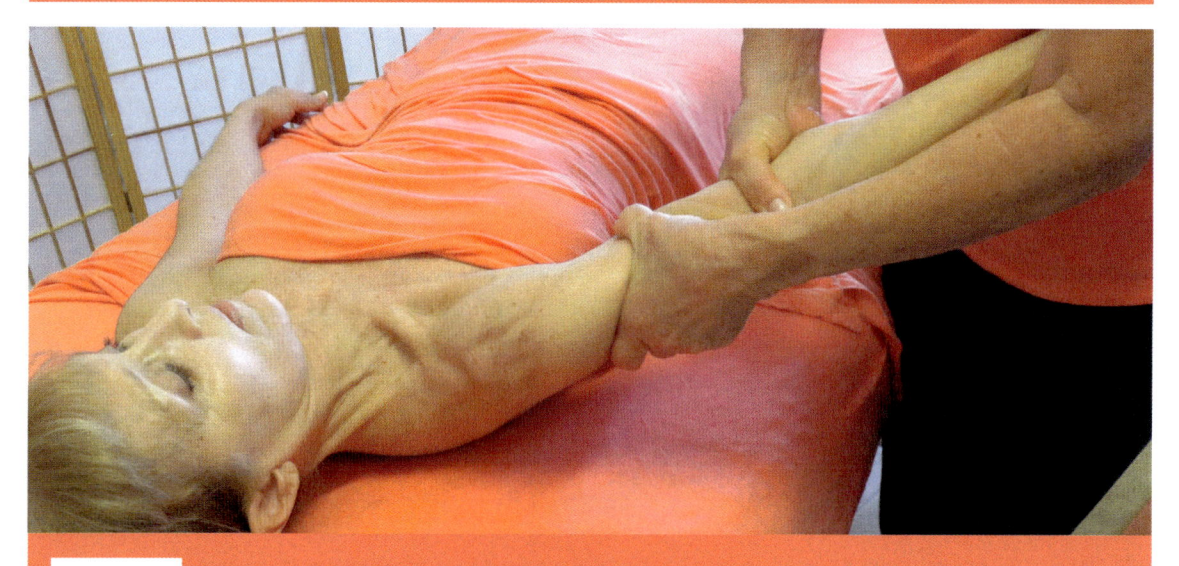

US 12

Arm Twist

Like you are wringing a towel, use both hands to twist in opposite directions starting from the axillary working distal toward the wrist.

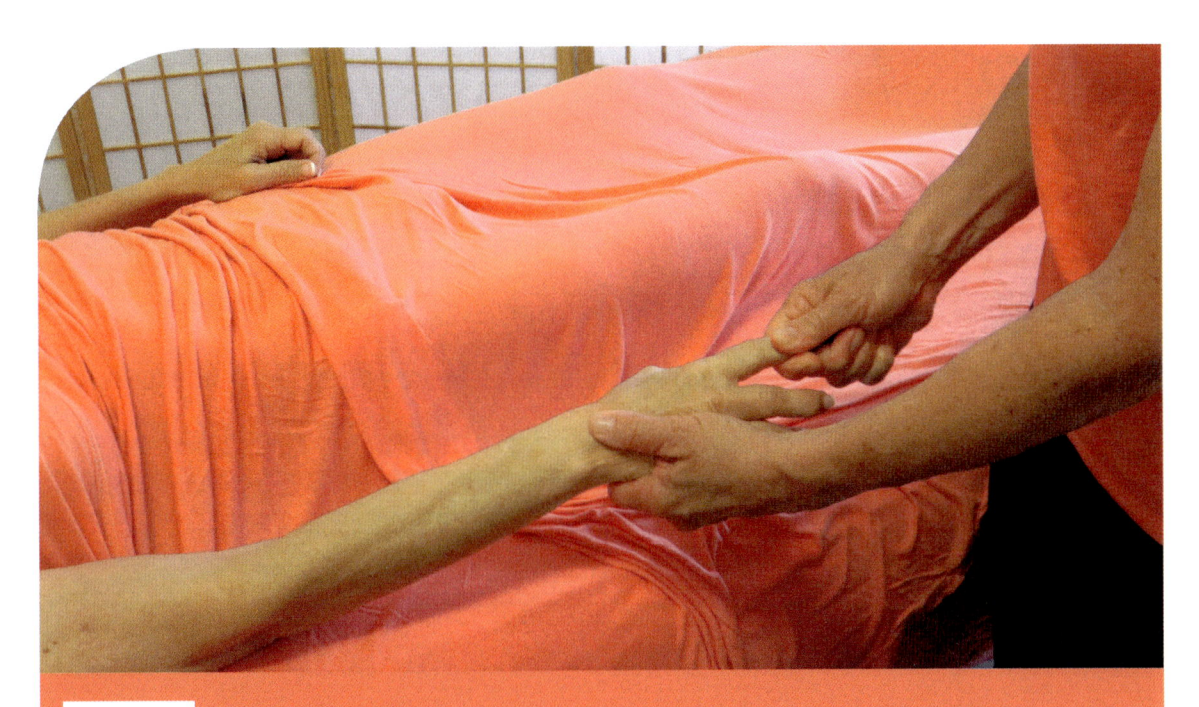

US 13
Finger Pull
Pull each finger with a gentle slow twisting motion.

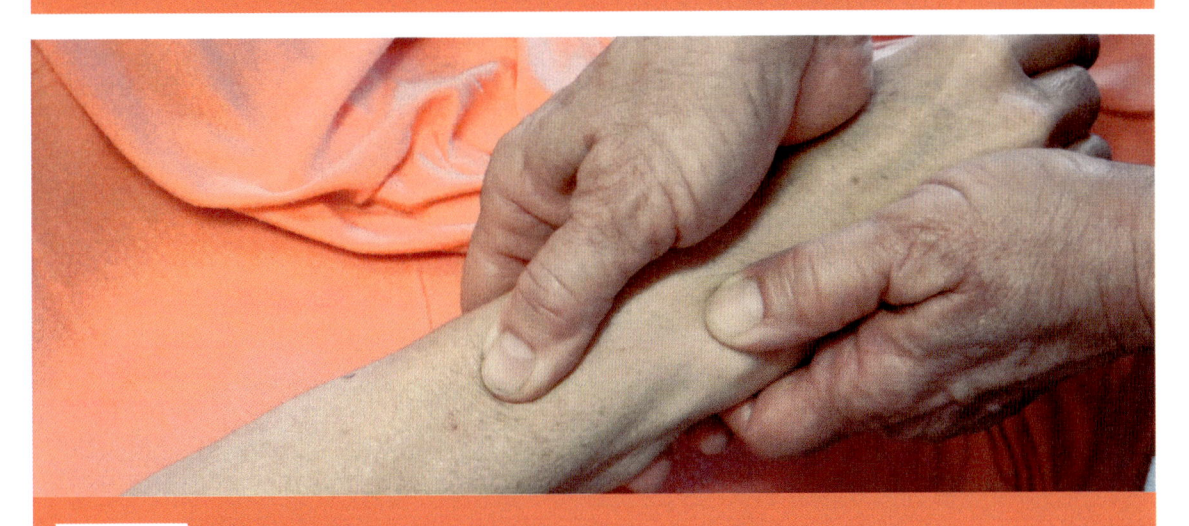

US 14
Wrist Extensor Acupressure Points
Massage and apply pressure to wrist and carpel acupressure points.

US 15

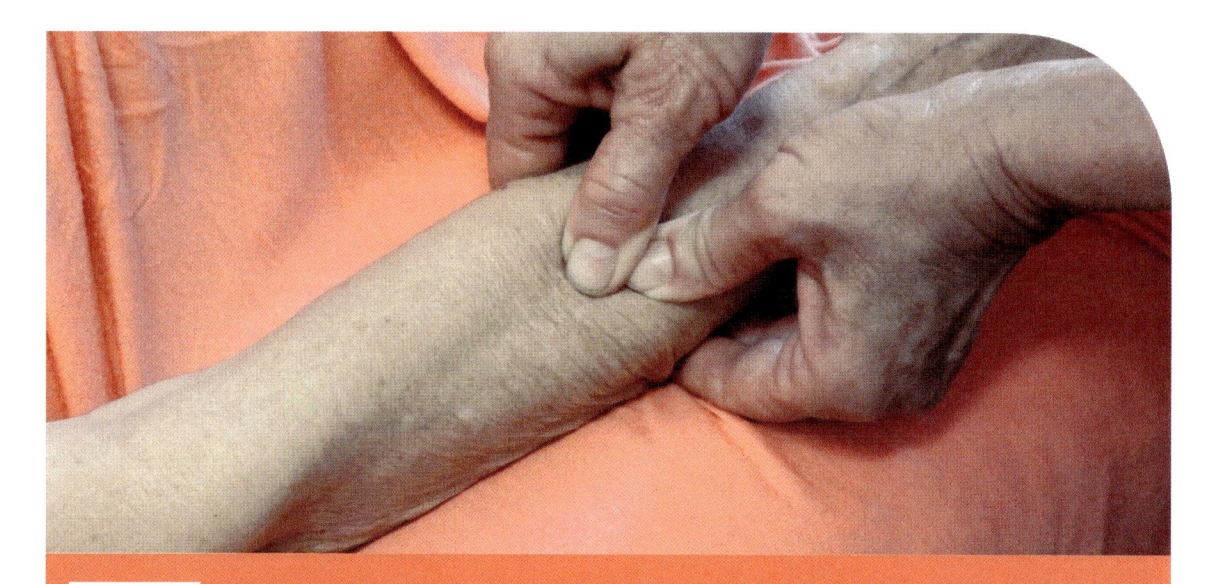

Forearm Wrist Extensor Separation

Using high friction glide, separate the valleys of the wrist extensor muscles from the wrist proximal to the elbow.

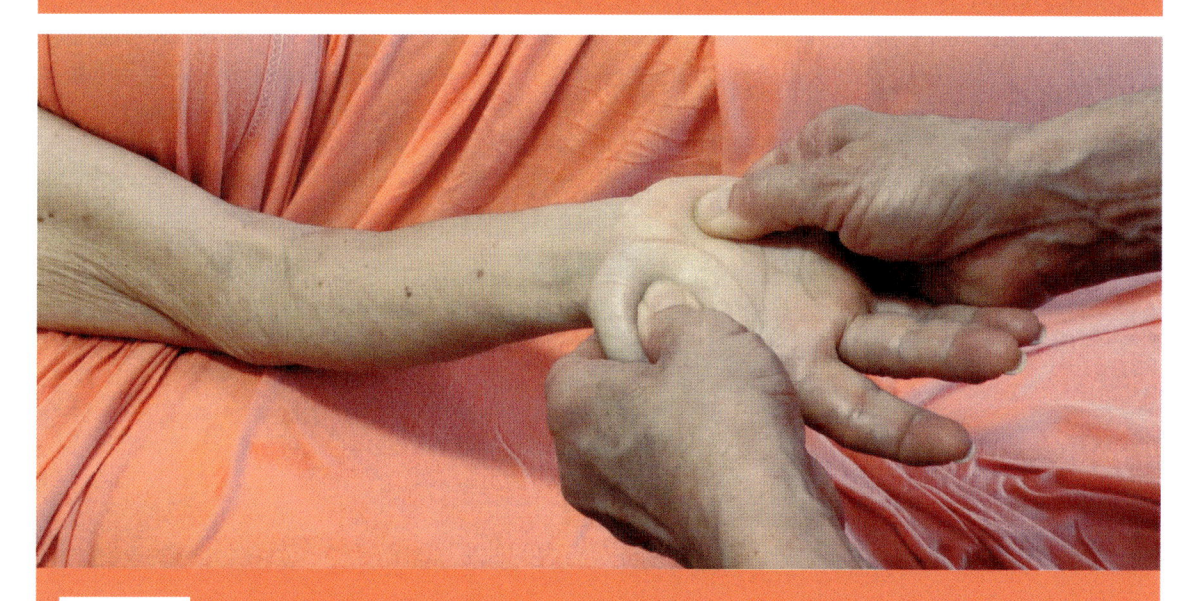

US 16

Thenar and Hypothenar Eminence Spread

Use your thumbs to spread the palm pads.

US 17

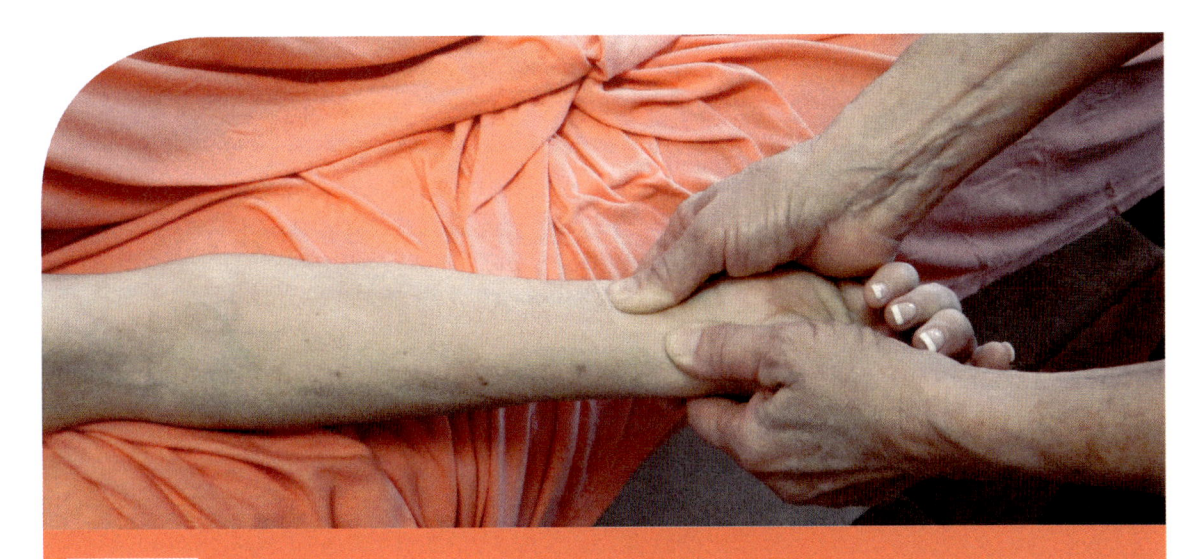

Wrist Flexor Acupressure Points
Massage and apply pressure to wrist and carpel acupressure points.

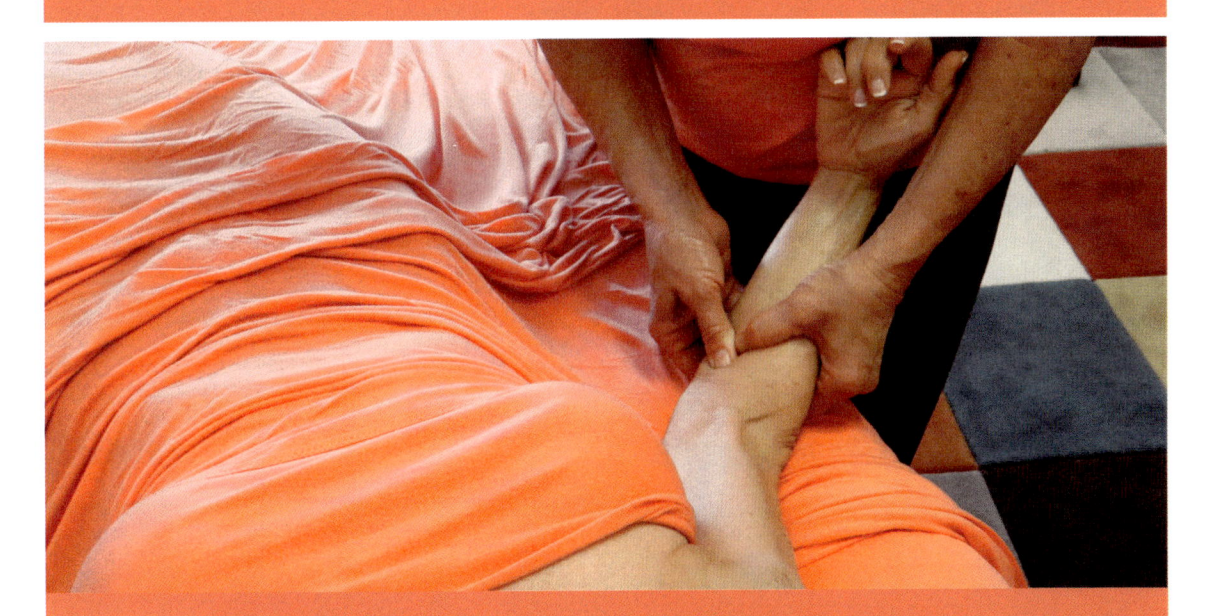

US 18

Forearm Wrist Flexor Separation
Using high friction glide, separate the valleys of the wrist flexor muscles, gliding proximal to the elbow.

US 19

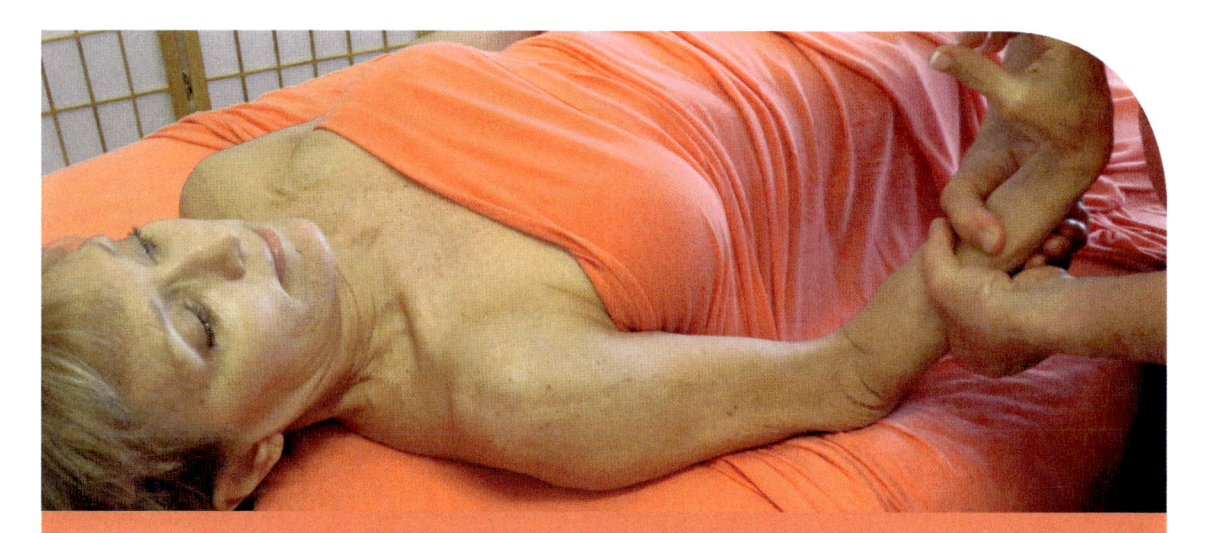

Forearm Twist
Like wringing a towel, use both hands to twist in opposite directions starting from the wrist proximal toward elbow.

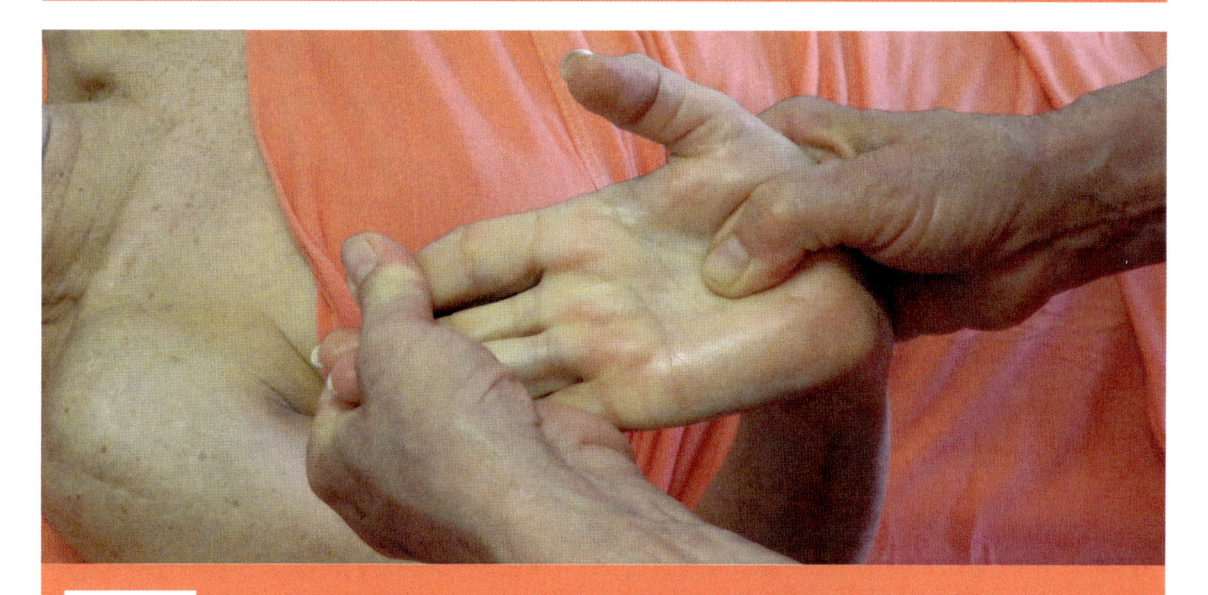

US 20

Fascial Finger Spread
Support the back of the hand with your fingers, placing your thumb in the client's palm; hyper-extend each finger one at a time as you spread the hand's fascia.

US 21

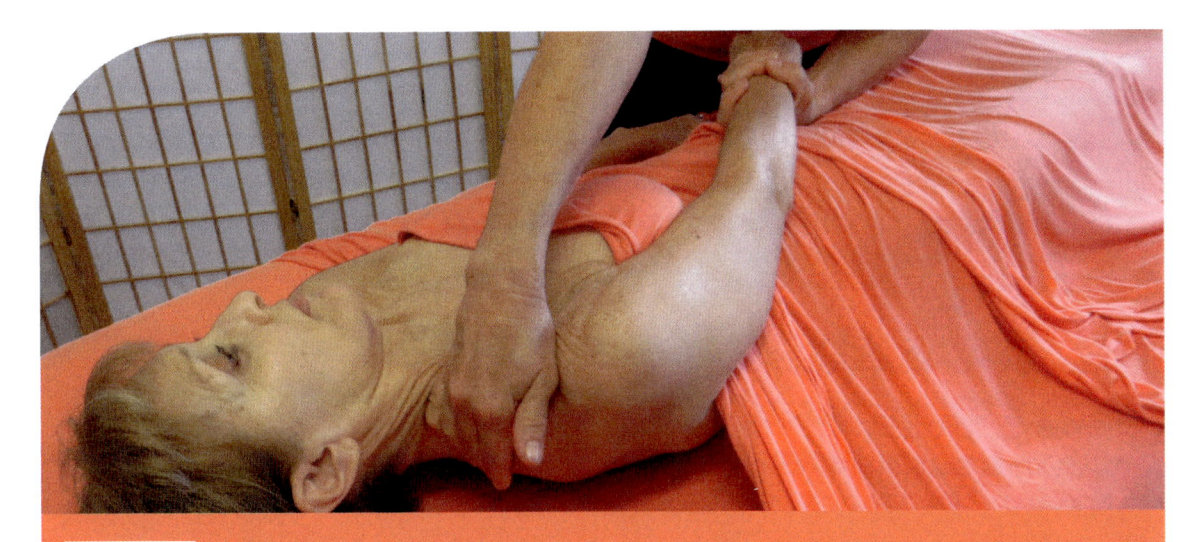

Trapezius Pull and Shear

Grab the client's wrist with your down table arm applying traction down and medially, just lateral to the pubic bone. As you pull, grab and shear the upper trapezius toward you.

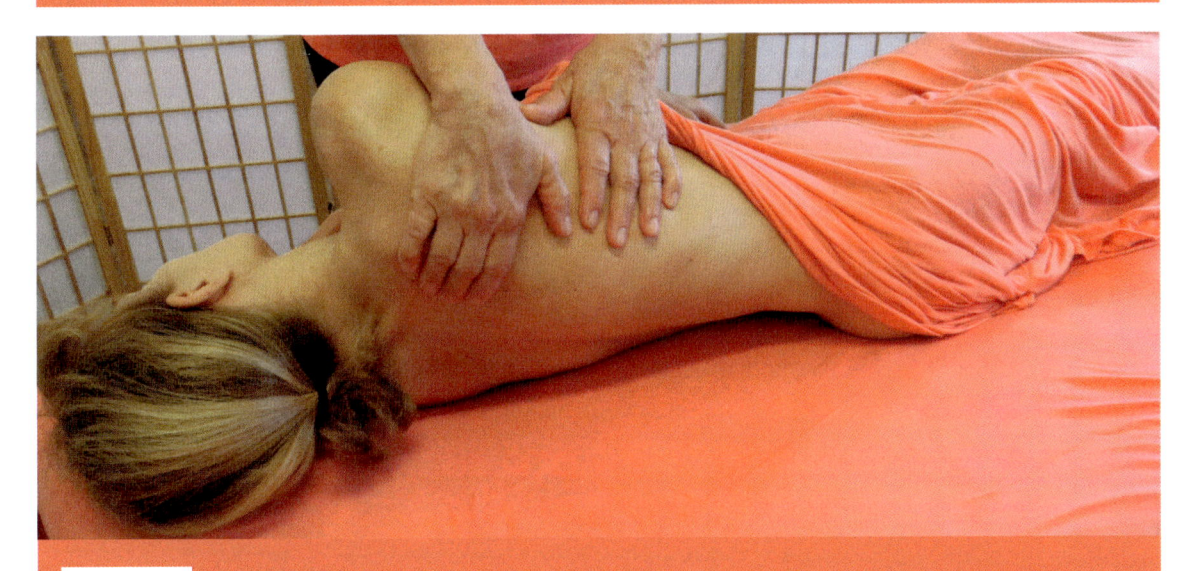

US 22

Cat Paw Spiral and Functional Lines

Use alternating "cat paw" shearing strokes as you pull tissue toward you, starting at the scapula, working down the side of the body toward the gluteus medius, then back to the scapula.

US 23

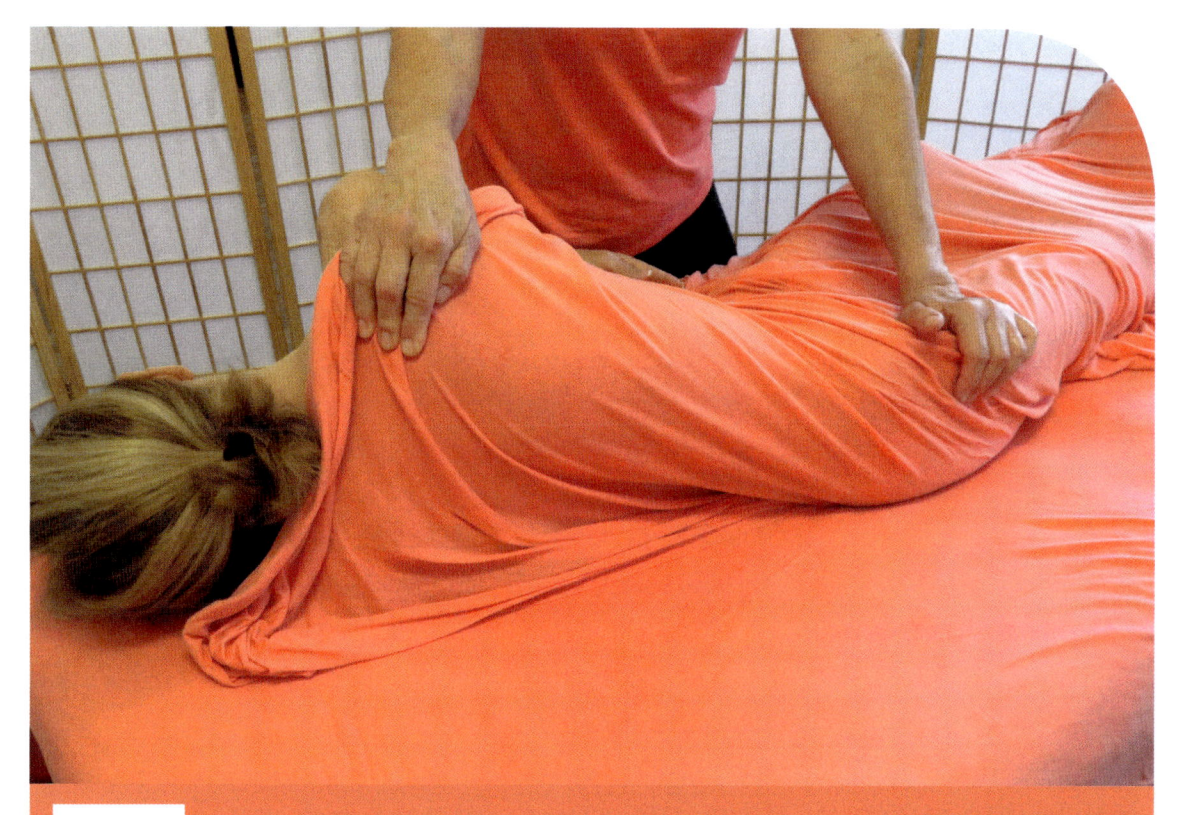

Internal External Oblique Twist

Firmly grasp the scapula with your up-table arm, securing the client's far ASIS with your down table palm, then use your body weight to gently lean back as you twist the client's torso.

Side Lying (SL) | SAGE-COLORED

Side lying is my favorite position to work on shoulders and the side of the neck. Using a large bolster, have the client lay stacked on their side, not leaning forward nor backward. With their lower leg straight, have the top bent leg rest on the bolster; use the up-table end of the bolster to help cover breasts. Place a hand towel on the lateral side of the breast to cover any exposed tissue.

Entire section okay for (*), except SL 12 and SL 13.

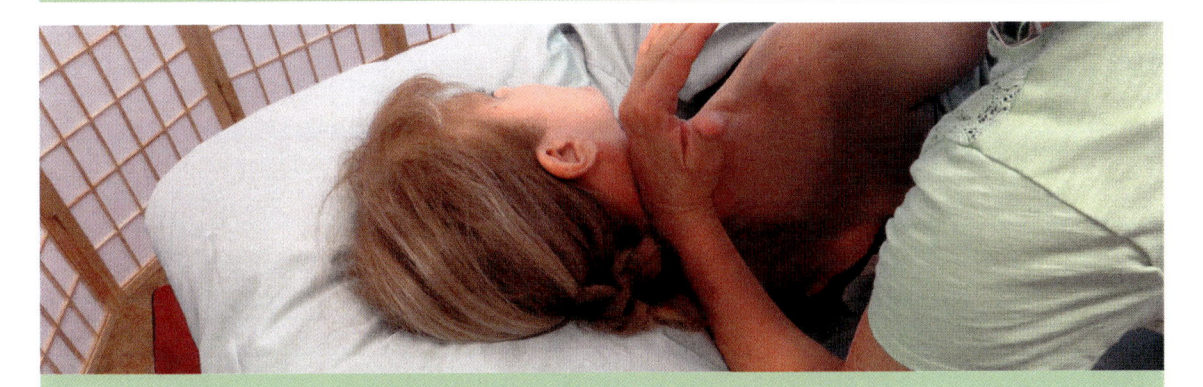

SL 1

Neck Myofascial Rake

With very little glide, use your forearm to shear the posterior scalene and trapezius in one long stroke from your elbow down to the side of the hand, making special note to "hook" with the side of your palm as you finish the stroke.

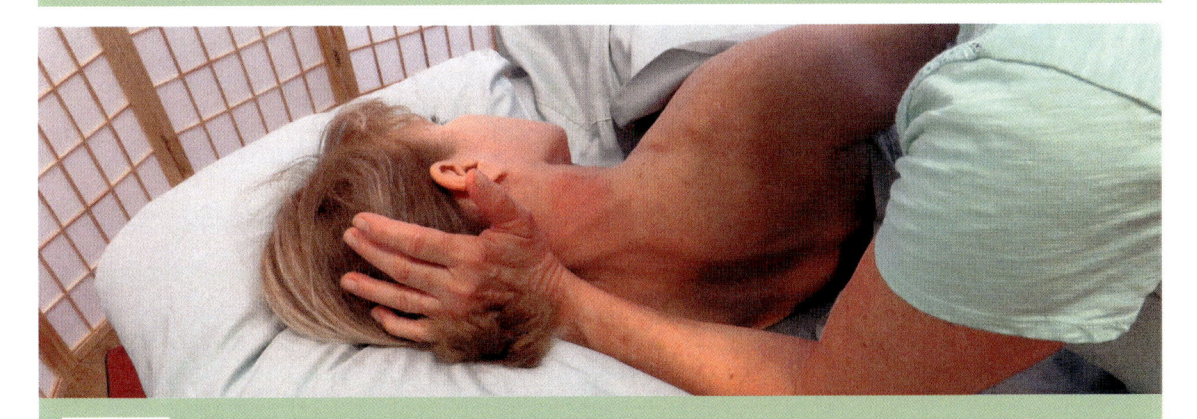

SL 2

Occipital Shear

Place the middle of your palm on the mastoid process and shear into the occipitals.

SL 3

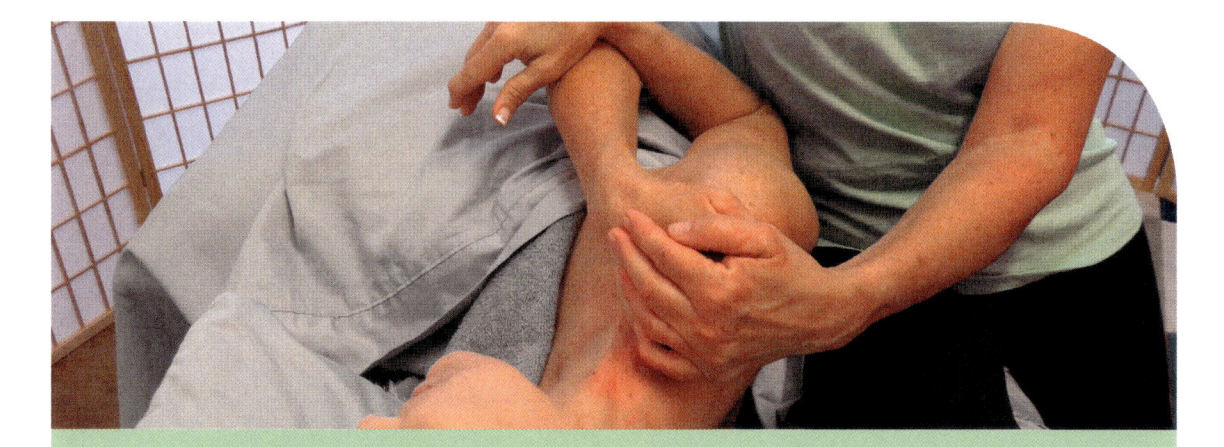

Trapezius Longitudinal Compressions

Sitting on the table behind the client, place both hands on top of the shoulder, lean back and forth with your bodyweight to massage and stretch the trapezius with the sides of your hands.

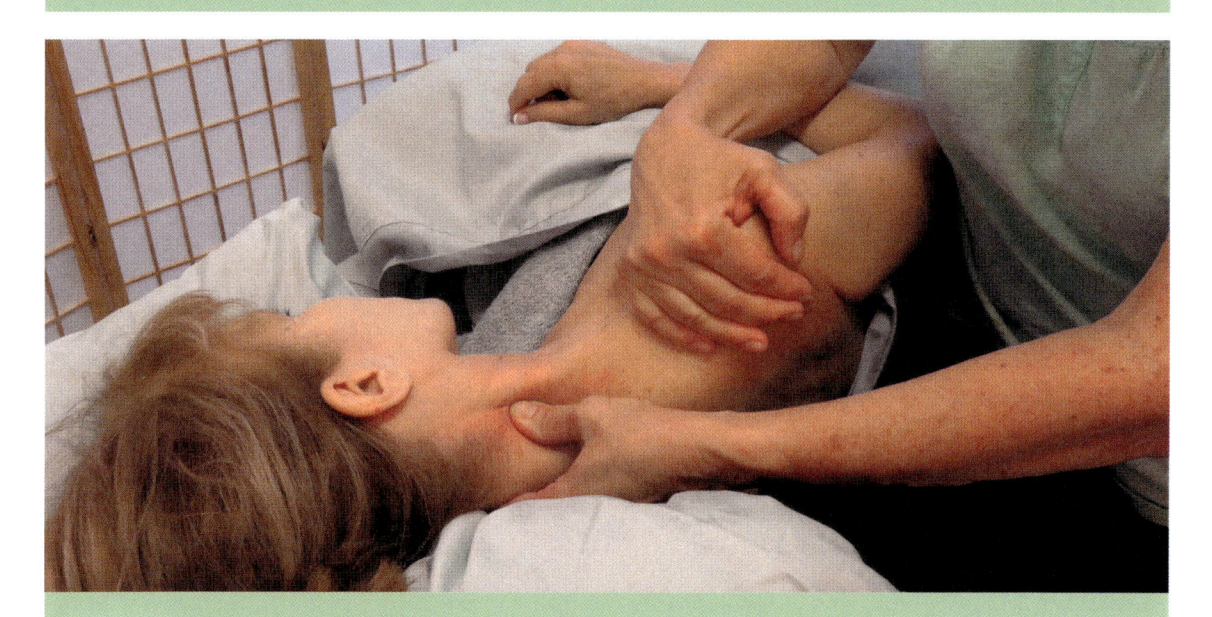

SL 4

Lamina Grove Stretch and Compression

Pull the shoulder down with your inside hand as you use your outside hand to pin and stretch the lamina groove from the mastoid process working inferiorly. Then with some glide, longitudinally glide inferior to superior along the lamina groove.

SL 5

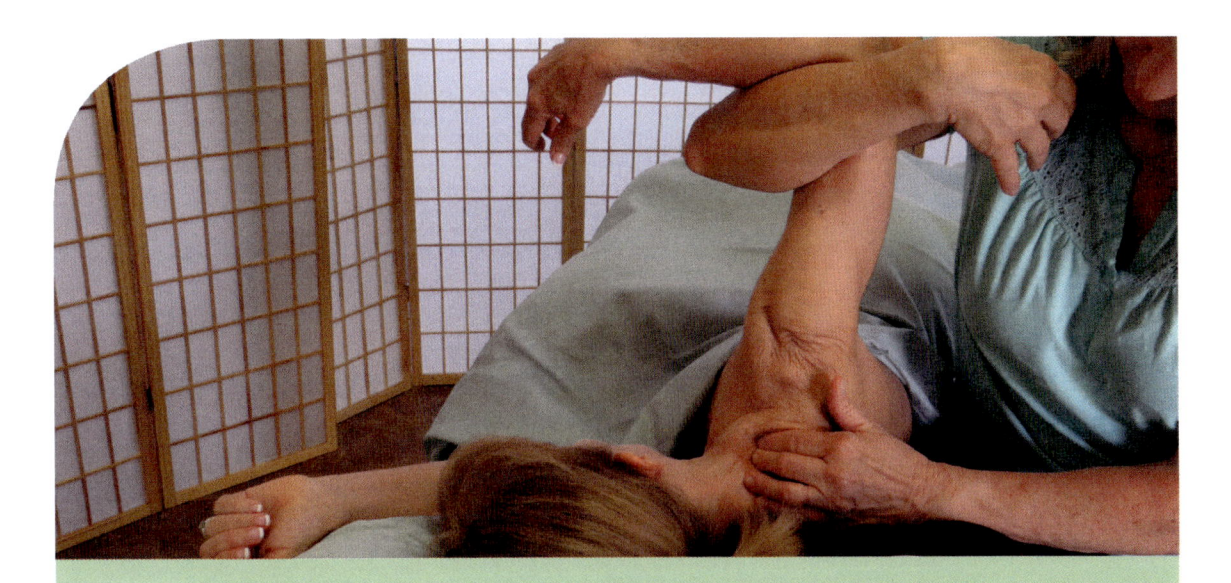

Splenius Capitus and Cervices Circles

Support the client's arm in the crook of your inside arm, while using the outside fingers to form compressive circles, working from the upper trapezius down into the splenius capitis and splenius cervicis muscles.

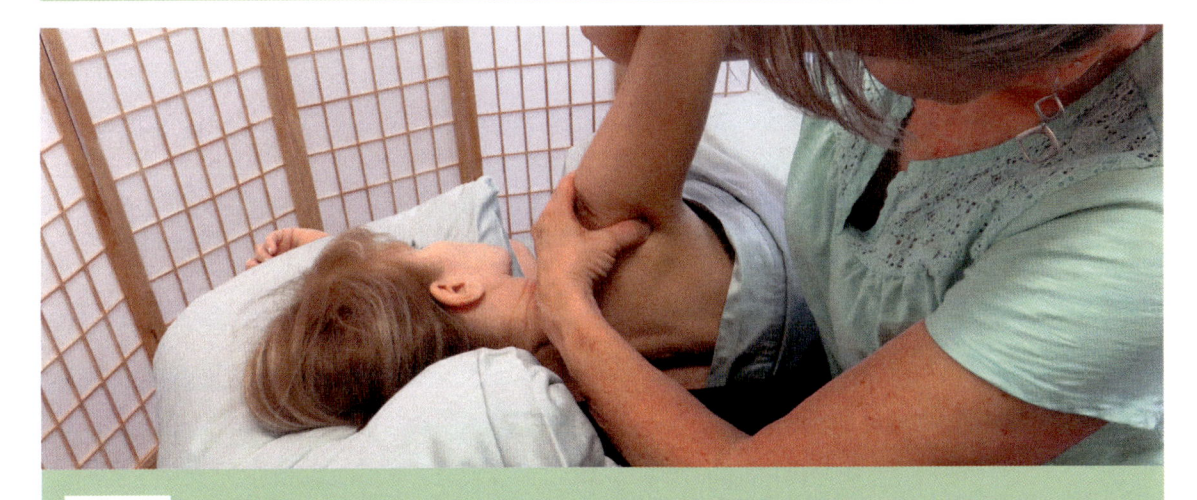

SL 6

Deltoid, Infraspinatus, and Teres Minor Rake

Support the client's arm in the crook of your inside arm, using some glide, massage deltoid with the outside hand, then twist deltoid, infraspinatus, and teres minor into the axilla.

SL 7

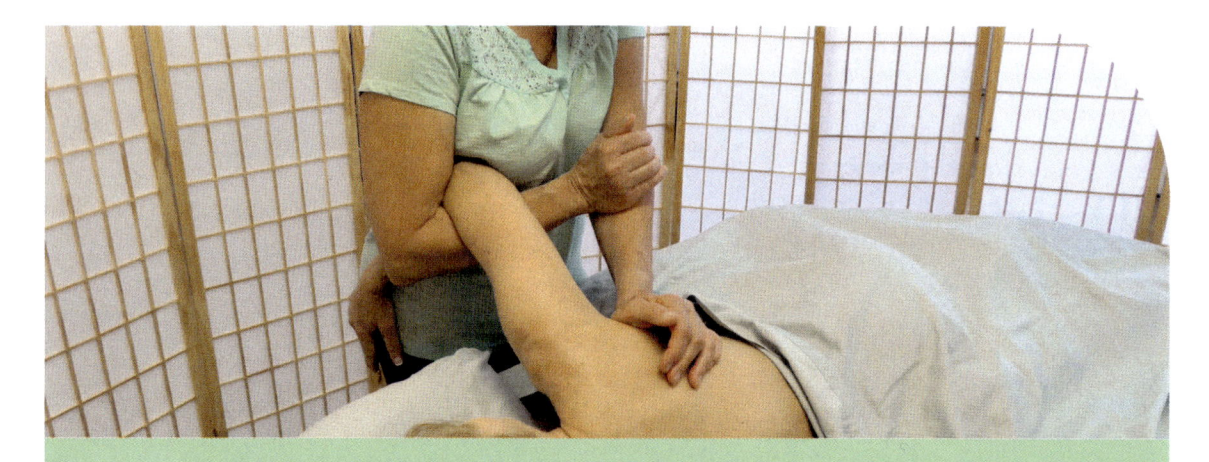

Latissimus Dorsi and Teres Major Compression

Hold the client's elbow in the crook of your elbow with your up-table arm; use broad firm, but gentle compressive strokes on the belly of the latissimus dorsi and the belly of the teres major using your forearm or hand.

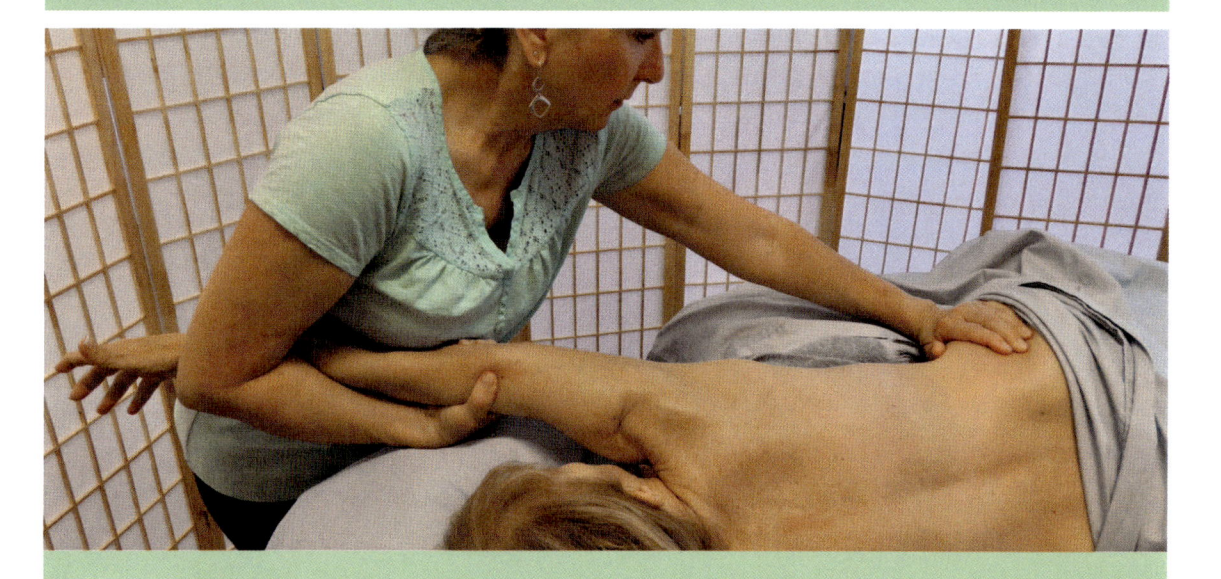

SL 8

Functional Line Stretch

Support the client's arm between your torso and up table arm. Using glide, slide your down table hand along the ribs, anchoring your palm into the anterior superior iliac spine. Then firmly pull the client's arm gliding from the axilla to the elbow (or wrist if your arms are long enough).

SL 9

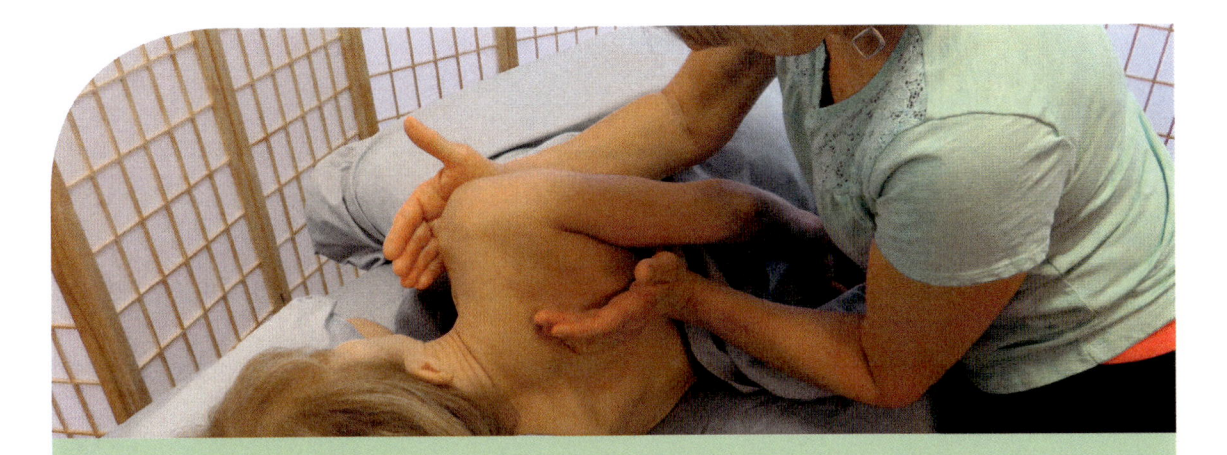

Anterior Posterior Shoulder Circles

Place the client's arm behind their lumbar. Put the side of your palm on the hollow between the deltoid and pectoralis major. Put the edge of your outside palm on the medial edge of the scapula. Move the shoulder in oscillating circles.

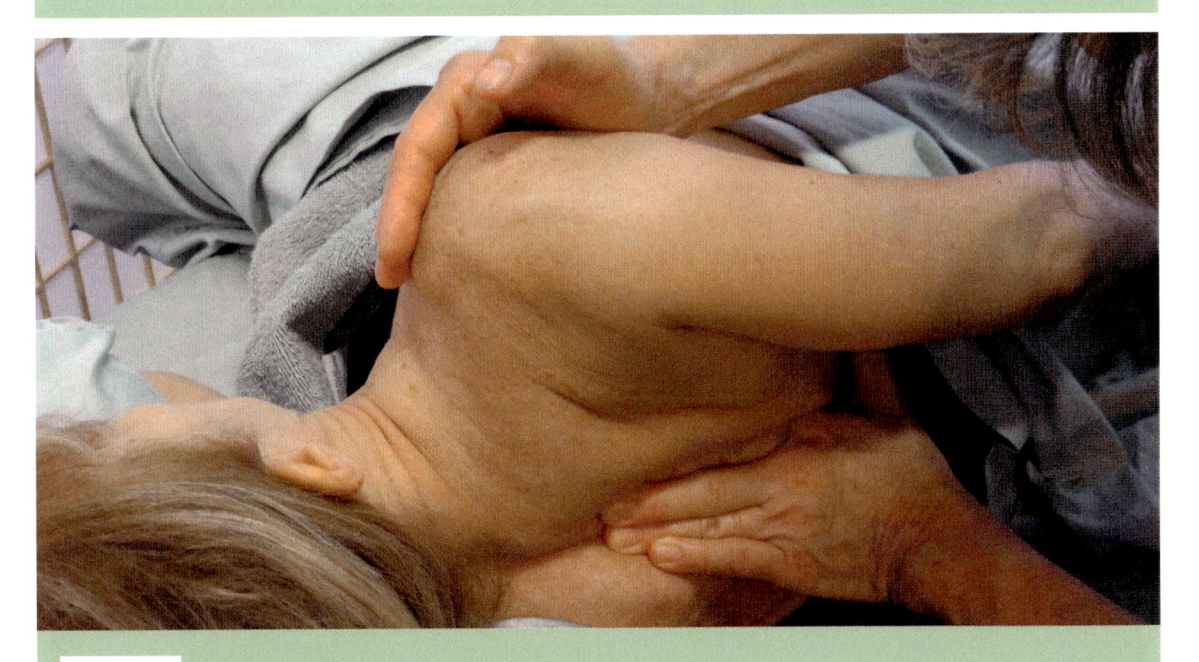

SL 10

Rhomboid Compression

Use the index finger or thumb of your outside hand to push underneath the medial border of the scapula, working inferior to superior just past the levator scapulae.

SL 11

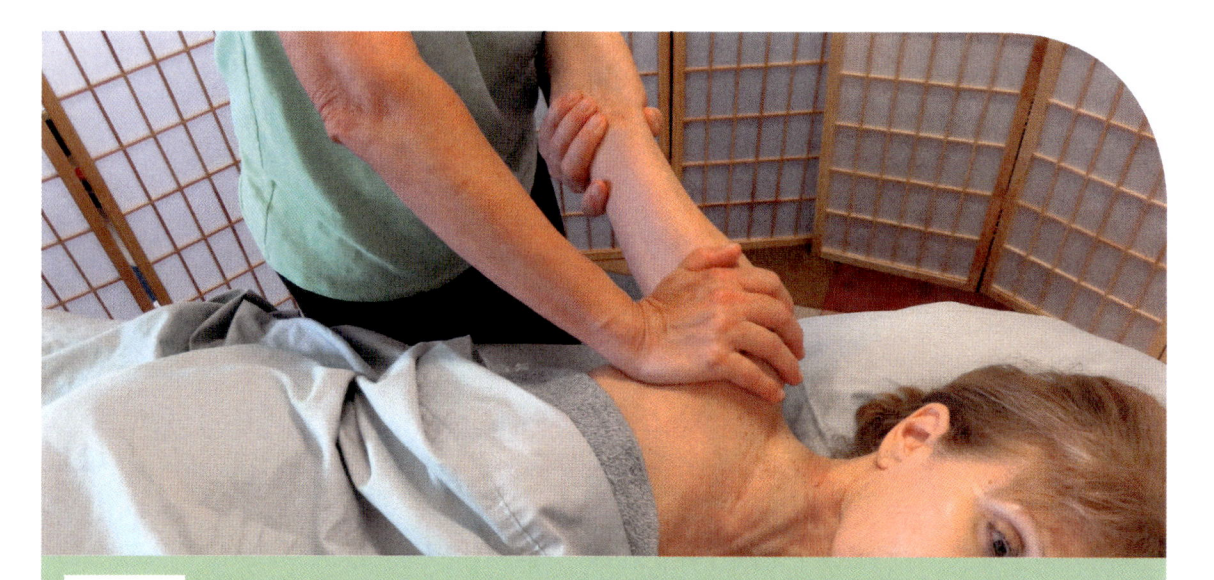

Pectoralis Major Stretch

Secure the client's arm between your up-table arm and your torso. With the pectoralis major in tension, gently hook the lateral border with the palm of your hand as you push medially into the muscle belly.

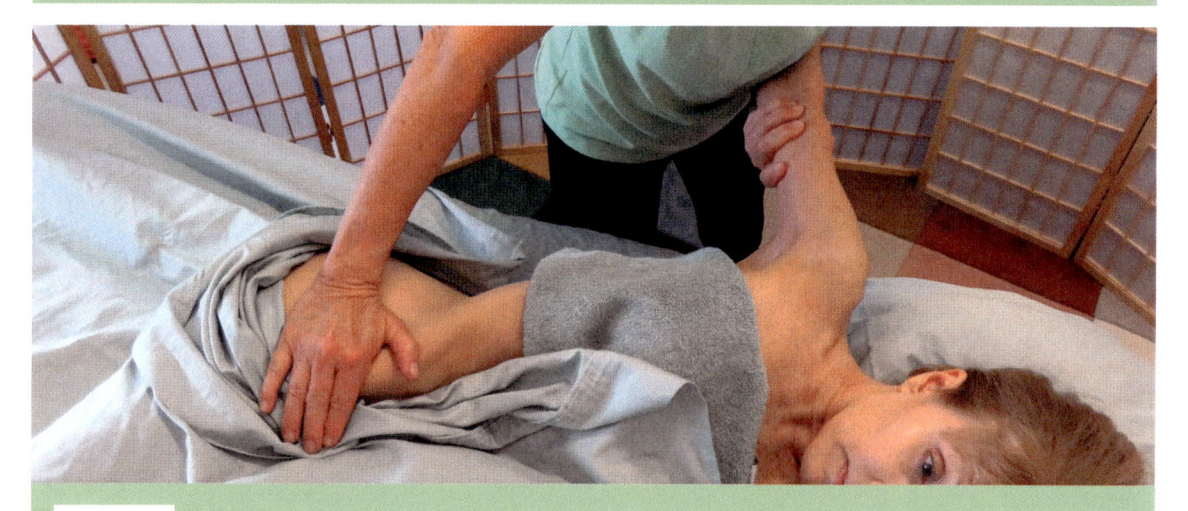

SL 12

Oblique Stretch

Secure the client's arm between your up-table arm and your torso; place your down table palm on the client's gluteus medius to provide an anchor. Gently lower your body to provide a stretch to the internal and external obliques and pectoralis major.

SL 13

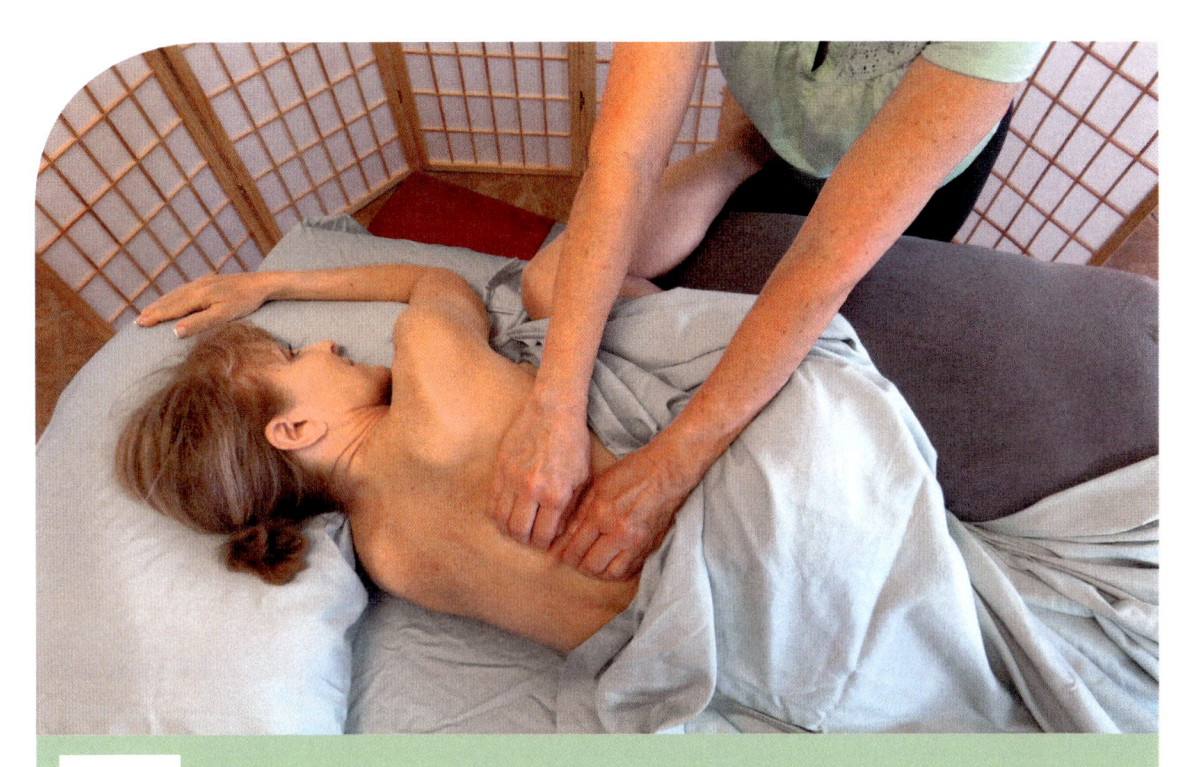

Fetal Superficial Back Line Scrunch

Place client's foot on your hip; using your fingertips, reach across and cross fiber the erector spinae group from the neck to the sacrum, and then from the sacrum just lateral to the sacral edge to the ischial tuberosity. Contraindicated for (*).

Sims' Lateral Recumbent (SLR) | LAVENDER-COLORED

Sims' Lateral Recumbent is my favorite position to help work deeply into the glutes and hips. The classic prone position has several disadvantages: it can actually create tension in the Sacro-lumbar region and buttock on some clients, it is uncomfortable for clients who have had augmentation mammoplasty (especially those with subpectoral implants), sinus drainage occurs during cold and allergy seasons, breathing restriction can occur, and some clients feel claustrophobic. The side lying and Sims' lateral recumbent are also excellent positions for those women who are pregnant. Some people fall asleep with one arm behind or under them, and one leg bent; hence, why I casually refer to this position as "sleepy" position. Place a small bolster under the hip of the bent leg to support the pelvis. Place a hand towel on the lateral side of the breast to cover any exposed tissue. Be careful of draping around the groin; use a towel for added security. Offer a pillow for the head. If the arm is behind client, watch for any kinks in the neck since the head is rotated.

Entire section okay for (*).

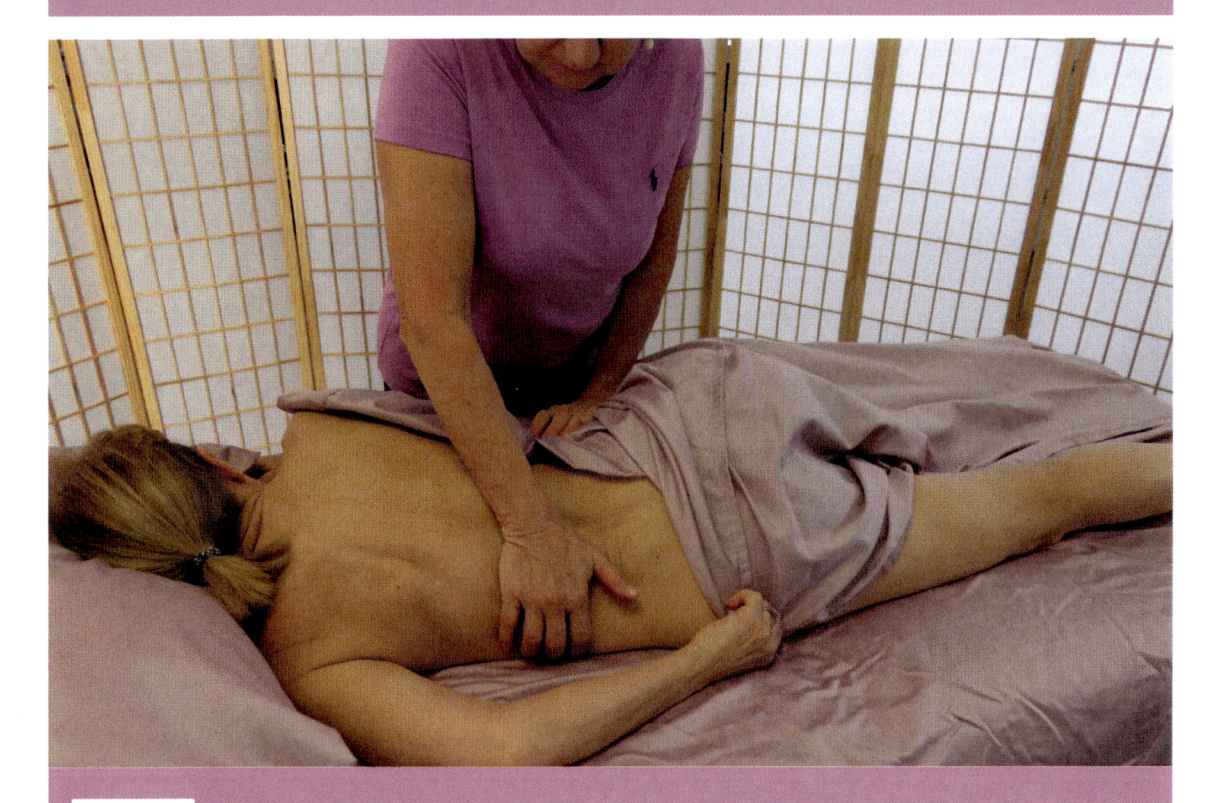

SLR 1

Erector Spinae Compression

With very little glide, use your palms to cross fiber shear the erector spinae group from the sacrum to the neck.

SLR 2

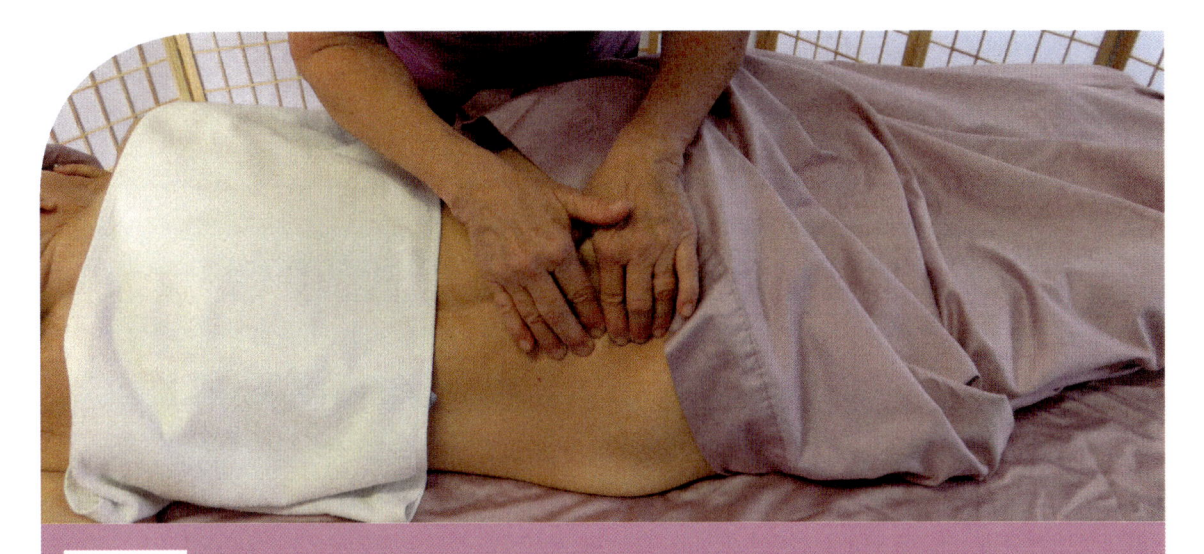

Sacrum Compression

With your fingertips, sink into the sacrum using cross-fiber compression strokes.

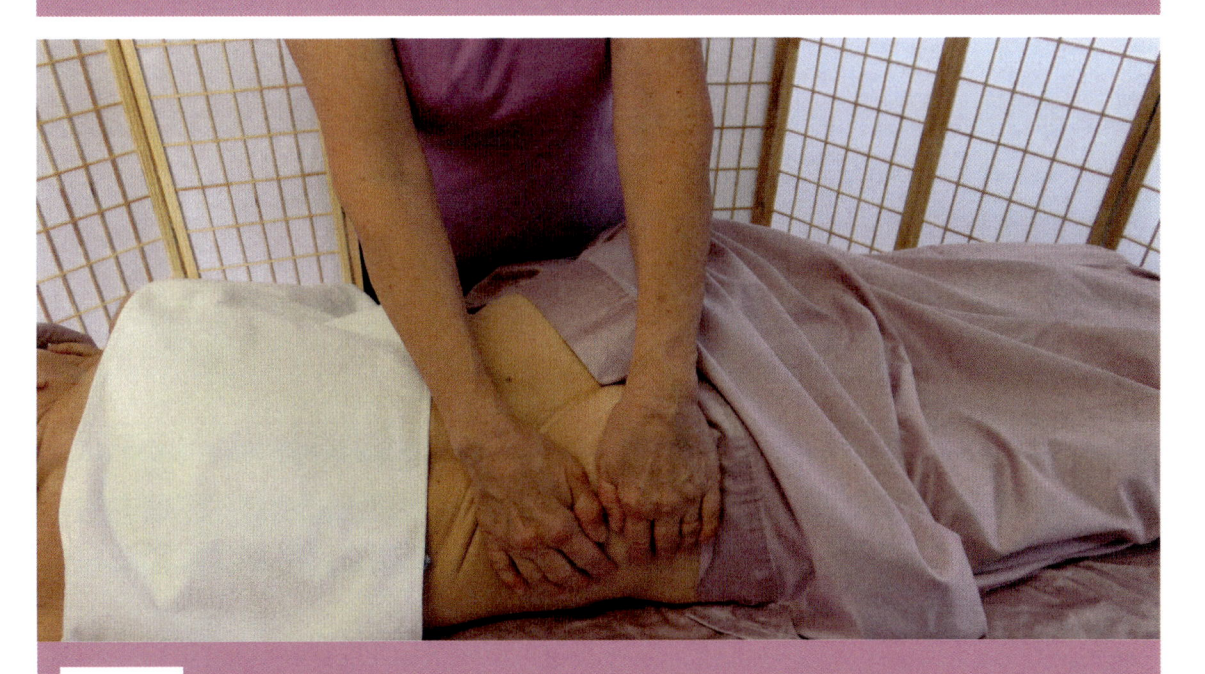

SLR 3

Sacral Band Pull

Use both hands to grab the far gluteus medius above the trochanter pulling lateral to medial across the piriformis to the sacrum, continuing into the near side piriformis.

SLR 4

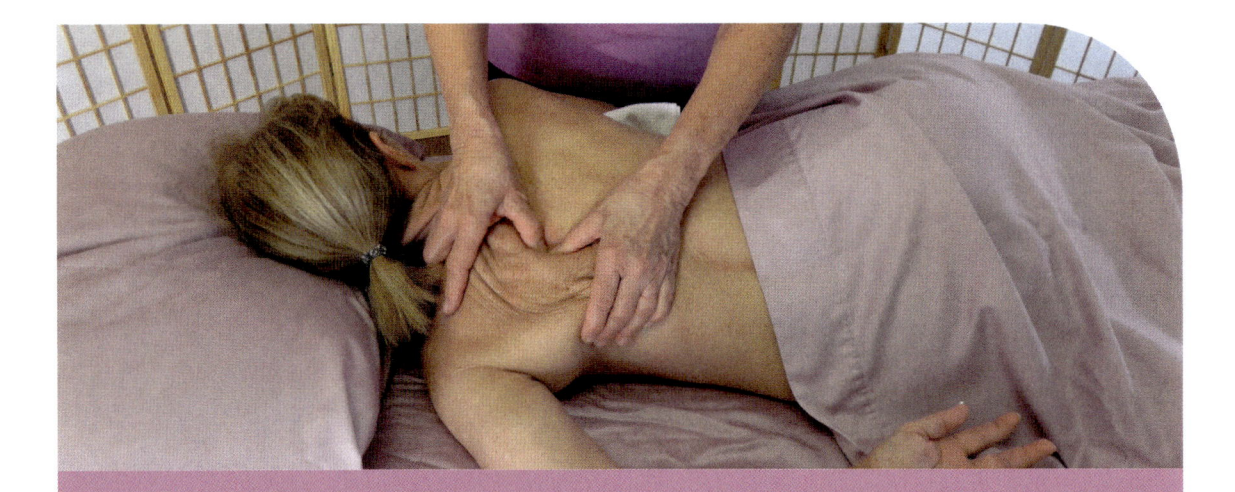

Rhomboid-Serratus Shear

Use thumbs or fingers to work under the medial border of the scapula. You can also massage the entire shoulder with particular attention to the infraspinatus.

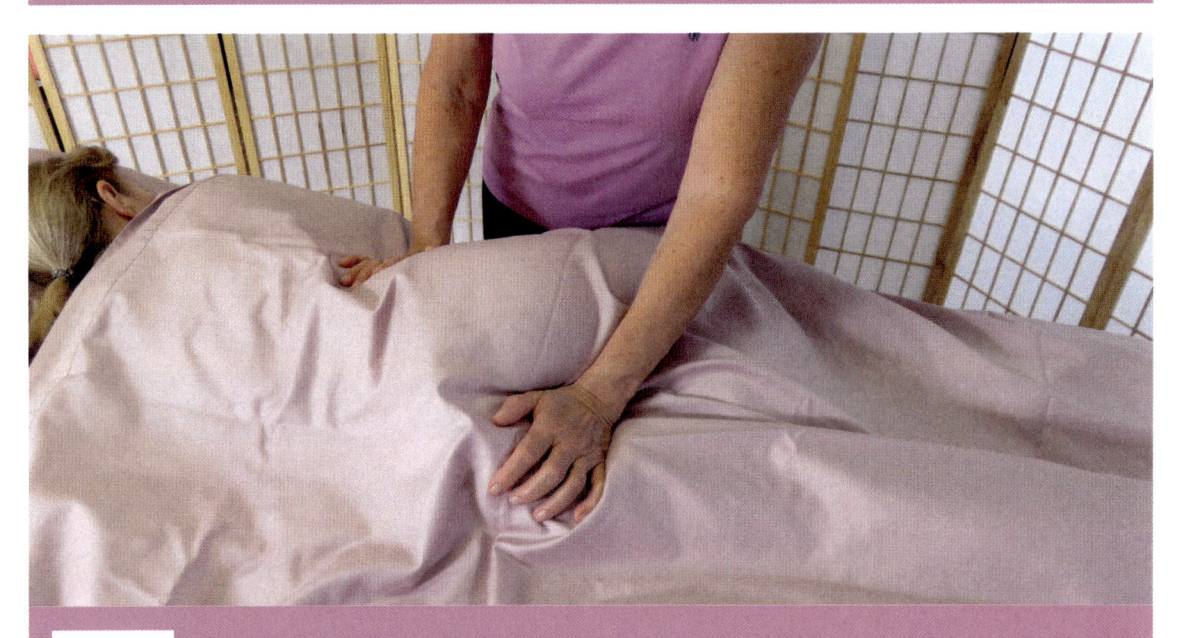

SLR 5

Sacrotuberous Shear

Using the drape, use the palm of your hand to gently shear the sacrotuberous ligament from medial to lateral, working inferior to the ischial tuberosity.

SLR 6

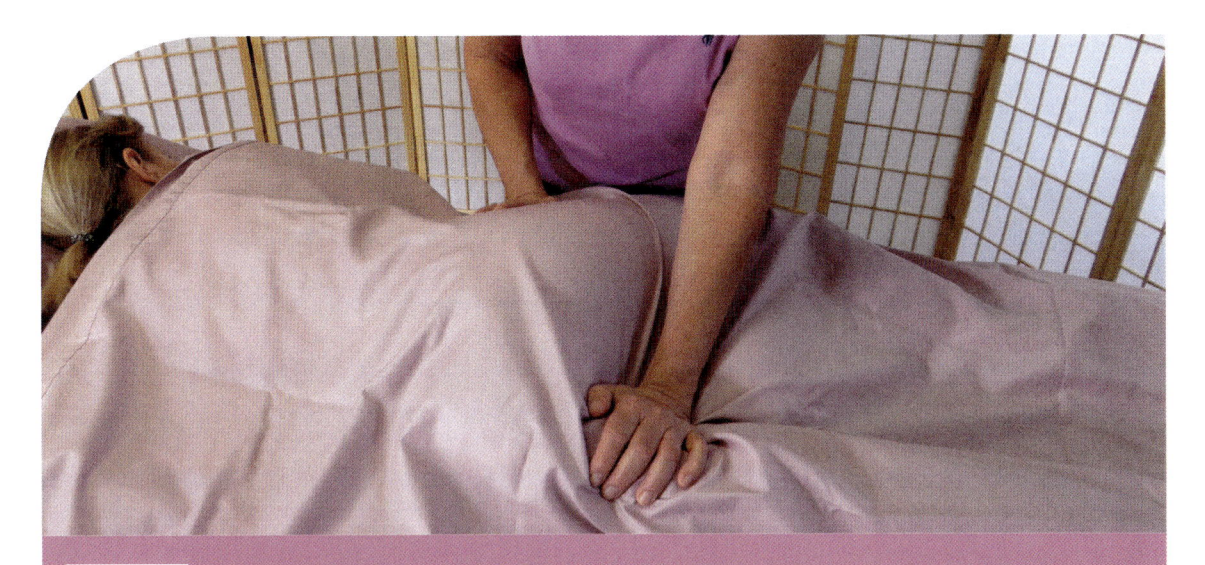

Adductor Magnus Compression and Shear

From the ischial tuberosity, continue gently compressing and shearing along the inside of the thigh distal to the knee.

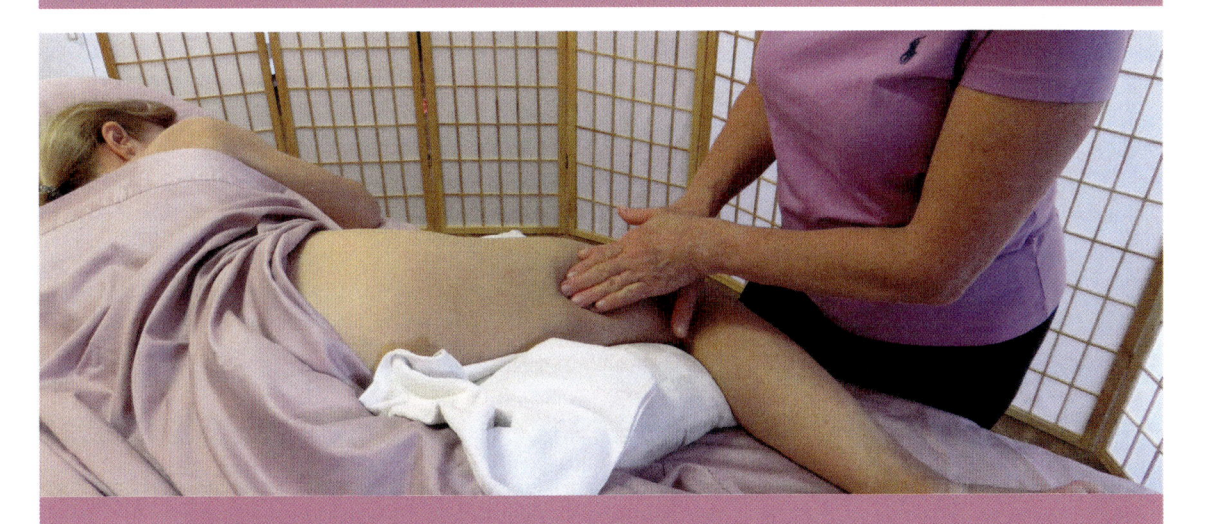

SLR 7

Trochanter Roundhouse, Up then Down

Using supported fingertips and some glide, find the valleys of the lateral thigh and use a longitudinal compression stroke from the knee gliding proximal around the greater trochanter, exiting at the gluteus medius. Do three passes lateral to medial. Then reverse the direction starting at the gluteus medius around the trochanter finishing at the knee.

SLR 8

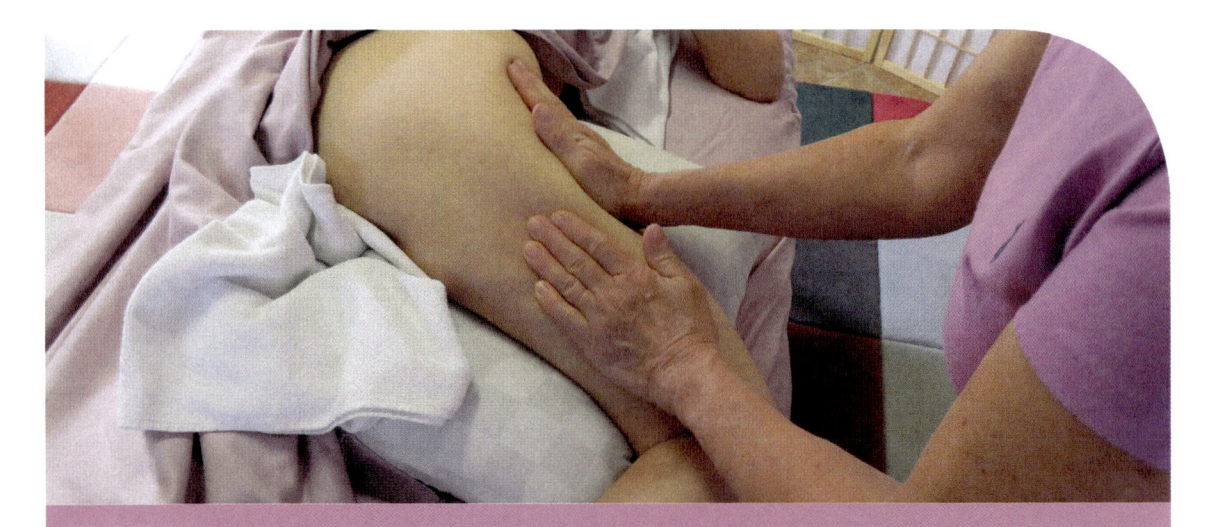

Iliotibial Band Shear
With open palms on either side of the femur and minimal glide, move hands in opposite directions, shearing the IT band.

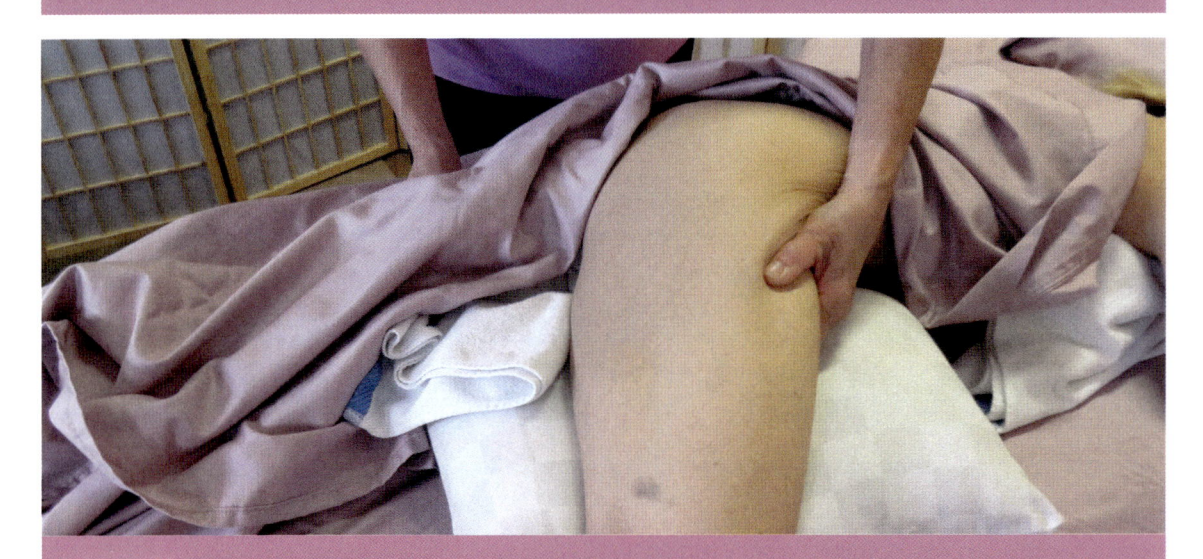

SLR 9

Rectus Femoris Pull
With glide, place your fingers under the rectus femoris at the knee and gently pull in one long stroke against gravity exiting at the tensor fascia latae, and then another stroke exiting around the anterior superior iliac spine. Use a towel to make sure groin area is covered.

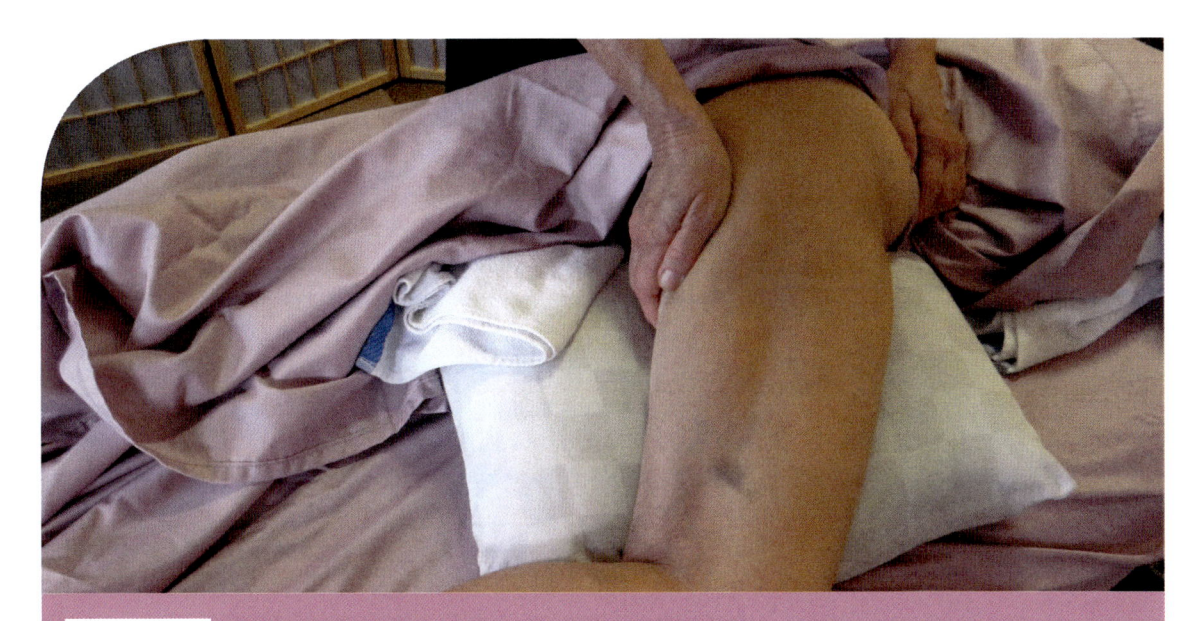

SLR 10

Medial Hamstrings Pull

With glide, place your fingers under the medial hamstrings and long adductors at the knee and gently pull in one long stroke against gravity stopping at the ischial tuberosity. Use a towel to make sure groin area is covered.

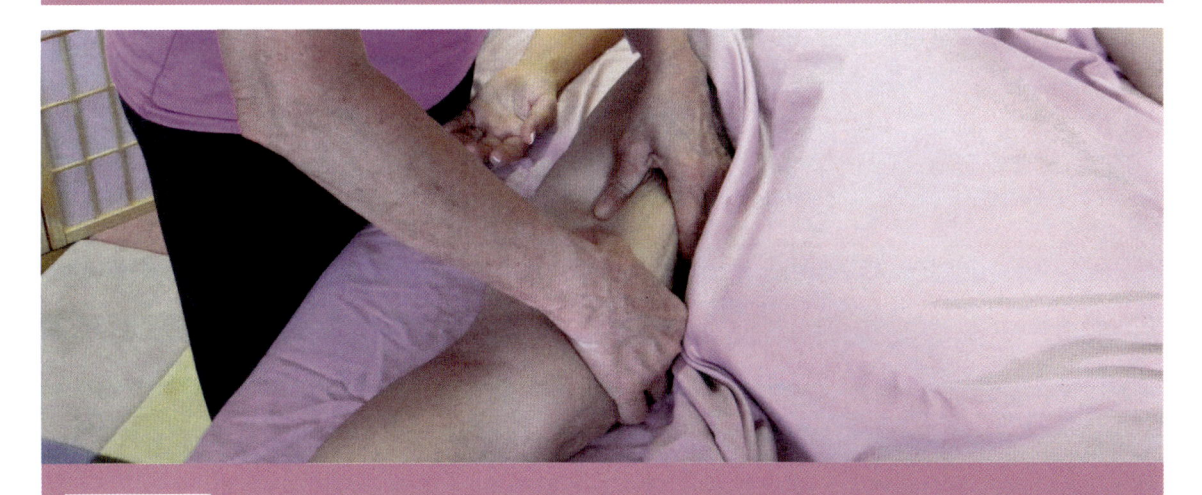

SLR 11

Petrissage Adductor Magnus

Petrissage the inside of the thigh from the drape working distal to the knee focusing on the medial adductors and adductor magnus. Use a towel to ensure groin area is covered.

SLR 12

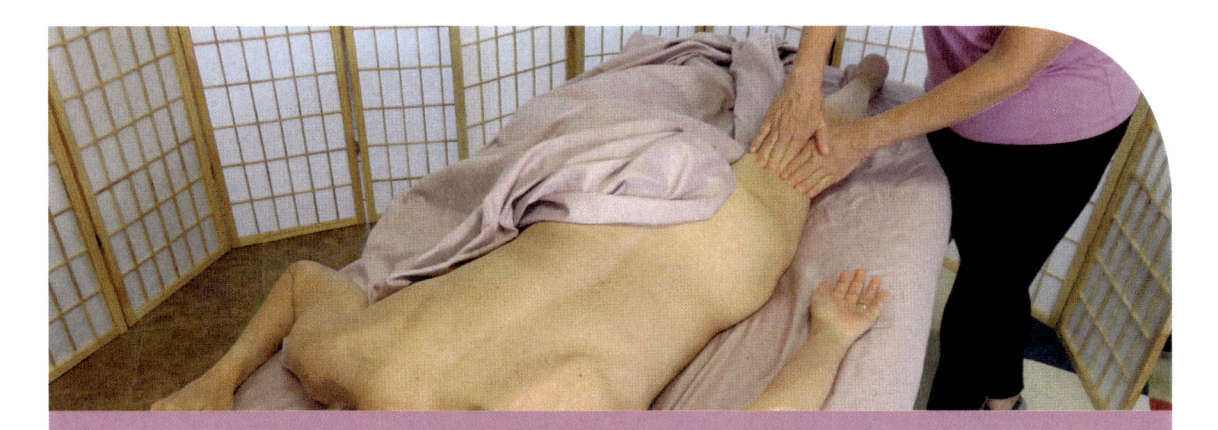

Superficial Back Line Compressions

With some glide, use supported fingers to sink in the muscles of the superficial back line, starting from the knee, with one long longitudinal compression stroke glide along the back of the leg, through the gluteus, along the erector spinae to the neck. Do three passes lateral to medial, staying lateral to the anal cleft.

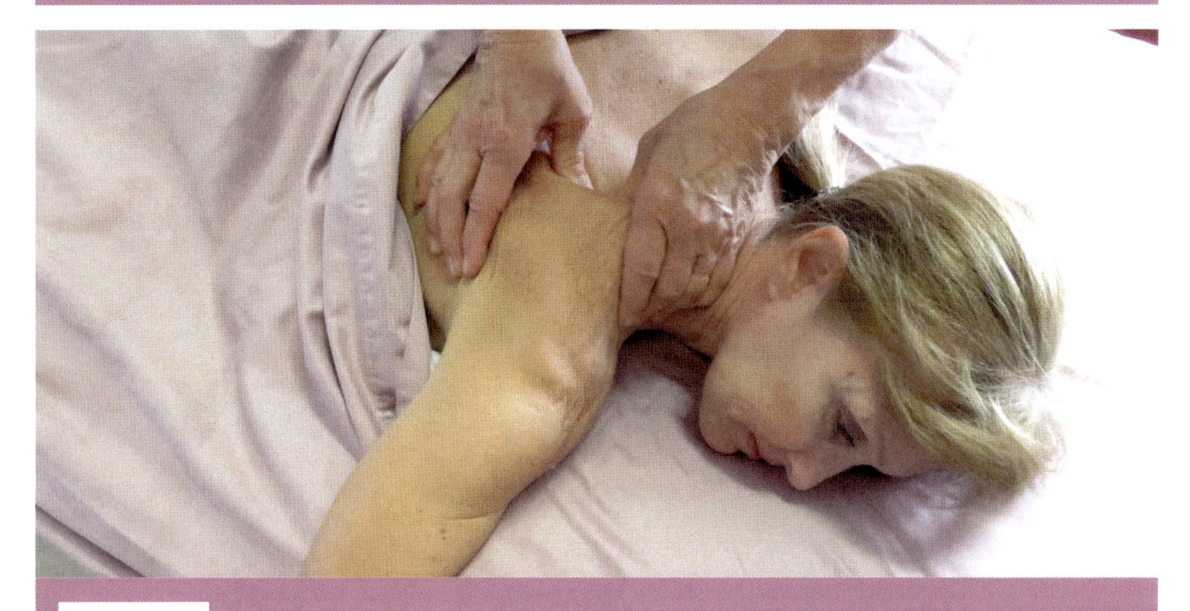

SLR 13

Up Shoulder Rhomboid-Serratus Shear

Use thumbs or fingers to work under the medial border of the scapula. You can also massage the entire shoulder with particular attention on the infraspinatus, teres minor, and teres major.

SLR 14

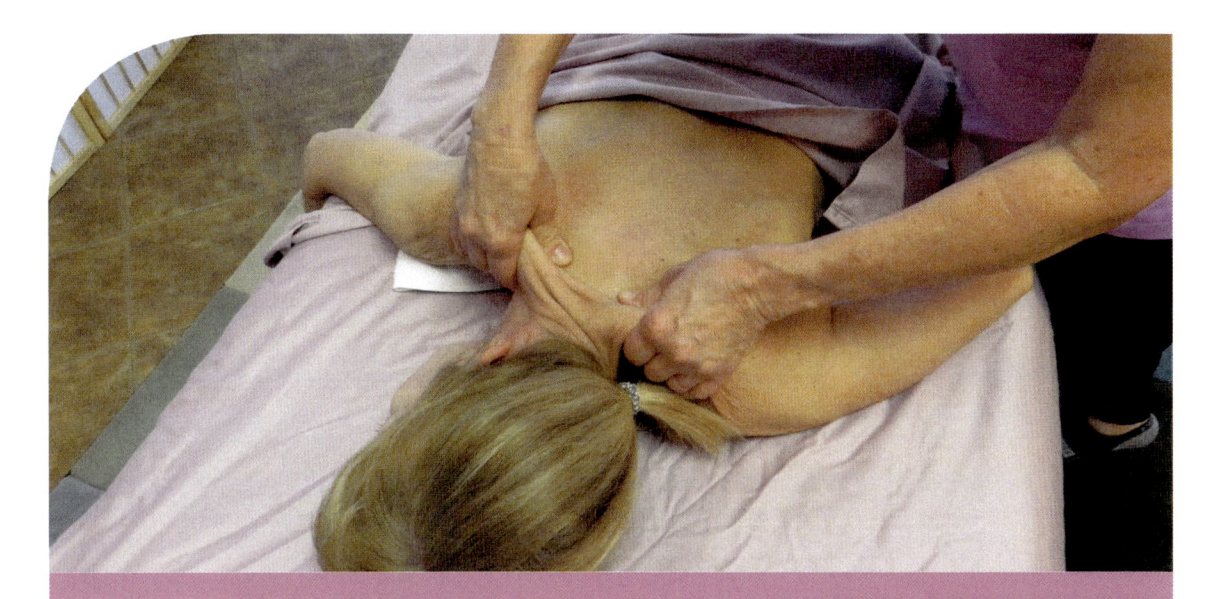

Trapezius Pull and Petrissage
Use both hands to grab and pull the upper trapezius against gravity, petrissage and shear as needed.

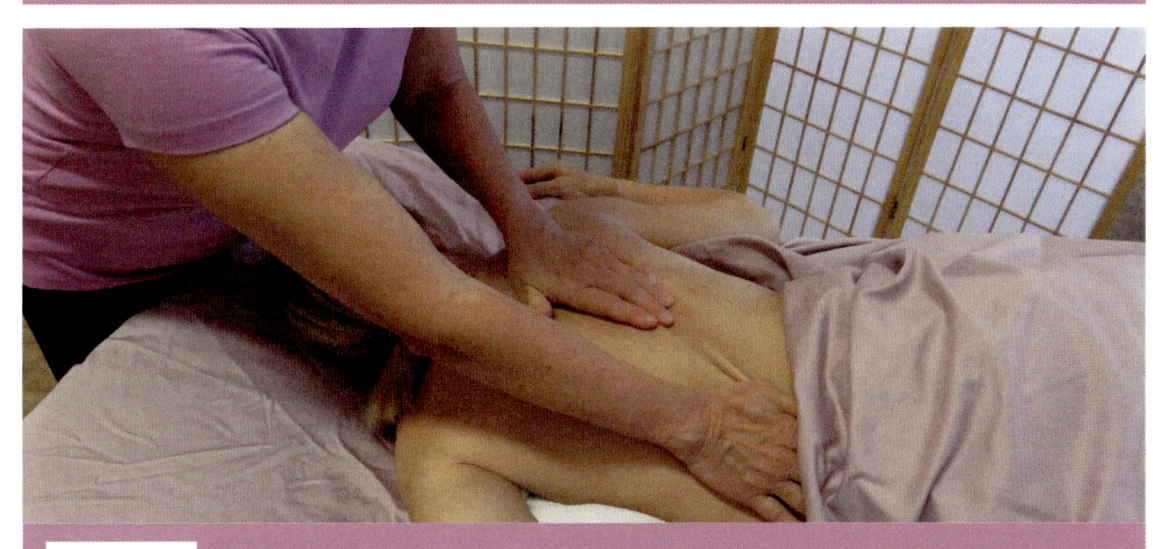

SLR 15

Myofascial Spread
With minimal glide, spread the superficial myofascia in an "X" pattern from shoulder to opposite gluteus medius.

Prone (P) | BLUE-COLORED

Facedown prone usually quiets a talkative client, and it's a nice relaxing way to finish the routine for most clients. I typically do the Sims' Lateral Recumbent Lavender-colored routine, or this routine, but not both due to time constraints. This classic two-dimensional Swedish position can be made 3-dimensional with some good simple Thai massage-inspired stretches shown at the end. I also like prone for cross fiber and compression of the "sacral belt" and the erector spinae group.

Entire section okay for (*) through P15 only; avoid final stretches

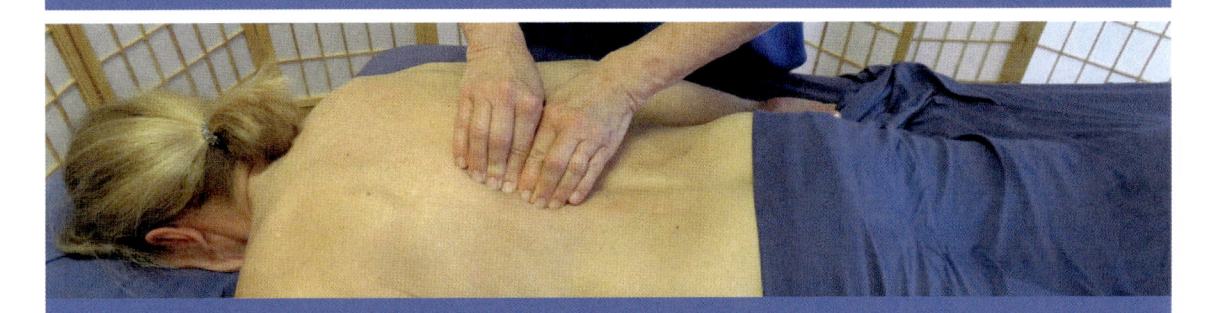

P1

Erector Spinae Compression

With very little or no glide, first use your palms to cross fiber shear the erector spinae group from the sacrum to the neck; then repeat using fingertips for deeper cross-fiber penetration.

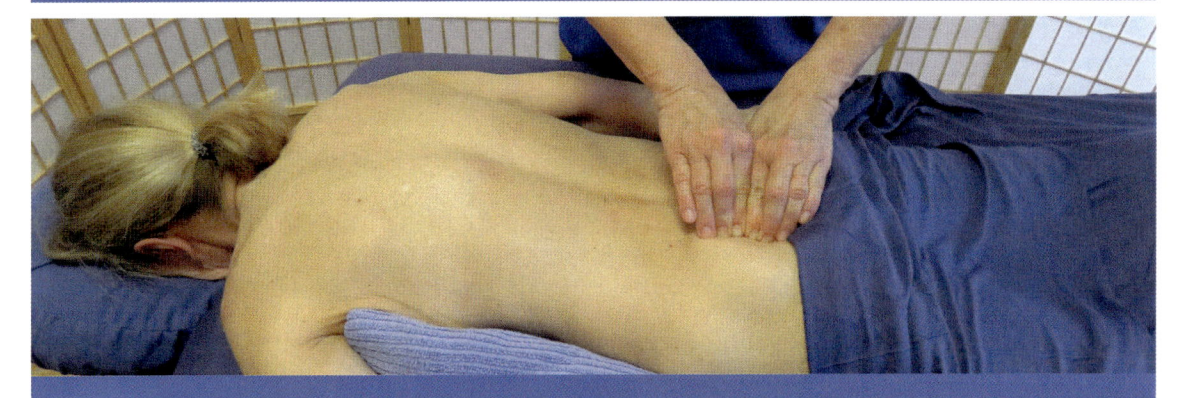

P2

Sacral Band Compression

With your fingertips, sink into the sacrum using cross-fiber strokes working lateral to the outside of the hip.

P3

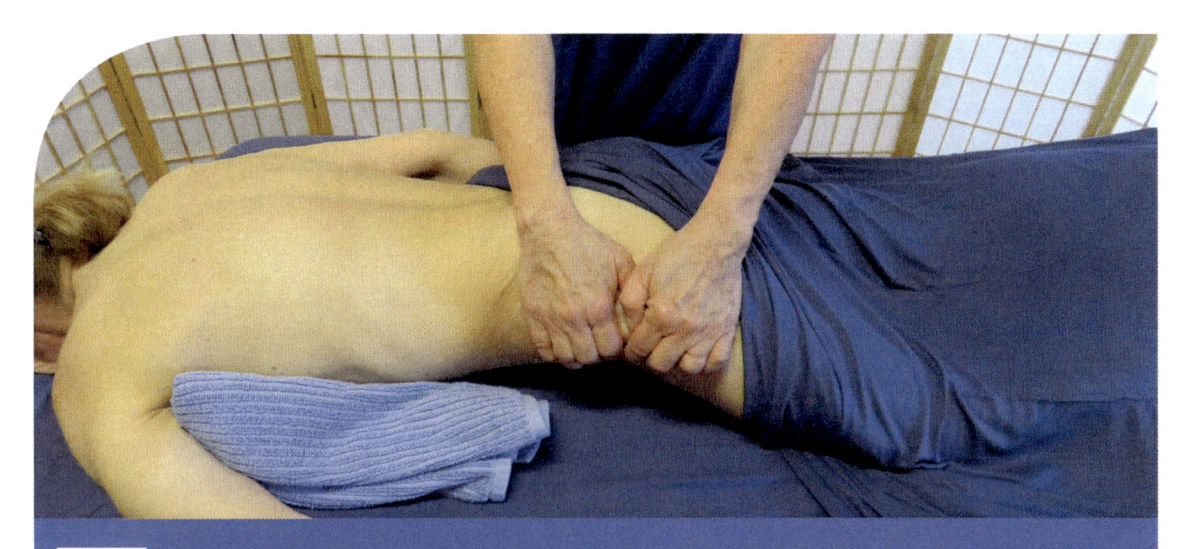

Gluteus Medius and Trochanter Pulls

Use both hands to grab the far gluteus medius above the greater trochanter pulling against gravity lateral to medial across the piriformis to the sacrum, continuing into the near side piriformis.

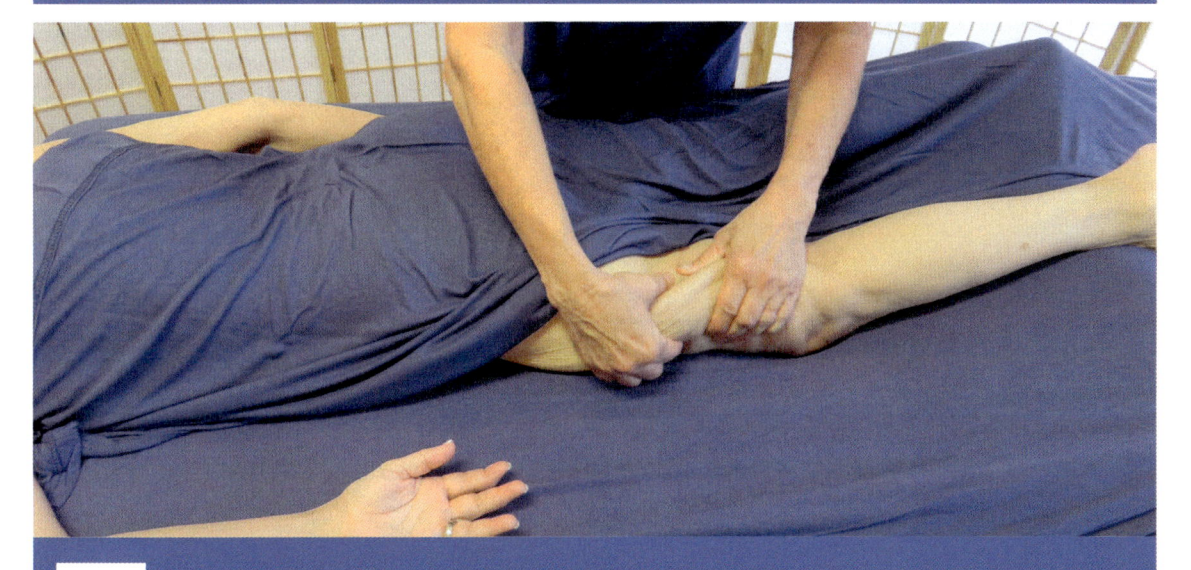

P4

Iliotibial Band Petrissage

Petrissage from the gluteus medius inferiorly to the iliotibial band continuing distal to the knee.

P 5

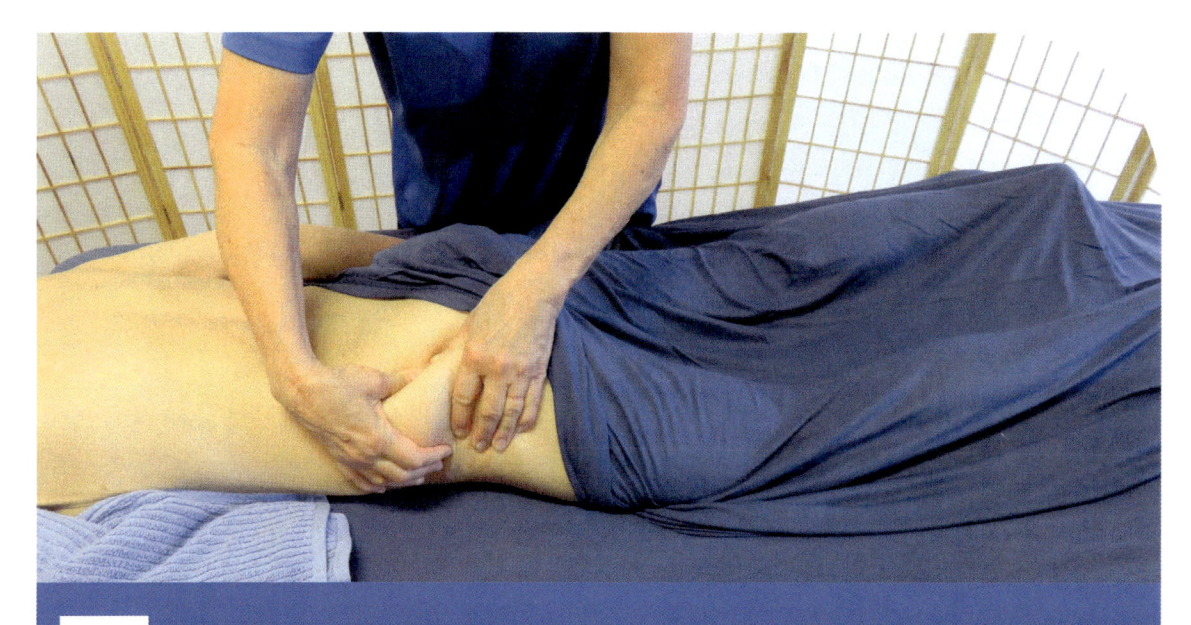

Gluteus Medius and Maximus Petrissage

Petrissage gluteus medius and the lateral aspect of the gluteus maximus.

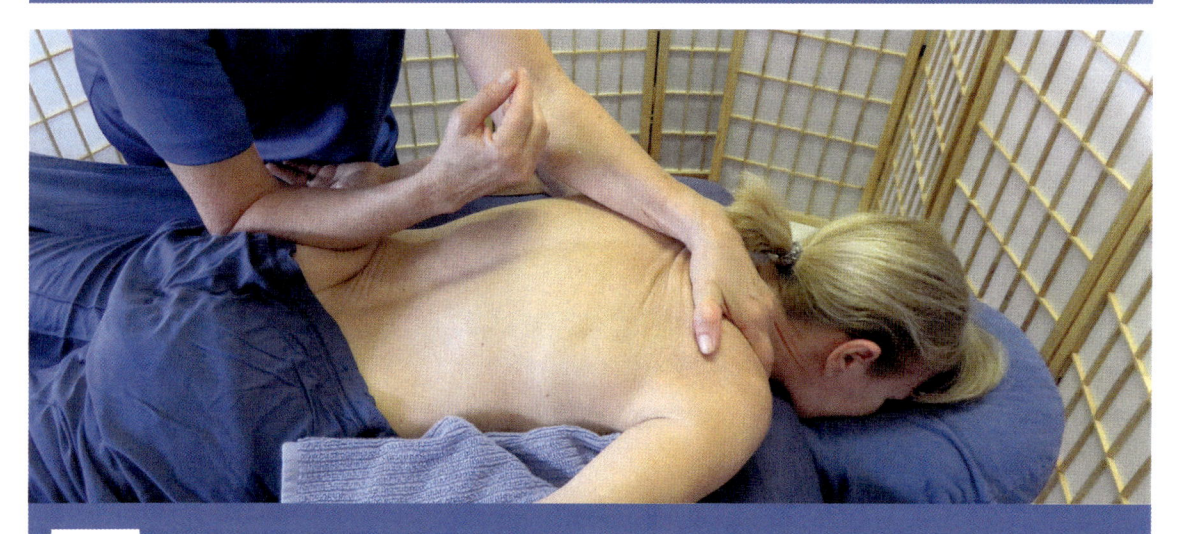

P 6

Opposite Upper Trapezius Pull

Use your forearm to sink into the gluteus medius while using your up-table hand to pull and shear the opposite side upper trapezius.

P 8

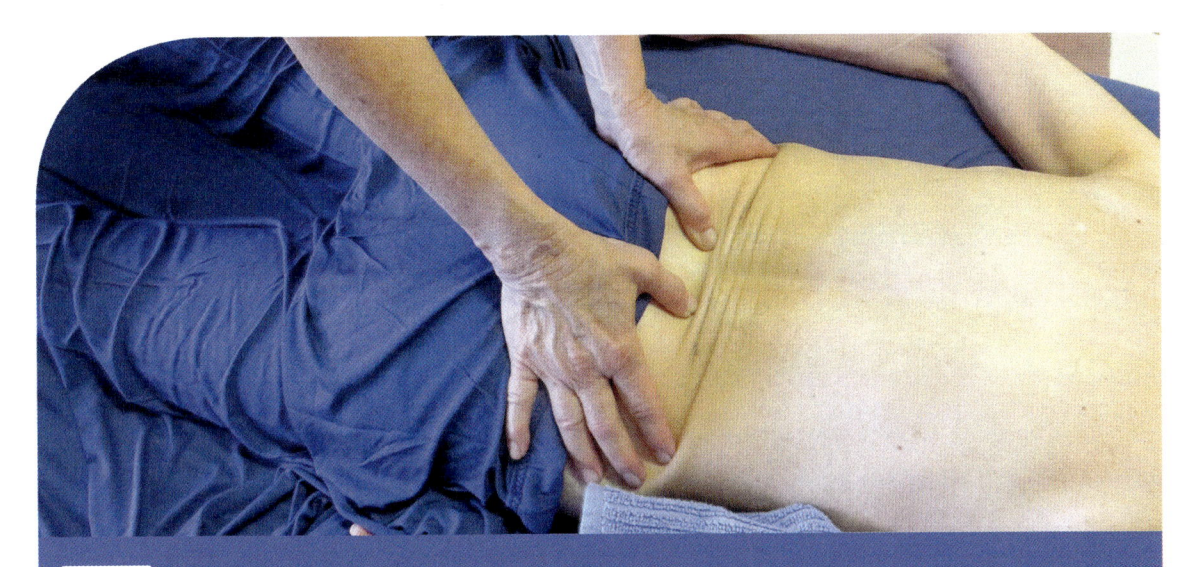

Sacrum to Erector Spinae Compression

Use friction strokes to longitudinally compress the sacrum, then use your fingers to longitudinally compress the erector spinae group on both sides of the spine gliding to the neck.

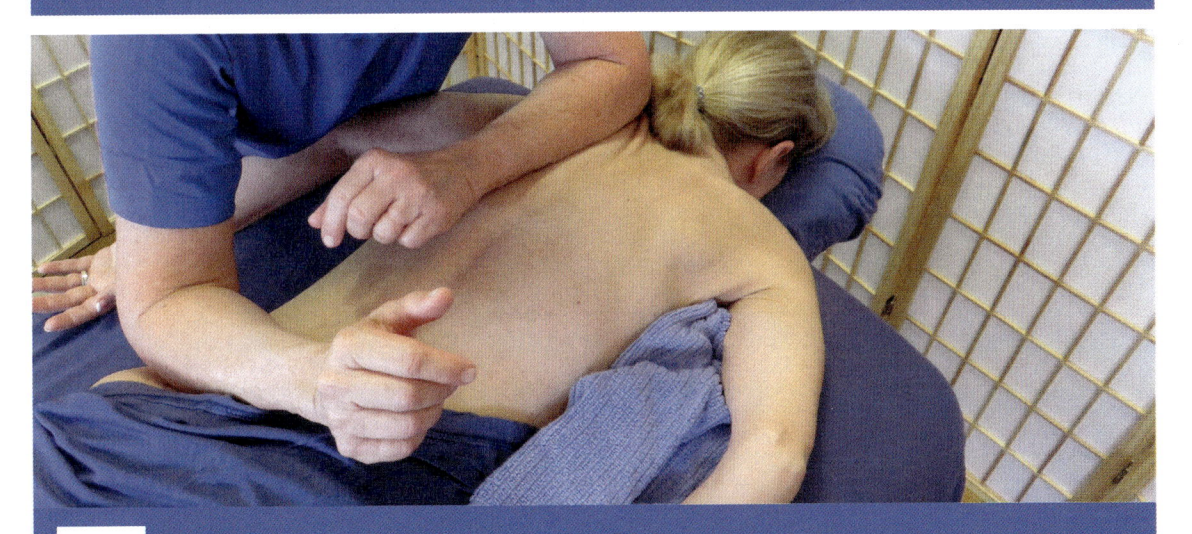

P 7

Myofascial Erector Spinae Spread

Use your forearm to lock down the myofascia lateral to the sacrum, sinking into the gluteus medius; then with minimal glide use your up-table forearm to spread the myofascia along the erector spinae, exiting down the upper trapezius.

P 9

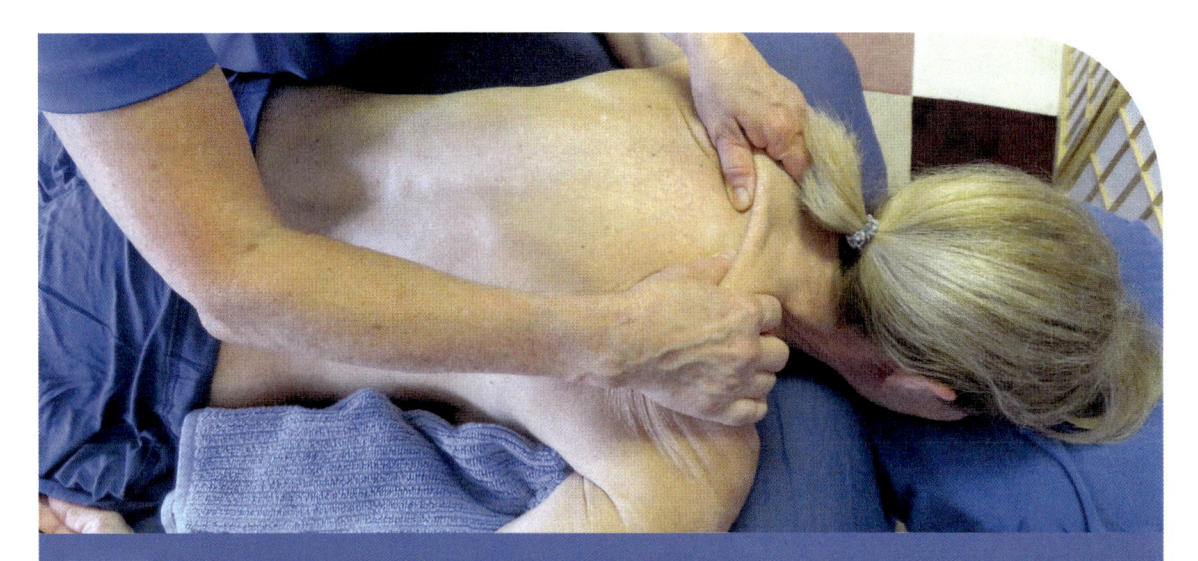

Trapezius Pull and Petrissage

Use both hands to grab and pull the upper trapezius against gravity, petrissage and shear as needed.

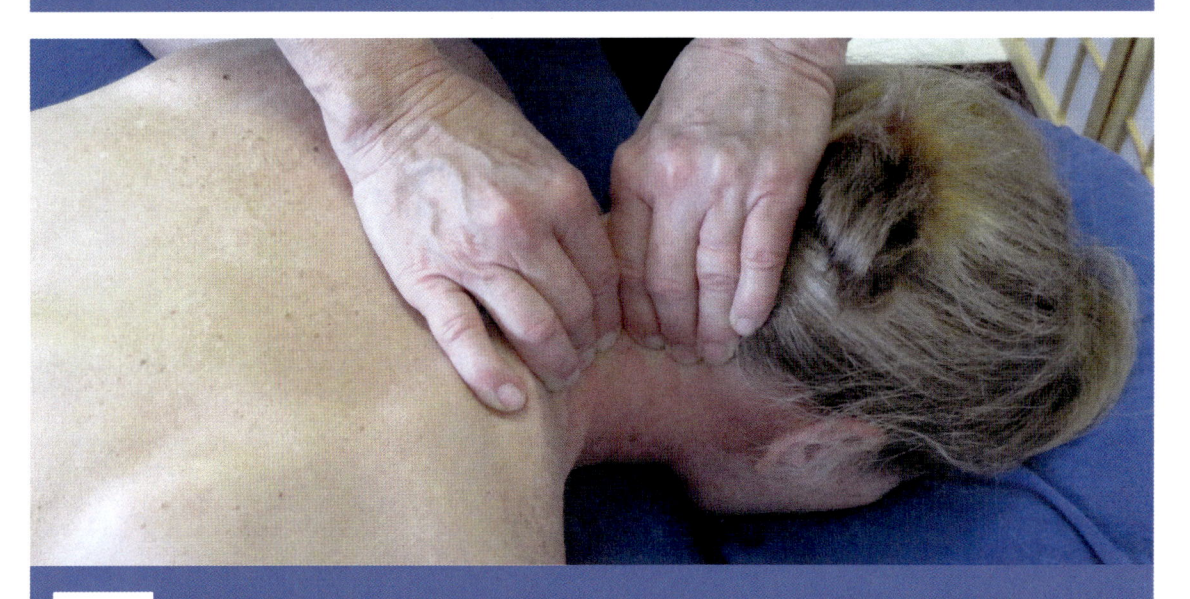

P 10

Upper Trapezius Grab

With fingertips, gently grab upper trapezius and posterior scalene and vertically pull away from cervical spine.

P 11

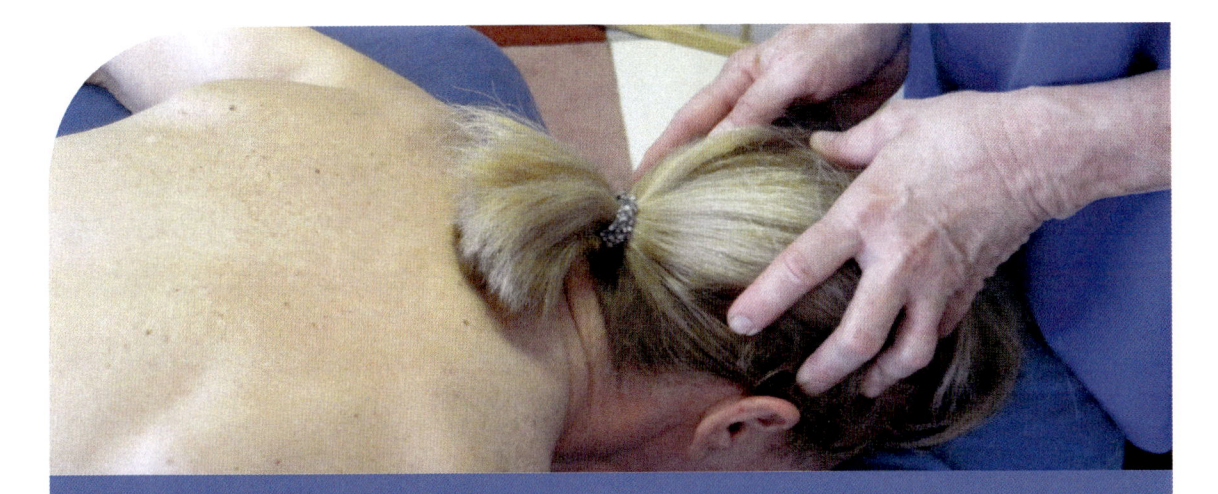

Epicranial Aponeurosis Circles

With no slippage, firmly place fingertips in the epicranial aponeurosis, temporal fascia, and occipital belly making deep slow circles. Then scratch head with fingernails to stimulate hair follicles.

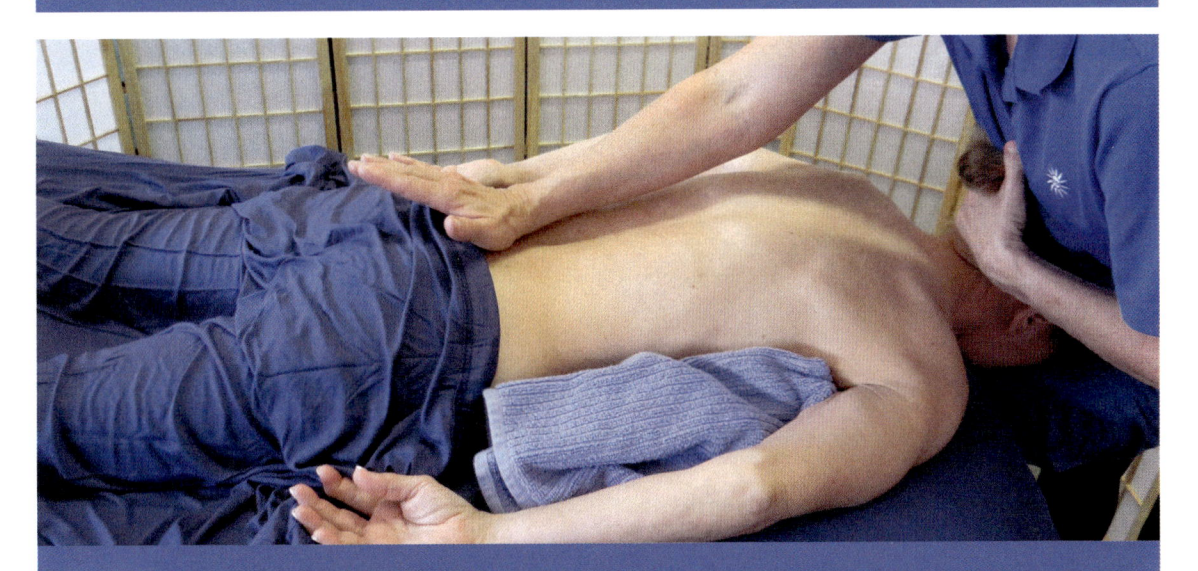

P 12

Cerebrospinal Stretch

Place side of palm on the occipital protuberance and gently pull toward you; simultaneously, place the other palm on the sacrum and gently push away creating spinal traction.

P 13

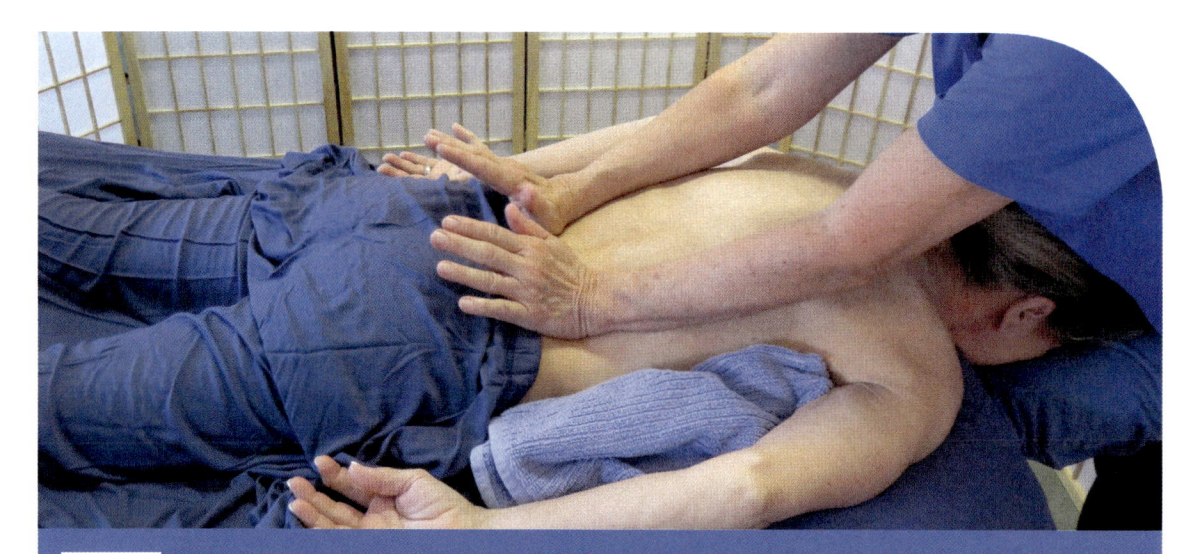

Oscillating Sacral Traction

Place both palms just superior to the iliac crest lateral to the sacrum and with rhythmic oscillations; push on one side then the other.

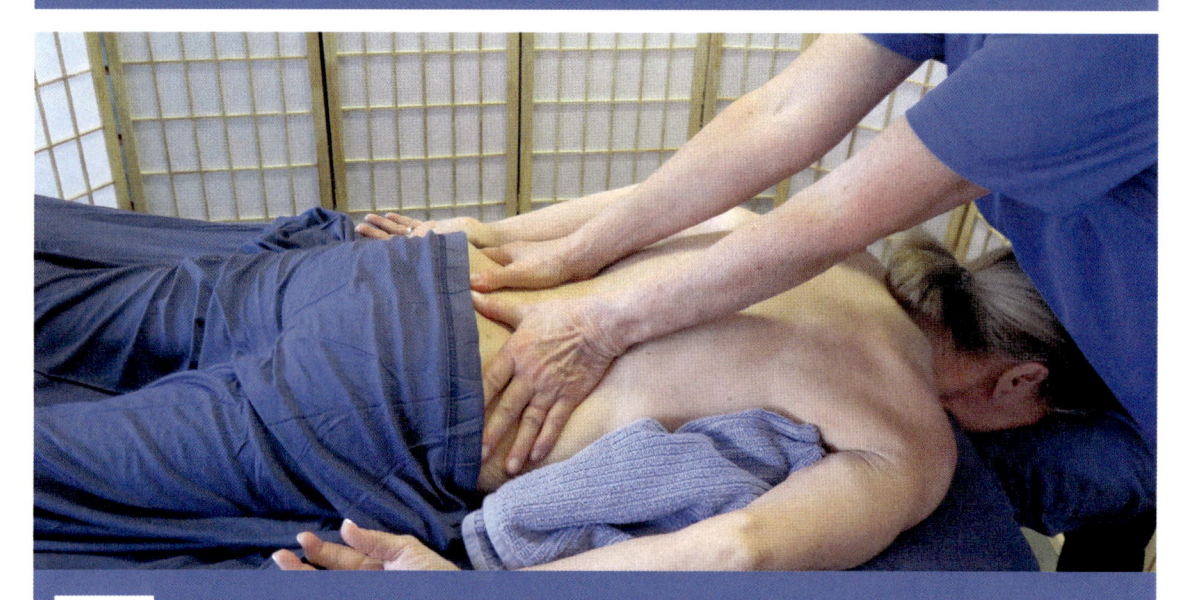

P 14

Swedish Effleurage

Effleurage the entire back and neck doing whatever strokes you learned in your Swedish massage class.

P 16

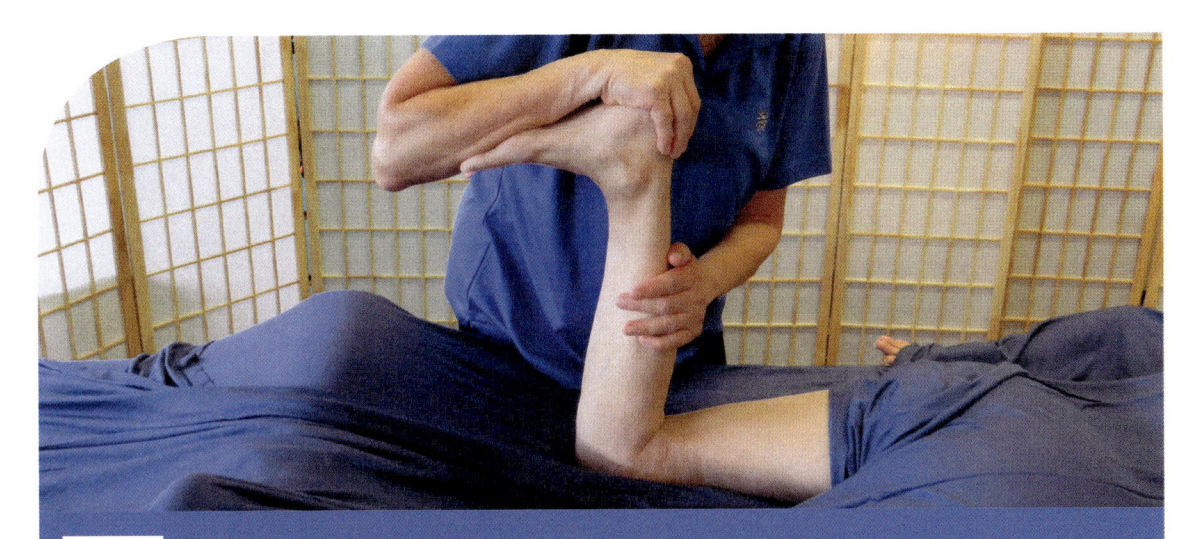

Calf Stretch

Place hand on heel and with your forearm push down on the ball of the foot to stretch calf muscles and Achilles tendon.

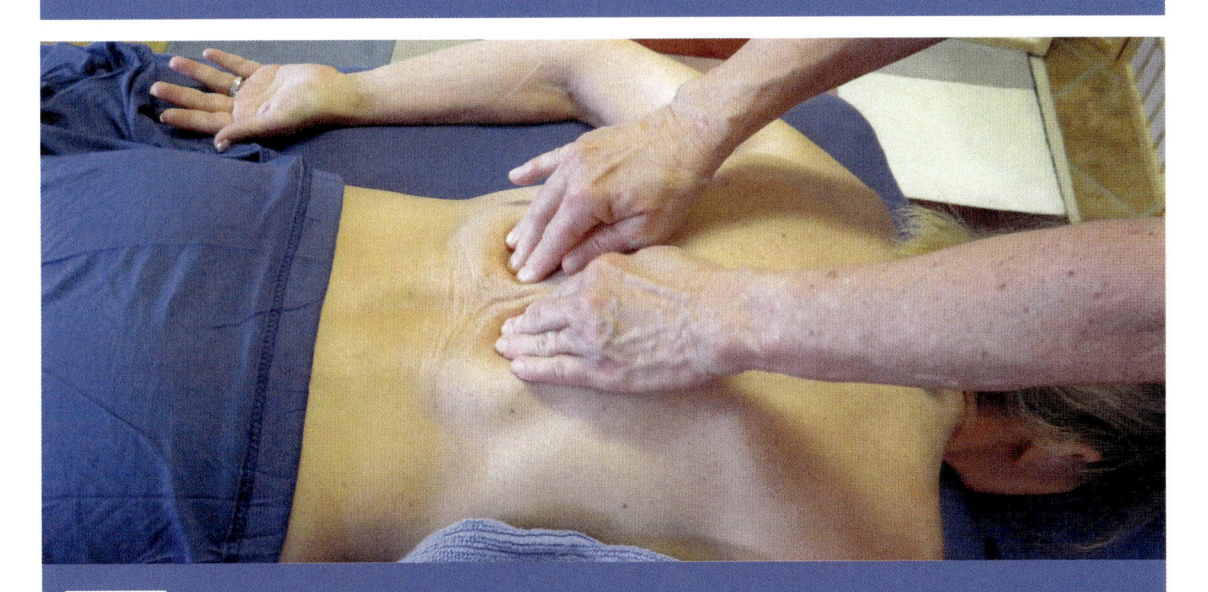

P 15

Erector Spinae "Bladder Shu Points"

With a nod to Chinese Meridians "Bladder Shu Points," sink your thumb or fingers into the erector spinae group on either side of the spine ("1.5 cun"), make individual outboard circles at each vertebra from T7 to the middle of the sacrum.

P 17

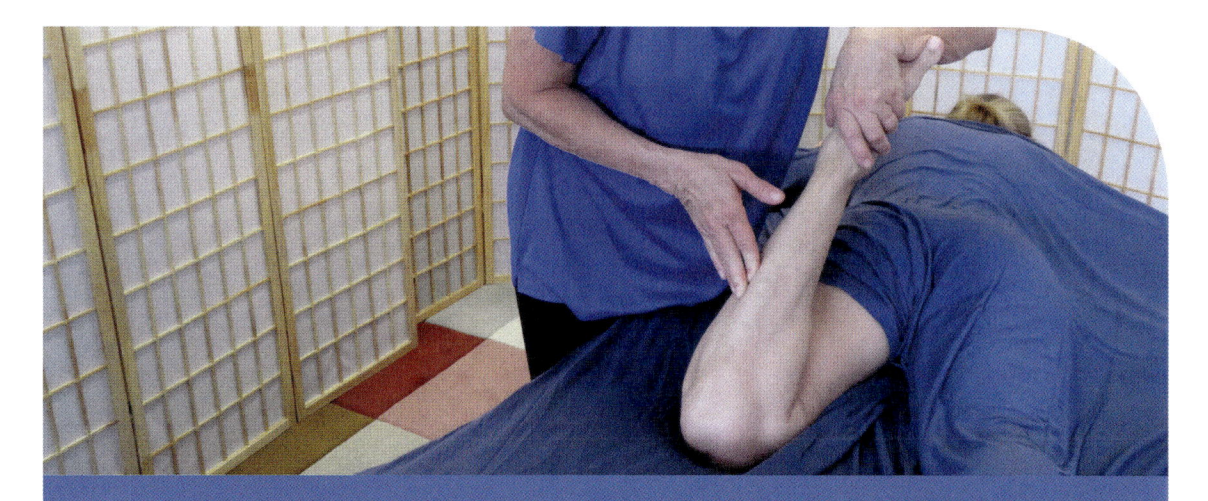

Quad Stretch and Tibialis Anterior Compression

Gently push heel toward buttock to stretch quadriceps, careful of any knee issue. Simultaneously, use your hand and forearm to plantar flex foot. With your down-table fingers, glide along the tibialis anterior from distal to proximal using a longitudinal compression stroke.

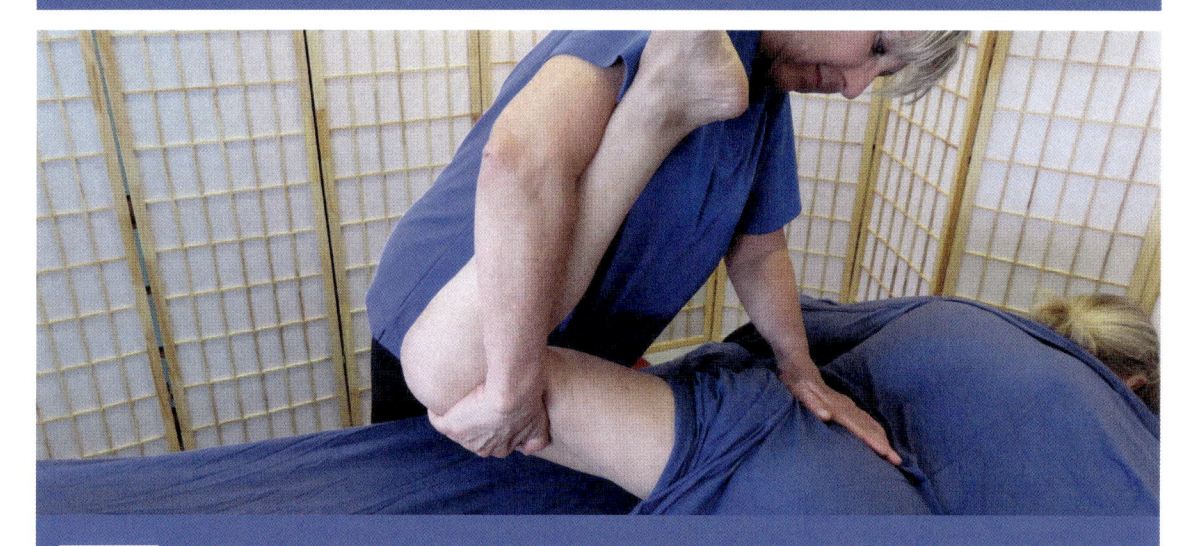

P 18

Iliopsoas Stretch

Place your up-table hand on the sacrum to lock down and stabilize the pelvis. Use your down-table hand and hold the client's thigh just superior to the knee. Pull up and lean your body forward. Watch for any pain in the lower back.

P 19

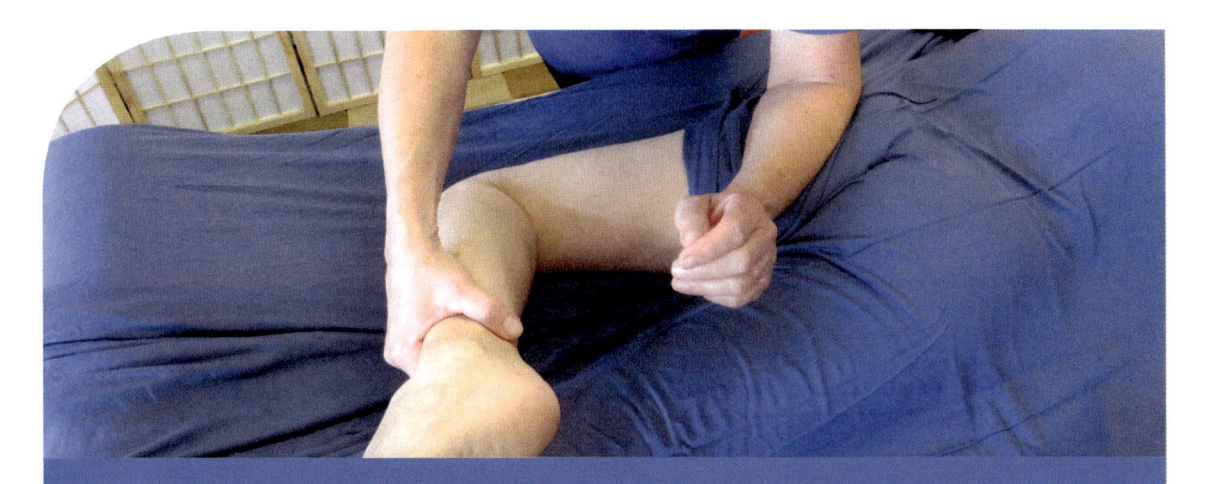

Hip Rotator Compression

Place your forearm in the "meaty groove" between the sacral edge and the greater trochanter. With client's leg vertically at 90 degrees, rotate leg away from you causing external hip rotation. Rotate back and forth while using your forearm to massage gluteus and hip rotator tissue.

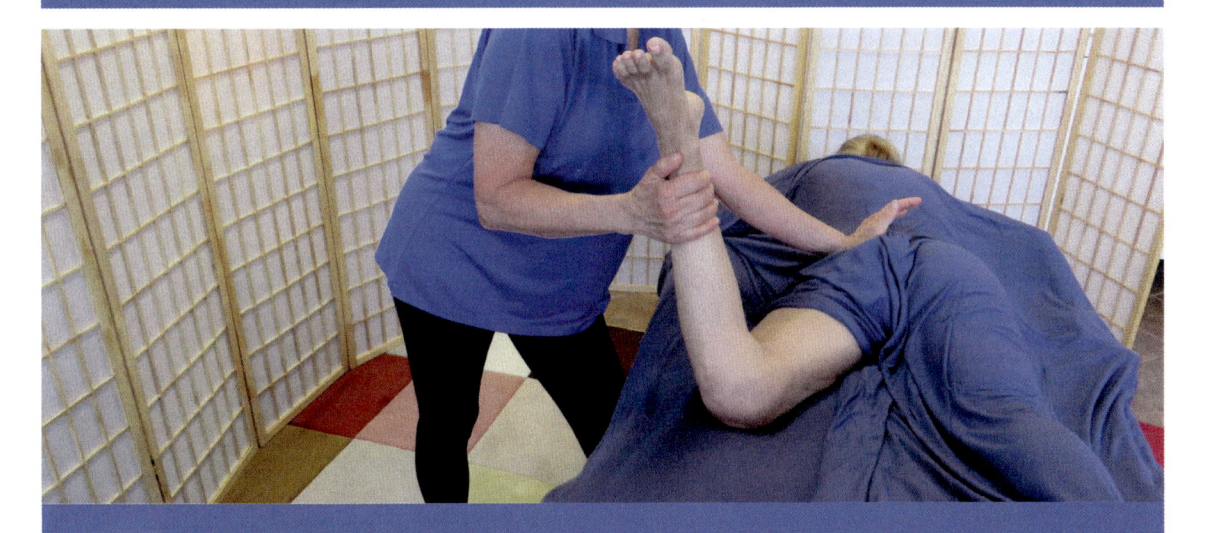

P 20

Hip Rotator and Gluteus Stretch

With the client's leg vertically at 90 degrees, place the palm of your hand in the "meaty groove" between the sacral edge and greater trochanter. Push away with your up-table hand, as the down-table hand gently pulls the client's leg toward you, causing hip internal rotation.

P 21

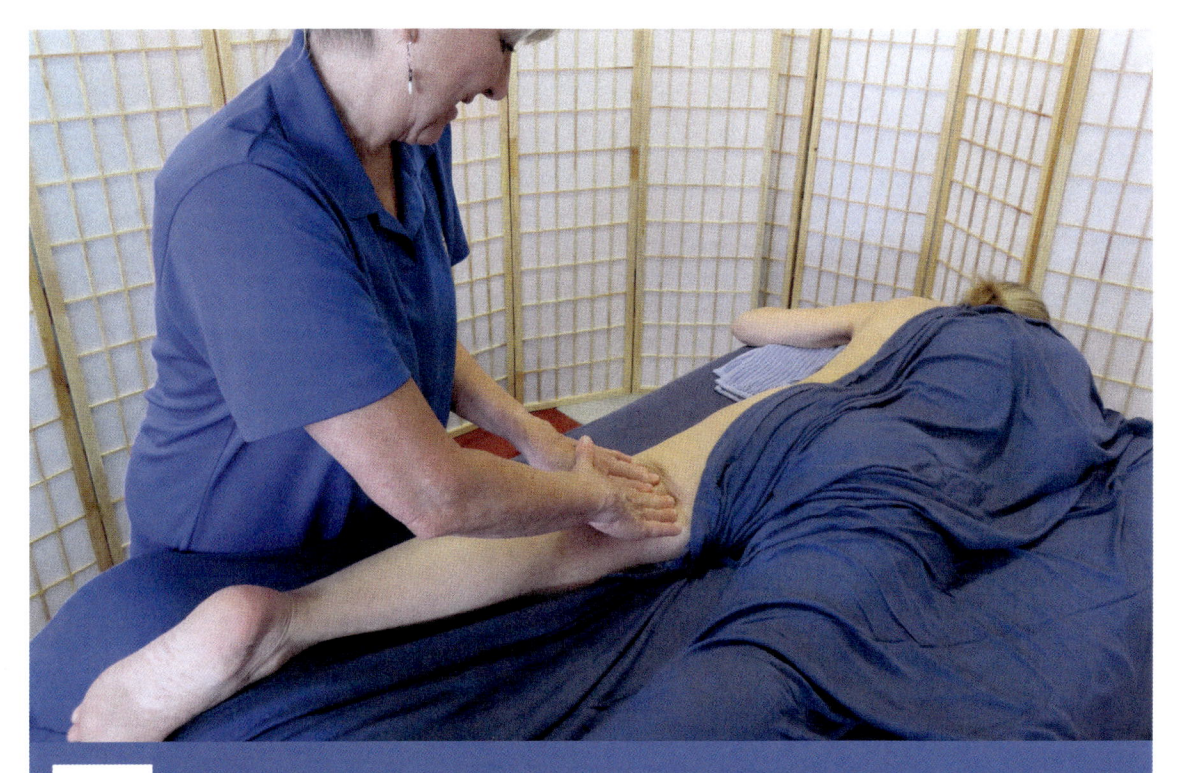

Superficial Back Line Compressions

With some glide, use supported fingers to sink in the muscles of the superficial back line, starting from the knee, with one long longitudinal compression stroke glide along the back of the leg, through the gluteus, along the erector spinae to the neck. Do three passes lateral to medial, staying lateral to the anal cleft.

APPENDIX A & APPENDIX B
(TRX® MOVEMENT PREPARATION ROUTINE)
(ViPR® MOVEMENT PREPARATION ROUTINE)

The following two appendices are extracted from my other book, *Mule Fitness: How to Turn a Mule into a Thoroughbred, Myofascial Network-based Strength and Conditioning*.

I include the two workouts because they stretch, extend, release, as well as activate the fascial networks, the myofascial meridians as described by Tom Myers.

Whatever myofascial release you accomplish on the table, it should be accompanied by a concomitant and complementary exercise program.

Fascia needs to be moved!

Your client should move their myofascial sacks. And you, the therapist, who works in a physically demanding job, needs to move your myofascia, too, and exercise self-care.

An exercise program, or rather an exercise program grounded in *proper movement patterns* often takes primacy over therapy. Consider this statement in Mosby's book, "more body fluids are moved by a 5-minute walk than by a 50-minute massage." And a body engaging in steady-state exercise increases lymph flow 2- to 3-times higher than at rest[20]. Obviously if a client can't walk because of pain or even get out of bed, then therapy becomes more important. But for most clients, and you the therapist: Move!

So feel free to use these routines for yourself, or pass them on to clients who can give them to their personal trainers for guidance. Each routine has a description page and a picture thumbnail page.

APPENDIX A

Column One SAGITTAL PLANE	Column Two FRONTAL PLANE	Column Three TRANSVERSE PLANE
ALTERNATING REVERSE LUNGE (start from standing, alternate reverse lunge, keeping arms and front leg at 90 degrees.)	**SIDE LUNGE** (side lunge keeping hip, knee, and foot in alignment, stationary foot "glued" to stretch adductors.)	**GOLF TROIKA 1** (from athletic stance, "look at ball" mobilizing shoulder joint.)
REPEATER REVERSE LUNGE WITH HIGH KNEE (start from standing, reverse lunge on same leg bringing thigh parallel to floor.)	**SIDE LUNGE** (side knee keeping hip, knee, and foot in alignment, stationary foot "toe up" to stretch calf and hams.)	**GOLF TROIKA 2** (from athletic stance, "eyes follow hand," allow opposite knee to collapse in for greater spiral stretch.)
FIGURE 4 SIT (keep knee toward floor, bring chest toward shin.)	**LATERAL LINE STRETCH** (hold straps with outside hand first.)	**GOLF TROIKA 3** (both hands stacked on grips, allow back leg to pivot on ball of foot.)
FORWARD HIP HINGE (wide stance, start with hands below navel, keep legs straight.)	**CRESCENT LUNGE** (arms overhead, back leg straight, float front knee across room until engagement, then lean L, R.)	**HELICOPTER** (from forward lunge with fly, spiral arms into forward leg only, look over hip to floor.)
LOW-STOOL SQUATS (low squat, glutes below knees.)	**SNOW ANGELS** (shoulder blades should move freely.)	**SKATER LUNGE** (reverse lunge, back leg at 3 and 9 clock positions.)
FORWARD LUNGE WITH FLY (big horse step, keep legs straight as arms come to a "T" then drop back knee toward floor as pecs stretch.)	**ARMPIT HANG SQUAT** (hand with head down, then turn torso and look under each armpit.)	**ROW AND PUSH UP** (row with pistol grip and "knuckle up" grip, stay on balls of feet during push up.)

3.1.1 TRX® Movement Preparation Thumbnails

Alternating Reverse Lunge	Side Lunge Foot Glued	Golf Troika 1
Repeater Reverse Lunge High Knee	Side Lunge Toe Up	Golf Troika 2
Forward Hip Hinge	Lateral Line Stretch	Golf Troika 3
Figure-4 Sit	Crescent Lunge	Helicopter
Low-stool Squats	Snow Angels	Skater Lunge
Forward Lunge with Fly	Armpit Hang Squat	Row and Push Up

A Systematic Approach to Myofascial Network Release

APPENDIX B

HIP HINGE ARMS OUT (from standing, tube tilts away as arms straighten, knees at 90 degrees as hip hinges in opposite direction of arms to stretch lats.)	**SIDE LUNGE RL, LR** (side lunge with foot, knee, and hip in alignment, hold tibe in opposite hand as lunge side, then "quick feet" for cardio)	**ARM PUNCH** (3 positions: punch middle, low, high, pivot, and drive off back foot.)
SIDE STRETCH (arms R, squat and sit back L, allow head to melt between arms, keep tube close at tip of toes.)	**INTERNAL AND EXTERNAL HIP ROTATION BOX STEPS** (step over imaginary box in to out, then out to in, balance on standing leg.)	**EGYPTIANS** (gold tube overhead, side lunge L shit tube R.)
ALTERNATING SIDE STRETCH (side stretch with alternating weight shift.)	**T-SPINE MOBILIZATION** (keep torso at 90 degrees to legs, open chest to far wall.)	**HAYLOFT** (step forward and internally rotate foot, then step back and to the side while externally rotating foot and punch high.)
FORWARD LUNGE (3 variations: tube vertical, tube forward, tube overhead then twist into forward leg.)	**SINGLE LEG PISTON ANKLE MOBILITY** (go "around the clock" at forward, side, skater positions, use plastic glider plate.)	**REVERSE LUNGE MOON ARCS** (reverse lunge then lateral arc L and R overhead.)
SIDE LUNGE RR, LL (side lunge with foot, knee, and hip in alignment, hold tube in same hand as lunge side, then "quick feet" for cardio.)	**BAZOOKAS** (hold each end of tube, lunge L while putting tube over L shoulder, then lunge R with tube over R shoulder.)	**VERTICAL LIFT WITH SQUATS** (pulsing squat throwing tube up and catching at all 4 smooth tube positions between tube hand cut outs.)

3.1.2 ViPR® Movement Preparation Thumbnails

Hip Hinge	Side Lunge RL, LR	Punch Mid, Low, High
Side Stretch	Box Steps	Egyptians
Alternating Side Stretch	T-spine Mobilization	Hayloft
Forward Lunge 3 Variations	Single Leg Piston Ankle Mobility	Reverse Lunge Moon Arcs
Side Lunge RR, LL	Bazookas	Vertical Tube Lift

A Systematic Approach to Myofascial Network Release

APPENDIX C
(3DB EXPECTATIONS)

3-DIMENSIONAL BODYWORK EXPECTATIONS

You've tried **stretching**, but asked yourself, "Is there more?"

You've tried **massage**, but asked yourself, "Is there more?"

3-Dimensional Bodywork (3DB) is highly therapeutic and relaxing. By using a unique combination of stretch and massage, it focuses on myofascial release of the body's sacks of muscle and tissue.

3DB is for those who want to take bodywork therapy to the next level.

This is fundamentally a massage, but it is done in three dimensions.

You should be comfortable with massage and bodywork. With therapeutic applications and athletic people in mind, limbs will be placed, and the body will be positioned to allow optimal muscle manipulation.

The muscle and connective tissue "highways" or myofascial meridians that run through the body will be massaged and stretched to release fascial adhesions, with emphasis on the major structural attachment points in the hips.

Therapeutically, it works best when only draping is used. That said; disrobe to the level of your comfort.

I hope you will find 3DB to be a very creative and unique integration of massage and stretch therapy. As one client commented, "It's the first 'real' massage I've ever had!"

APPENDIX D

(WAIVER AND RELEASE)

WAIVER AND RELEASE

I declare that I have informed *(your company name)* about any health or medical issue that might be exacerbated or contraindicated by participation in exercise or therapy, and regardless of any underlying said health or medical issue, known or unknown to me or *(your company name)*, **I assume sole risk and that (your company name) shall not be liable** for any pain, injuries, accidents, or death occurring to me, including those resulting from *(your company name's)* services and/or negligence, arising directly or indirectly out of my participation in *(your company name's)* services. I for myself, on behalf of my executors, administrators, heirs, and assigns, do hereby expressly release, discharge, waive, relinquish, and covenant not to sue *(your company name)*, its affiliates, officers, directors, agents, or employees for all such claims, demands, injuries, damages, or courses of action.

Date _____

Signature _____

Printed Name _____

APPENDIX E
INFORMED CONSENT

INFORMED CONSENT

1. Therapeutic Massage sessions are in full compliance with California state laws and regulations.
2. Disrobe to the level of your comfort.
3. You may stop the massage at any time if you feel uncomfortable. Immediately verbalize this request.
4. Massage sessions that include stretching (e.g., 3-Dimensional Bodywork which includes massage and stretch) can be done at any level of draping or clothed. Underwear, swimsuit bottoms, or running shorts are good options if you are new to therapy techniques that place the body and limbs in optimal positions for manipulation.
5. Clients who choose therapy modalities unclothed and draped understand that secure draping will be used. Further, they will be shown how to control the drape to their comfort level. The client must feel relaxed during the technique.
6. Stretch (only) sessions are done in workout attire, are considered a "sports stretch," and do not fall under any California state laws or regulations governing therapeutic massage.

Date _____

Signature _____

APPENDIX F

PERMISSIONS, BOUNDARIES, AND CONSENT

CHECKLIST

- ☐ Focus on gluteus and hips ("all trains run through mid-town Manhattan")
- ☐ Sacrum and coccyx (where latissimus and spinal muscles start)
- ☐ Ischial tuberosity (sitz bones where hamstrings start)
- ☐ Sacrotuberous ligament (therapeutic need only), (bony gluteus ligament, force transmission path)
- ☐ Lesser trochanter (therapeutic need only), (inside thigh where hip flexor connects)
- ☐ Ischial pubic ramus (therapeutic need only), (torso where adductors start)
- ☐ Iliiopsoas (deep hip flexor muscles under your intestines that runs by pubic bone to inside thigh)
- ☐ Pubic insertion of rectus abdominus (lower insertion of 8-pack abdominal muscle)
- ☐ Femoral triangle and Inguinal Ligament (lymph glands, insertion of oblique abdominal muscles)
- ☐ Sternum (breast plate, where pecs start)
- ☐ Lateral border of pectoralis major (outside border of pec)

Client Initials _____

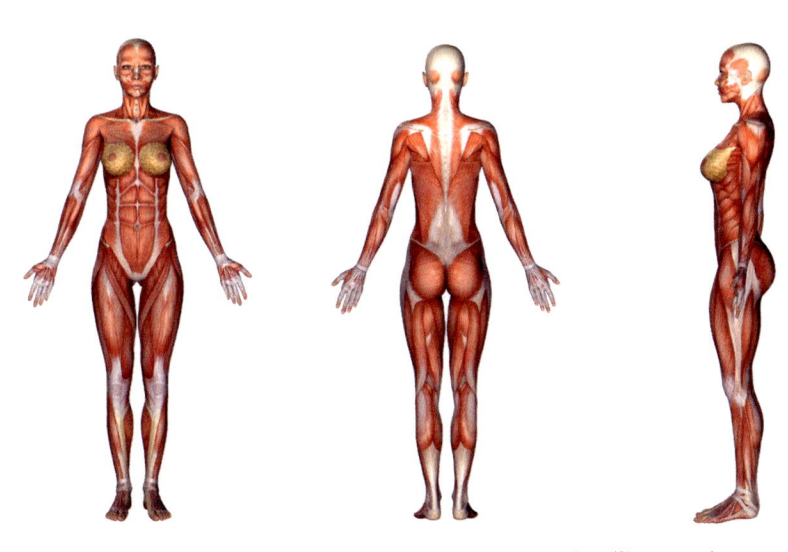

Image credit: TreesTons/Shutterstock.com

APPENDIX G
COURSE SYLLABUS

MYOFASCIAL RELEASE

_____ 40 CLOCK HOURS
(SEMESTER AND YEAR)

REQUIRED TEXT

3-Dimensional Bodywork: A Systematic Approach to Myofascial Network Release for Massage Therapists, by Robert W. McCarthy

RECOMMENDED REFERENCE

Anatomy Trains: Myofascial Meridians for Manual and Movement Therapists, by Thomas W. Myers

INSTRUCTOR

Robert W. McCarthy, MS, CMT, CSCS, CPT, CFSS

COURSE OVERVIEW

There are many Myofascial Release (MFR) techniques and devices. MFR resides within the connective tissue branch of massage therapy, which includes Rolfing, Structural Integration, etc. In these techniques, your goal is to "mechanically" release fascial adhesions and restrictions. The concept of myofascia, and fascia in particular, is a rapidly evolving concept. You should appreciate that fascia is inseparable from muscle. Together, they form a three-dimensional web, or network, that runs through the body and surrounds every cell in the body. The approach in this course takes this three-dimensional "global" view and will give you a repeatable technique that can be used in a standard 60- to 90-minute massage session. You will also learn less traditional massage positions and bolstering, such as side lying and Sims' lateral recumbent. Your goal is to release or free-up fascial restrictions to alleviate discomfort and allow for the proper extensibility of fascial networks that run through the body. These networks, or meridians, as defined by Thomas Myers, give us an anatomical organization, or starting point to address fascial restrictions – and the local, distant, or referred pain they cause. The systematic MFR technique that you will learn combines elements of tension (stretch), torsion, shear, and compression of myofascial tissue. Every stroke has therapeutic intent; every stroke should feel good to the client. Since you will be placing a client's body in optimal three-dimensional positions to perform manual manipulation, the technique is not appropriate for first-time, only-time spa clients, but rather, for clients who desire: therapeutic relief of discomfort, therapeutic change of a condition, condition management, greater physical function, or enhanced sports performance.

COURSE OBJECTIVES AND COMPETENCIES

1. Upon completing the Myofascial Release course, students will be able to demonstrate knowledge of the following:
2. The main physiological components and properties of myofascia.
3. Rudimentary understanding of the organizing myofascial meridians.

4. The concept of fascia's "global sensory network."
5. Causes of dysfunction in the fascial system.
6. Concept of Therapeutic Change versus Condition Management.
7. Appropriate application of the technique and routine to include tension, torsion, shear, and compression.
8. Appropriate application of the technique and routine to include proper three-dimensional body placement.
9. Critical assessment of routine application on more difficult cases.
10. Indications and contraindications for performing myofascial release techniques.
11. Integration of myofascial techniques with other forms of bodywork.
12. Increased awareness of tissue texture and mobility.
13. Proper body mechanics allowing the technique to be performed safely and effectively.

COURSE REQUIREMENTS

1. Attend all class sessions.
2. Practice sequence techniques at least three times each week outside of class.
3. Read assigned chapters from the textbook.
4. Actively participate in class discussions and practicum.
5. Optional periodic quizzes on homework reading material.
6. Pass a practical examination on the final day of class.
7. Adhere to all school polices and procedures.

COURSE SYLLABUS

(LO = Learning Objective)

Class 1
MONTH AND DAY

FIRST HOUR
- Introduction of class and students
- Slide presentation overview of myofascia, Myofascial Meridians, myofascial release (MFR), and 3-Dimensional Bodywork (3DB)
- Learning Objective 1 (LO1): What are the differences and similarities between 3DB versus other myofascial release techniques?

SECOND & THIRD HOUR
- LO2: Where would you use 3DB? Review appendices: SOAP, waiver, informed consent, and permissions.
- LO3: Practical Exercise – "Global Sensory Snowsuit" observations: body overview, tissue assessment, end-feel, first point of resistance, compression, rebounding, skin rolling; round-robin comparison of other students.
- LO4: Practical Exercise - Draw Superficial Back Line (SBL) on each other (note landmarks and muscles involved)

FOURTH HOUR
- LO5: Learn 3DB draping and cautions of Lower Supine routine

FIFTH HOUR
- ☐ LO6: Practicum: Learn 3DB Lower Supine LS 1 through LS 8

HOMEWORK
- ☐ Read 3DB Chapter 1
- ☐ Practical Assignment: Manipulate the "Global Sensory Snowsuit" of a client, significant other, friend, cat, dog, or packaged chicken breast
- ☐ Practical Assignment: Practice LS 1 – LS 8 on a client, friend, or significant other

Class 2
MONTH AND DAY

FIRST HOUR
- ☐ LO7: discuss Chapter 1 fascial restrictions, condition management vs. therapeutic change, "Rule of Thumb." (Optional quiz)

SECOND HOUR
- ☐ LO8: Draw Superficial Front Line (SFL) on each other

THIRD HOUR
- ☐ LO9: Learn 3DB Lower Supine LS 1 through LS 12

FOURTH HOUR
- ☐ LO10: Learn 3DB Lower Supine LS 13 through LS 24

FIFTH HOUR
- ☐ LO11: Practicum: LS 1 through LS 24

HOMEWORK
- ☐ Read 3DB Chapter 2
- ☐ Practical Assignment: Practice LS 1 – LS 24 on a client, friend, or significant other

Class 3
MONTH AND DAY

FIRST HOUR
- ☐ LO12: Read course overview. Discuss Chapter 2 mechanical versus energy work, what are we really doing when we "release " myofascia? Demonstrate iliopsoas release (stretch vs. manual manipulation) (Optional quiz)

SECOND HOUR
- ☐ LO13: Draw Deep Front Line (DFL) on each other (adductors only)

THIRD HOUR
- ☐ LO14: Learn 3DB Lower Supine routine LS 25 through LS 37

FOURTH HOUR
- ☐ LO15: Practice 3DB Lower Supine routine LS 1 through LS 37

FIFTH HOUR
- ☐ LO16: Practicum: LS 1 through LS 37

HOMEWORK
- ☐ Read 3DB Chapter 3
- ☐ Practical Assignment: Practice LS 1 – LS 37 on a client, friend, or significant other

Class 4
MONTH AND DAY

FIRST HOUR
- ☐ LO17: Discuss 3DB Chapter 3, Hallmarks of the Routine; practice Hallmarks of the Routine on each other. (Optional quiz)

SECOND HOUR
- LO18: Discuss Arm Lines. Instructor draw Back Functional Line, Pectoralis Major, Pectoralis Minor, "Serratus Sling," and Teres Major on a student.

THIRD HOUR
- LO19: Learn 3DB Upper Supine US 1 through US 12

FOURTH HOUR
- LO20: Learn 3DB Upper Supine US 13 through US 23

FIFTH HOUR
- LO21: Practicum: US 1 through US 23

HOMEWORK:
- Read 3DB Chapter 4. Review appendices including exercise routines
- Practical Assignment: Practice US 1 – US 23 on a client, friend, or significant other

Class 5
MONTH AND DAY

FIRST HOUR
- LO22: Discuss 3DB Chapter 4 types of clients, when the technique is appropriate.
- LO23: Discuss all appendices incl. exercise routines. (Optional quiz)

SECOND HOUR
- LO24: Instructor draw Lateral Line (LL) on student from ankle to ribs; prosciutto ham as int./ext. oblique demonstration (optional); demonstrate side lying stretch; demonstrate TRX® lateral line stretch (optional).

THIRD HOUR
- LO25: Learn 3DB Side Lying SL 1 through SL 13

FOURTH HOUR
- LO26: Practicum: SL 1 through SL 13

FIFTH HOUR
- LO27: Practicum: Open time to practice LS, US, SL

HOMEWORK
- Read 3DB Chapter 6 Case Studies 1, 2 and 3
- Practical Assignment: Practice SL 1 – SL 13 on a client, friend, or significant other

Class 6
MONTH AND DAY

FIRST HOUR
- LO28: Discuss 3DB Chapter 6 Case Studies 1, 2, and 3. (Optional quiz)

SECOND HOUR
- LO29: Draw Superficial Back Line (SBL) and Deep Front Line adductors on each other with new perspective. Observe how they relate to SLR 1 - SLR 15.

THIRD HOUR
- LO30: Learn 3DB Sims' Lateral Recumbent SLR 1 through SLR 10

FOURTH HOUR
- LO31: Learn 3DB Sims' Lateral Recumbent SLR 11 through SLR 15

FIFTH HOUR
- LO32: Practicum: SLR 1 through SLR 15

HOMEWORK
- Read 3DB Chapter 6 Case Studies 4 and 5, and "First, do no harm" discussion
- Practical Assignment: Practice SLR 1 – SLR 15 on a client, friend, or significant other

Class 7 _{MONTH AND DAY}

FIRST HOUR
- ☐ LO33: Discuss 3DB Chapter 6 Case Studies 4 and 5. (Optional quiz)
- ☐ LO34: Practical Transverse Asymmetry Test.
- ☐ LO35: Discuss "First Do No Harm" and contraindications. Open student/teacher discussion on previous pathologies encountered, and if the issues could have been helped (or worsened) by the 3DB technique and routine.

SECOND HOUR
- ☐ LO36: Instructor draw Spiral Line (SL) on student. Demonstrate TRX® transverse plane exercises (optional). Instructor then draws dermatomes (L4-S1) on a second student, and Chinese meridian bladder and stomach lines on a third student. Discuss integrative concepts of 3DB.

THIRD HOUR
- ☐ LO37: Learn 3DB Prone P 1 through P 11

FOURTH HOUR
- ☐ LO38: Learn 3DB Prone P 12 through P 21

FIFTH HOUR
- ☐ LO39: Practicum: P1 through P 21

HOMEWORK
- ☐ Practical Assignment: Practice P 1 – P 21 on a client, friend, or significant other
- ☐ Practical Assignment: Practice all five routines (about 2 hours) on a client, friend, or significant other

Class 8 _{MONTH AND DAY}

FIRST HOUR
- ☐ LO40: Instructor demonstrates routine positions, one side of body only, with half of class following along.

SECOND HOUR
- ☐ LO41: Same as above but with other half of class.

THIRD & FOURTH HOURS
- ☐ Final Practical Exam: Instructor randomly pick sequential steps from two of the five routine positions; have each student demonstrate the routine on the instructor to assess intuitive grasp of the technique, rhythm, body mechanics, and draping and bolstering.

FIFTH HOUR
- ☐ Class wrap-up and evaluations.

APPENDIX H
RECOMMENDED CLASS MATERIALS

DRAPING
- Any type of sheet will do, sheets with some elastic stretch work best.

TOWELS
- A bath towel and several hand towels to cover sensitive areas.

BOLSTERS
- Pillow for the head
- King-size extra-firm pillow for Side Lying
- Small pillow for Sims' Lateral Recumbent
- Various standard bolsters for knees and ankles

GLIDE
- Small amounts of lotion are recommended. No oil.

BODY DRAWING
- Washable markers
- Paper towels and hand sanitizer for clean up

TRX® SUSPENSION TRAINER (OPTIONAL)
- For self-care exercise demonstration, Lateral Line demonstration, and Spiral Line demonstration. Only recommended if the instructor (or student) is a Certified Personal Trainer (CPT).

REFERENCES

1. Myers, Thomas W., et al. *Anatomy Trains: Myofascial Meridians for Manual and Movement Therapists, 3rd Edition. (2014).* Churchill Livingstone/Elsevier, p 12.

2. Fritz, Sandy, *Mosby's Fundamentals of Therapeutic Massage, 6th Edition.* (2017) Elsevier/Mosby, pp. 411-427.

3. Vizniak, N. A. (2018). *Quick reference evidence informed muscle manual.* Canada: Professional Health Systems, pg. 25.

4. Fritz, Sandy, *Mosby's Fundamentals of Therapeutic Massage, 6th Edition.* (2017) Elsevier/Mosby, p. 199. Citing Day, J. A., Stecco, C., & Stecco, A. (2009). Application of Fascial Manipulation© technique in chronic shoulder pain—Anatomical basis and clinical implications. *Journal of Bodywork and Movement Therapies*, 13(2), 128-135. doi:10.1016/j.jbmt.2008.04.044

5. Ushiki, T. (2002). Collagen Fibers, Reticular Fibers and Elastic Fibers. A Comprehensive Understanding from a Morphological Viewpoint. *Archives of Histology and Cytology*, 65(2), 109-126. doi:10.1679/aohc.65.109

6. Fritz, Sandy, *Mosby's Fundamentals of Therapeutic Massage, 6th Edition.* (2017) Elsevier/Mosby, p. 198.

7. Duncan, Ruth A. *Myofascial Release.* Human Kinetics, (2014), citing Jacob C. Van Der Wal, Md, Phd. (2009). The Architecture of the Connective Tissue in the Musculoskeletal System - An Often Overlooked Functional Parameter as to Proprioception in the Locomotor Apparatus. *International Journal of Therapeutic Massage & Bodywork: Research, Education, & Practice*, 2(4). doi:10.3822/ijtmb.v2i4.62

8. Marieb, E. N., & Hoehn, K. (2019). *Human anatomy & physiology.* Hoboken, NJ: Pearson, The Peripheral Nervous System.

9. Duncan, Ruth A. *Myofascial Release.* Human Kinetics, 2014, p. 70.

10. Fritz, Sandy, *Mosby's Fundamentals of Therapeutic Massage, 6th Edition.* (2017) Elsevier/Mosby, p 120.

11. Fritz, Sandy, *Mosby's Fundamentals of Therapeutic Massage, 6th Edition.* (2017) Elsevier/Mosby, pp. 238.

12. Fritz, Sandy, *Mosby's Fundamentals of Therapeutic Massage, 6th Edition.* (2017) Elsevier/Mosby, p 438.

13. Fritz, Sandy, *Mosby's Fundamentals of Therapeutic Massage, 6th Edition.* (2017) Elsevier/Mosby, p 42.

14. Fritz, Sandy, *Mosby's Fundamentals of Therapeutic Massage, 6th Edition.* (2017) Elsevier/Mosby, p 370.

15. Myers, Thomas W., et al. *Anatomy Trains: Myofascial Meridians for Manual and Movement Therapists, 3rd Edition.* (2014). Churchill Livingstone/Elsevier, p 41.

16. Fritz, Sandy, *Mosby's Fundamentals of Therapeutic Massage, 6th Edition.* (2017) Elsevier/Mosby, p 371.

17. Fritz, Sandy, *Mosby's Fundamentals of Therapeutic Massage, 6th Edition.* (2017) Elsevier/Mosby, p 361.

18. J. Marion Sims. (2019, July 04). Retrieved from https://en.wikipedia.org/wiki/J._Marion_Sims

19. Fritz, Sandy, *Mosby's Fundamentals of Therapeutic Massage, 6th Edition.* (2017) Elsevier/Mosby, p 437.

20. Lane, K., Worsley, D., & Mckenzie, D. (2005). Exercise and the Lymphatic System. *Sports Medicine*, 35(6), 461–471. doi: 10.2165/00007256-200535060-00001

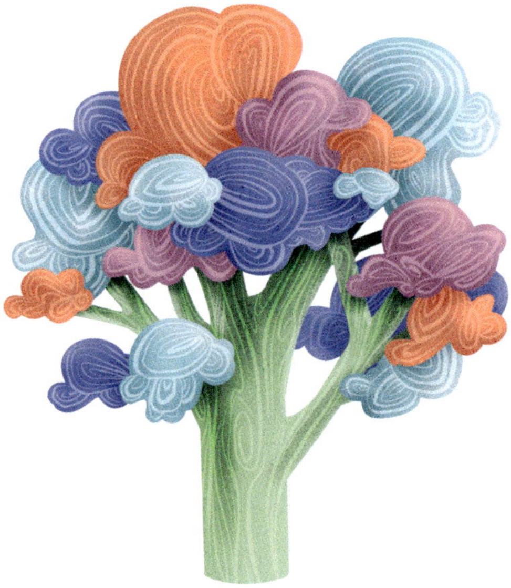

Made in the USA
Middletown, DE
29 December 2019